# THE AVENGERS

# THE ONCE AND FUTURE KANG

## WRITERS
### ROGER STERN, DANNY FINGEROTH & STEVE ENGLEHART
### WITH JIM SHOOTER & MARK BRIGHT

## PENCILERS/BREAKDOWNS
### JOHN BUSCEMA, STEVE DITKO & MARK BRIGHT

## INKERS/FINISHERS
### TOM PALMER, KLAUS JANSON & GEOF ISHERWOOD

## COLORISTS
### CHRISTIE SCHEELE, ELAINE LEE & PETRA SCOTESE

## LETTERERS
### JIM NOVAK, LOIS BUHALIS, KENNY LOPEZ & TOM ORZECHOWSKI

## ASSISTANT EDITORS
### HOWARD MACKIE & MICHAEL HIGGINS

## EDITOR
### MARK GRUENWALD

## COVER ARTISTS
### JOHN BUSCEMA & TOM PALMER

## FRONT COVER COLORIST
### CHRIS SOTOMAYOR

## BACK COVER COLORIST
### THOMAS MASON

COLLECTION EDITOR
**NELSON RIBEIRO**

ASSISTANT EDITOR
**ALEX STARBUCK**

EDITORS, SPECIAL PROJECTS
**MARK D. BEAZLEY & JENNIFER GRÜNWALD**

SENIOR EDITOR, SPECIAL PROJECTS
**JEFF YOUNGQUIST**

RESEARCH & LAYOUT
**JEPH YORK**

PRODUCTION
**COLORTEK**

SENIOR VICE PRESIDENT OF SALES
**DAVID GABRIEL**

EDITOR IN CHIEF
**AXEL ALONSO**

CHIEF CREATIVE OFFICER
**JOE QUESADA**

PUBLISHER
**DAN BUCKLEY**

EXECUTIVE PRODUCER
**ALAN FINE**

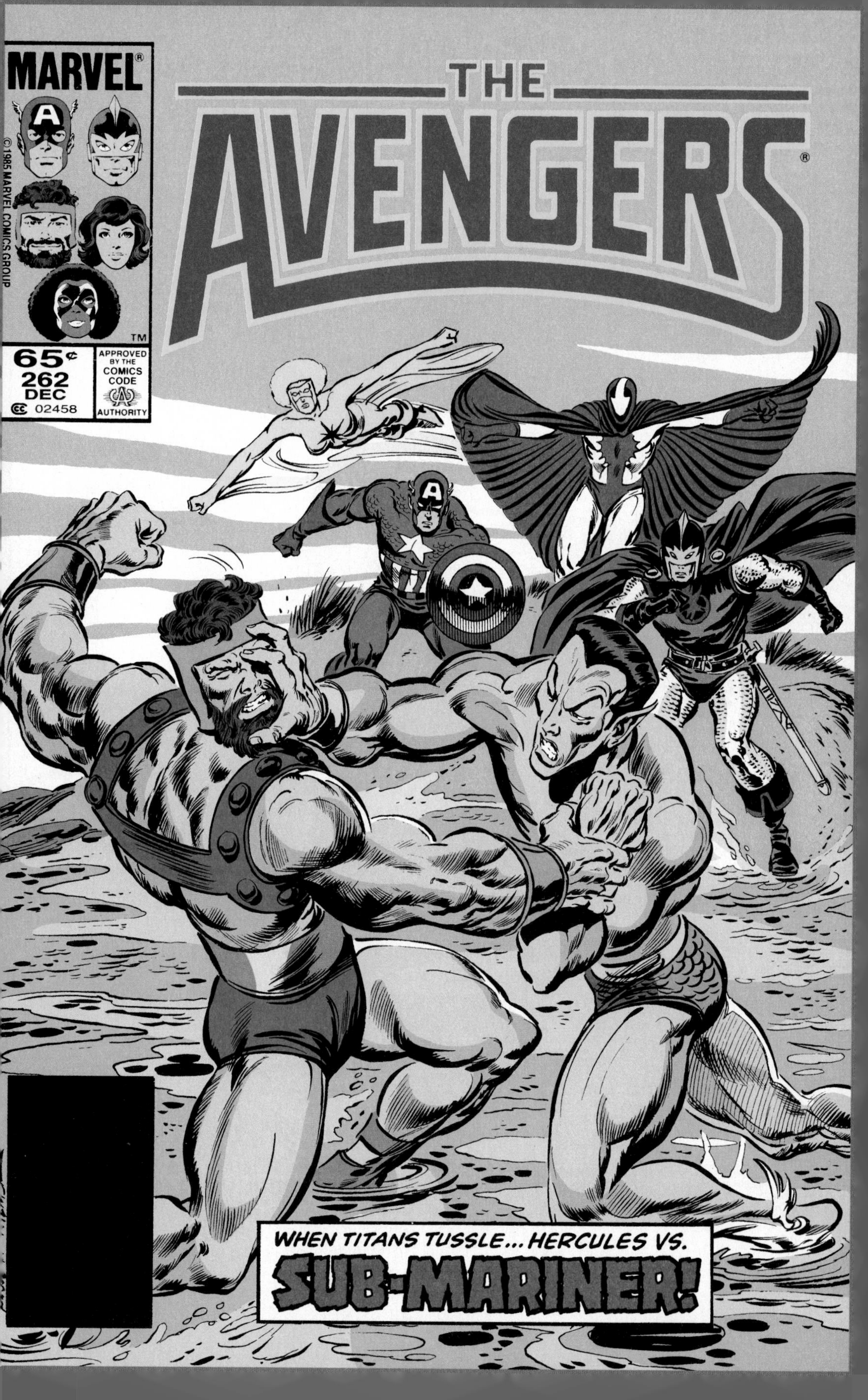
MARVEL
© 1985 MARVEL COMICS GROUP
THE AVENGERS
TM
65¢
262
DEC
02458
APPROVED BY THE COMICS CODE AUTHORITY
WHEN TITANS TUSSLE... HERCULES VS.
SUB-MARINER!

STAN LEE PRESENTS: "MANY BRAVE HEARTS..."

SOME FIFTY MILES TO THE SOUTHEAST OF LOWER NEW YORK BAY, A LIGHT CABIN CRUISER CUTS ACROSS THE WAVES OF THE ATLANTIC, WHEN SUDDENLY...

AHOY, THE SHIP! THIS IS *STINGRAY*... PREPARE TO BE BOARDED!

AG7A

ROGER STERN-WRITER    JOHN BUSCEMA-BREAKDOWNS
TOM PALMER-FINISHER    JIM NOVAK-LETTERER
CHRISTIE SCHEELE-COLORIST    MARK GRUENWALD-EDITOR
JIM SHOOTER-EDITOR IN CHIEF

"PREPARE TO BE BOARDED"?! OH, AYE-AYE, SIR! SHIVER ME TIMBERS AND YO-HO-HO!

"PREPARE TO BE BOARDED"...*REALLY*, WALT! HOW CORNY CAN YOU GET?

GIVE ME A BREAK, DIANE! I'LL BET HALF THE *OCEANO-GRAPHERS* ALIVE DREAMED OF BEING *PIRATES* WHEN THEY WERE KIDS.

LET ME GUESS... YOU WERE IN THAT HALF, RIGHT?

RIGHT AS RAIN, ME PROUD BEAUTY! AH, FOR THE ROMANCE OF THE OPEN SEAS!

ALL ACES! MY IMPROVED *PROPULSION UNIT* GOT ME UP TO 60 KNOTS ON LOW POWER!

WHAT'S THIS?

YESTERDAY'S *DAILY BUGLE!* THE LEAD STORY MIGHT INTEREST YOU!

I'LL DRINK TO THAT! MMMM—MMHH!

HOW'D YOUR TESTING GO?

WOW! I'LL SAY IT DOES! PRETTY HEAVY NEWS...

...AND IT COULD BE JUST THE BREAK WE NEED!

DAILY BUGLE
THE PICTURE NEWSPAPER®

FAA CLIP AVENGERS' WINGS

LANDING RIGHTS REVOKED

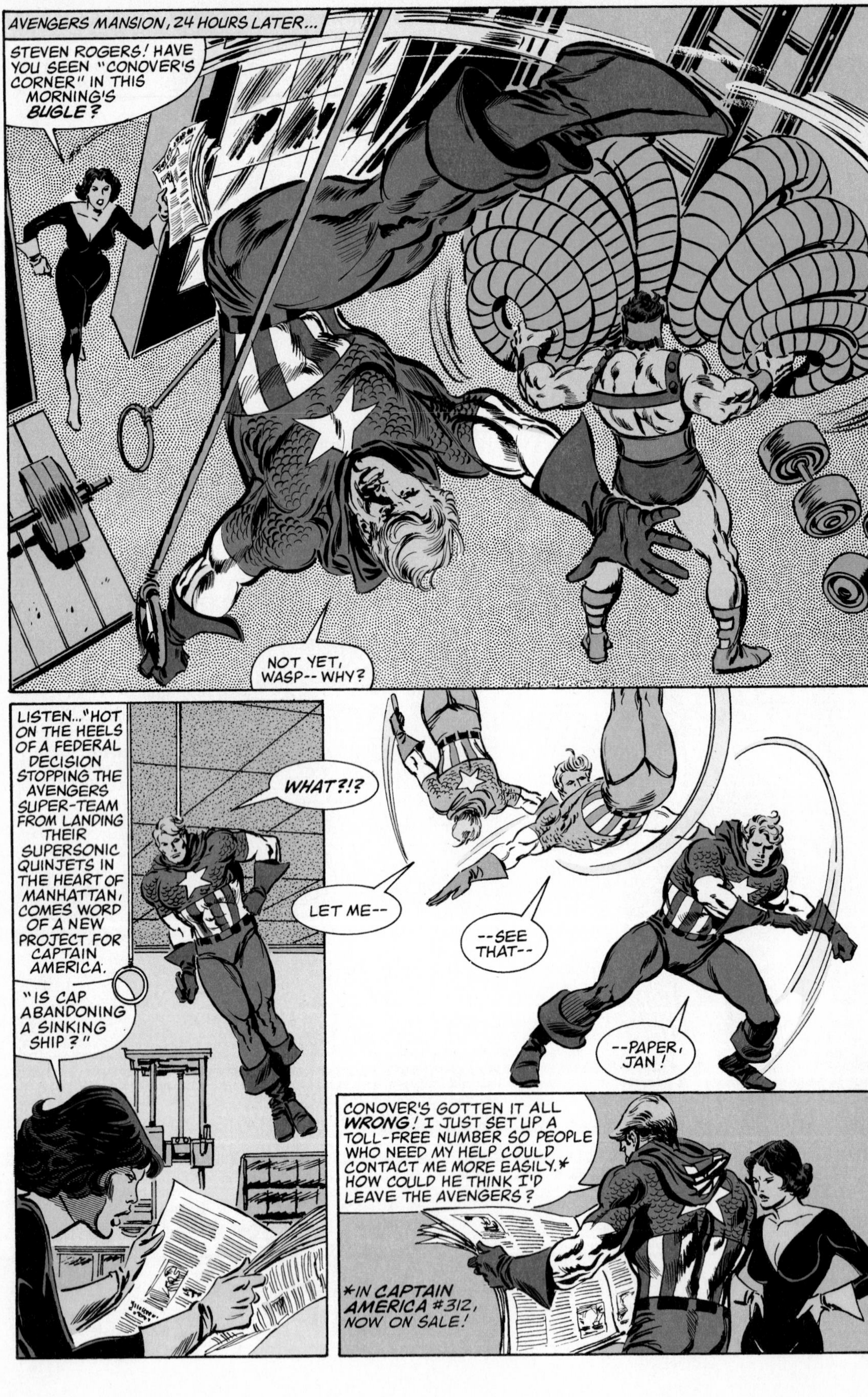
AVENGERS MANSION, 24 HOURS LATER...
STEVEN ROGERS! HAVE YOU SEEN "CONOVER'S CORNER" IN THIS MORNING'S BUGLE?
NOT YET, WASP-- WHY?
LISTEN..."HOT ON THE HEELS OF A FEDERAL DECISION STOPPING THE AVENGERS SUPER-TEAM FROM LANDING THEIR SUPERSONIC QUINJETS IN THE HEART OF MANHATTAN, COMES WORD OF A NEW PROJECT FOR CAPTAIN AMERICA.
"IS CAP ABANDONING A SINKING SHIP?"
WHAT?!?
LET ME--
--SEE THAT--
--PAPER, JAN!
CONOVER'S GOTTEN IT ALL WRONG! I JUST SET UP A TOLL-FREE NUMBER SO PEOPLE WHO NEED MY HELP COULD CONTACT ME MORE EASILY.* HOW COULD HE THINK I'D LEAVE THE AVENGERS?
*IN CAPTAIN AMERICA #312, NOW ON SALE!

IF THIS MISCREANT IS SPREADING *LIES* ABOUT THE MIGHTY AVENGERS, THEN HERCULES SHALL TEACH HIM THE ERROR OF HIS WAYS!

AT EASE, HERC. THE MAN'S JUST EXPRESSING AN OPINION, AND HE HAS EVERY RIGHT TO DO THAT... MISTAKEN THOUGH HE MIGHT BE. IT'S PARTLY MY FAULT--

--I SHOULD HAVE MADE IT CLEARER THAT MY PHONE-IN SERVICE WAS *IN ADDITION* TO MY AVENGERS ACTIVITIES. BUT THEN, I DIDN'T KNOW THE *FAA* WAS GOING TO LEAK THE NEWS THAT THEY'D RESCINDED OUR *LANDING PERMIT.*

KA-TUUNG

IF YOU WANT, JAN, I COULD CALL CONOVER AND SET HIM STRAIGHT.

NO, AT THIS POINT A DENIAL WOULD ONLY MAKE THINGS LOOK WORSE.

THIS COULDN'T HAVE COME AT A WORSE TIME! THE NATIONAL SECURITY COUNCIL IS RESTRUCTURING OUR PRIORITY CLEARANCE... THE BEYONDER IS LOOSE ON EARTH... AND, SINCE *STAR-FOX* LEFT, WE'RE *SHORT* AN AVENGER!*

NO NEED TO WORRY! THE SON OF ZEUS CAN PULL THE WEIGHT OF TWO AVENGERS! AND HAS NOT THE BLACK KNIGHT DEVISED A WAY TO TRACK DOWN THE BEYONDER?

SO HE SAYS. HOW'S IT WORKING, DANE?

OH, *IT* IS WORKING FINE, JAN. HOWEVER, IT APPEARS THAT THE *BEYONDER* ISN'T!

*LAST ISSUE.

7

HERE WE GO TO ALL THE TROUBLE OF SETTING UP THIS *DETECTION-WEB* NETWORK WITH PROJECT PEGASUS TO TRACE THE BEYONDER VIA HIS COSMIC EMISSIONS-- AND THEN HE SUDDENLY STOPS *EMITTING!*

ARE YOU SURE? MAYBE HE'S LEFT THE EARTH!

WE COULDN'T POSSIBLY BE THAT LUCKY, STEVE!

THAT WOULDN'T NECESSARILY BE *LUCK*, JAN! THE BEYONDER DESTROYED A WHOLE GALAXY... YOU AND CAP AND I SAW THAT FIRSTHAND! HE COULD DECIDE TO DO IT AGAIN... TO *OURS!*

CAPTAIN MARVEL'S RIGHT, JAN! SAY, DANE... PERHAPS HE'S DISGUISED HIS TRAIL SOMEHOW, WHAT IF...

I'VE BEEN AN AVENGER ONLY A SHORT TIME, BUT THESE PEOPLE AREN'T JUST THE BLACK KNIGHT AND THE WASP AND CAPTAIN AMERICA TO ME ANYMORE--

--THEY'RE *DANE* AND *JAN* AND ...*STEVE*. BUT THEY STILL KNOW ME ONLY AS *CAPTAIN MARVEL.* AVENGERS BY-LAWS DON'T REQUIRE ME TO REVEAL MY TRUE *IDENTITY* TO THEM ...BUT WE'VE BEEN THROUGH SO MUCH, MAYBE I *SHOULD--!*

*UMMPH!* I BEG ALL OF YOUR PARDONS, BUT I REALLY MUST HAVE SOME *ASSISTANCE* WITH THIS! IT'S MORE THAN ONE BUTLER CAN HANDLE!

*JARVIS?!* WHAT ON EARTH--?

...THIS IS BARELY A *TENTH* OF THE MORNING MAIL, MADAME! THESE ARE INVITATIONS FROM CITIES AND TOWNS ACROSS THE COUNTRY...

...ALL OFFERING THE AVENGERS SPACE TO RELOCATE! IT'S BEEN LIKE THIS EVER SINCE THAT STORY HIT THE *WIRE SERVICES* THE OTHER DAY.

OH, FINE!

TWO DAYS LATER...

'MORNING, ALL. STILL NO *LET UP?*

NO. IN FACT, NOW WE'RE STARTING TO GET FOLLOW-UP ORDERS!

*DETROIT?* THEY'VE GOTTA BE KIDDING?

8

BAH, THESE SCRAPS OF PAPER MAKE THE SAME MEANINGLESS OFFERS OVER AND OVER! I WILL HAVE NO FURTHER *PART* OF THIS FOOLISHNESS!

BUT, HERCULES, DIDN'T I HEAR YOU SAY YOU COULD PULL THE WEIGHT OF TWO AVENGERS?

I AM IN NO MOOD TO BE *MOCKED*, WASP!

I STILL CAN'T BELIEVE THAT SO MANY *MAYORS* WANT US TO SET UP SHOP IN THEIR HOME TOWNS. HAVING THE AVENGERS AROUND WOULDN'T EXACTLY LOWER THEIR *INSURANCE RATES*, AFTER ALL!

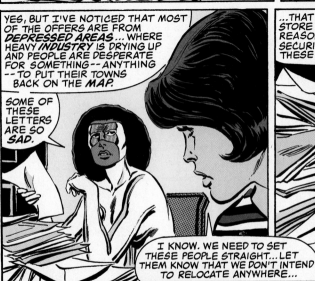

YES, BUT I'VE NOTICED THAT MOST OF THE OFFERS ARE FROM *DEPRESSED AREAS*... WHERE HEAVY *INDUSTRY* IS DRYING UP AND PEOPLE ARE DESPERATE FOR SOMETHING -- ANYTHING -- TO PUT THEIR TOWNS BACK ON THE *MAP*.

SOME OF THESE LETTERS ARE SO *SAD*.

I KNOW. WE NEED TO SET THESE PEOPLE STRAIGHT... LET THEM KNOW THAT WE DON'T INTEND TO RELOCATE ANYWHERE...

...THAT ALL WE NEED IS A PLACE TO STORE OUR *QUINJETS* -- SOMEPLACE REASONABLY *CLOSE* WITH GOOD SECURITY. SO FAR, NOTHING IN THESE OFFERS FILLS THE BILL.

THAT'S TOO BAD. WE HAVE LESS THAN A MONTH TO COMPLY WITH THE *FAA'S* ORDER. IF YOU WANT, I COULD SEE ABOUT GETTING US SOME HANGAR SPACE AT McGUIRE AIR FORCE BASE. IT'S NOT TOO FAR AND--!

WAIT-A-MINUTE! OH, THIS IS TOO GOOD TO BE *TRUE*, BUT...

...I THINK WE MAY HAVE A *WINNER!*

9

AT THAT MOMENT, THOUSANDS OF MILES AWAY...

THE PETTY UNREASONING FOOLS! THEY MUDDLE ALONG, EACH DAY BRINGING CIVILIZATION CLOSER TO *EXTINCTION*--

--WHILE *I*, ONE OF THE FEW GREAT MINDS CAPABLE OF *SAVING* THEM, AM LOCKED AWAY... LIKE A COMMON *CRIMINAL*!

MORLAK!

EH? THAT VOICE... *ZOTA*?

YES, OVER HERE!

I'LL SOON HAVE YOU FREE OF THIS CELL!

YOU'RE REALLY *HERE*! I'M NOT HALLUCINATING! THANK HEAVENS, I--!

MORLAK, FOR ONCE IN YOUR LIFE, BE STILL!

IF WE WANT TO GET OUT OF HERE, IT HAS TO BE *NOW*!

WHILE, SOMEWHERE IN THE HEART OF BROOKLYN...

WHAT IS KEEPING THEM?! THE *TRANSFER GRID* WON'T HOLD UP MUCH LONGER!

MORLAK... ZOTA... AT LAST!

*SHINSKI*, YOU OLD CURMUDGEON! I SHOULD HAVE KNOWN YOU WOULDN'T LET US DOWN!

SHUT UP AND MOVE! THE GRID IS GOING TO BLOW--

10

ZOW

--ANY SECOND!

ARE YOU ALL RIGHT?

I THINK SO.

YOU RESCUED ME WITH JURY-RIGGED EQUIPMENT ...OPERATING OUT OF A DIRTY WAREHOUSE?! IS THIS WHAT THE EN-CLAVE HAS SUNK TO...

...WE WHO ESTABLISHED THE GREATEST CENTER FOR SCIENTIFIC RESEARCH EVER TO GRACE THIS PLANET?!? WE WHO SET OUT TO SAVE CIVILIZA-TION FROM ITS IGNORANCE--

"-- BY CREATING A NEW RACE OF PERFECT HUMAN BEINGS... BEINGS WHICH WOULD HAVE RECOGNIZED US AS THE EARTH'S SAVIORS... AND MASTERS!

"SURELY, WE EARNED THE RIGHT TO RULE THIS WORLD! IT TOOK YEARS OF EXPERI-MENTATION TO DEVELOP THE PROTOTYPE OF OUR PERFECT MAN WITHIN THE LIFE-CELL TANK. IF ONLY WE HAD BEEN LESS EAGER!

"WE BROUGHT HIM ALONG TOO QUICKLY AND HE ESCAPED FROM THE TANK, WREAKING HAVOC THROUGHOUT OUR CITADEL..."

THAT UNEARTHLY GLOW... IT'S HIM! HE'S FOUND US!

THE MONSTER HAS CAUGHT US --AT LAST!

"YES, HE WAS A MASTERPIECE OF FACE AND FORM --BUT WHAT HE DID WAS MONSTROUS, INDEED!

11

"HE REFUSED TO SEE OUR WISDOM...HE DARED EVEN CALL US *EVIL.* IN TAKING HIS LEAVE, HE UNLEASHED SUCH ENERGIES THAT I THOUGHT THE CITADEL WOULD BE DESTROYED!*

"YET WE MANAGED A SECOND ATTEMPT AT CREATING A *PERFECT HUMAN.* THAT, TOO, ENDED DISASTEROUSLY**, BUT OUR FORTUNES WERE STILL GREAT ENOUGH--

*FANTASTIC FOUR #67. **HULK ANNUAL #6.

"--TO FORGE AN ALLIANCE WITH THE RENEGADE INHUMAN *MAXIMUS* AND INVADE THE HIDDEN CITY OF *ATTILAN.*

"THAT *CITY* AND ALL ITS AMAZING *TECHNOLOGY* WOULD HAVE BEEN *OURS,* IF MAXIMUS HADN'T LOST HIS SENSES AND *TURNED* ON US!

"TRUE, AFTER THE INHUMANS MOVED THEIR CITY TO THE MOON, MAXIMUS TRIED TO MAKE AMENDS... HELPING US SET UP A SECRET LUNAR BASE.

"BUT THAT OPERATION WAS ENDED BY THE INHUMANS AND THEIR FRIENDS, THE AVENGERS.* WE WERE RETURNED TO EARTH AND IMPRISONED..."

*IN AVENGERS ANNUAL #12.

...ONLY *YOU* REMAINED FREE, SHINSKI-- BECAUSE YOU WERE TOO *INFIRM* TO HAVE GONE TO THE MOON WITH ZOTA AND ME! I SPENT ENOUGH TIME IN THAT CELL TO THINK YOU'D *ABANDONED* US!

PERHAPS I SHOULD HAVE! I *WARNED* YOU AGAINST THOSE ALLIANCES WITH *MAXIMUS,* BUT NEITHER OF YOU WOULD LISTEN!

NOW, YOU SEE THE RESULTS OF YOUR FOOLISH ESCAPADES... OUR RESOURCES HAVE BEEN ALL BUT EXHAUSTED! IT TOOK ME *MONTHS* TO COBBLE TOGETHER THE TRANSFER GRID THAT MADE YOUR ESCAPES POSSIBLE!

SO DON'T POINT YOUR FINGER AT *ME,* MORLAK!

I HATE TO ADMIT IT, BUT HE'S *RIGHT!*

OF COURSE, I'M RIGHT. BUT THIS IS NO TIME FOR US TO BE ARGUING!

I HAVE MANAGED--THROUGH THE FRUGAL USE OF OUR REMAINING FUNDS--TO MAKE QUITE A FORTUITOUS *BREAKTHROUGH!* OBSERVE!

AND AS THE ENCLAVERS GATHER AROUND THE PARTIALLY OPENED CRATE, THEIR EYES GLEAM FROM THE *GLOW* WITHIN!

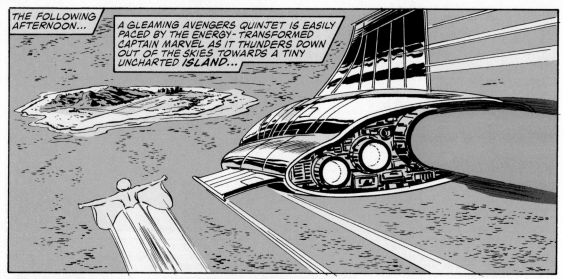

THE FOLLOWING AFTERNOON...

A GLEAMING AVENGERS QUINJET IS EASILY PACED BY THE ENERGY-TRANSFORMED CAPTAIN MARVEL AS IT THUNDERS DOWN OUT OF THE SKIES TOWARDS A TINY UNCHARTED *ISLAND*...

AND, WAITING TO GREET THE HEROES AT THE END OF AN ISLAND AIRSTRIP...

HELLO, I'M *DR. WALTER NEWELL* -- AND THIS IS MY WIFE, *DIANE!*

WELCOME TO *HYDROBASE!*

IN MINUTES...

SO... DID YOU HAVE ANY TROUBLE FINDING THE PLACE?

NOT AT ALL. YOUR DIRECTIONS WERE VERY GOOD.

GLAD TO HEAR IT! I THINK YOU'LL FIND THAT OUR LITTLE ISLAND WILL MAKE AN *IDEAL BASE* FOR YOUR QUINJETS!

I UNDERSTAND THAT YOU'VE BEEN USING THIS ISLAND AS A BASE FOR OCEANO-GRAPHIC RESEARCH.

THAT'S RIGHT, CAPTAIN MARVEL. WE HAD A GRANT FROM THE PACIFICA INSTITUTE OF TECHNOLOGY... EMPHASIS ON THE "HAD".

WE'D BEEN LOOKING FOR A NEW SOURCE OF *FUNDING*, WHEN WE HEARD ABOUT YOUR PROBLEMS WITH THE FAA... AND WE FIGURED, WHY NOT LEASE YOU SOME OF OUR SPACE? WE HAVE *PLENTY!*

OH, ONE THING I SHOULD MENTION... STRICTLY SPEAKING THIS *ISN'T* AN ISLAND! YOU SEE, IT *FLOATS!*

I BEG YOUR PARDON?

I KNOW IT'S HARD TO BELIEVE, BUT IT'S TRUE! *HYDROBASE* IS REALLY A HUGE OCEAN-GOING VESSEL. IT WAS CREATED BY A CRAZED SURVIVALIST WHO CALLED HIMSELF DR. HYDRO.

I CAN'T BEGIN TO TELL YOU ALL THE *TROUBLE* HE CAUSED. SUFFICE IT TO SAY THAT EVENTUALLY THINGS WERE PUT RIGHT, AND I WOUND UP WITH *OWNERSHIP* OF THE PLACE-- THANKS TO AN OBSCURE MARITIME SALVAGE LAW.

WELL, HERE WE ARE... THESE *HANGAR* BUILDINGS HAVE BEEN *VACANT* FOR MONTHS. I'M SURE THEY COULD BE ADAPTED TO YOUR NEEDS.

THE REAL NERVE CENTER OF THE ISLAND, THOUGH, IS UNDER-GROUND. IF YOU'LL STEP THIS WAY, I'LL--!

JUST A MOMENT, DO YOU HEAR SOMETHING? IT SOUNDS AS IF--!

YES... *LOOK!* SOME-THING'S APPROACHING HYDROBASE FROM THE *AIR!*

NOT SOME-*THING,* C.M.-- SOME*ONE!* THAT'S--

"--PRINCE NAMOR, THE *SUB-MARINER!*"

EH? WHAT ARE THOSE *AVENGERS* DOING ON HYDROBASE? IS THAT THE BLACK KNIGHT AMONG THEM?

NAMOR... *HI!* LONG TIME, NO SEE!

WHAT BRINGS THE SEA-LORD HITHER?

AS THE SUB-MARINER TOUCHES DOWN, THE WASP ASSUMES THE POWERS OF HER NAMESAKE AND...

HOLD IT RIGHT THERE, NAMOR! IF YOU'VE COME HERE TO CAUSE TROUBLE--!

YES, HE'S AN OLD DEAR FRIEND!

I KNOW THERE'S BEEN BAD BLOOD BETWEEN YOU FOLKS AND NAMOR, BUT--!

WE'VE HAD A TRUCE FOR SOME TIME NOW, DOCTOR.

FOR MY MONEY, IT'S STILL IN EFFECT!

NO, WASP. I'VE MERELY COME TO VISIT THE NEWELLS.

THANK YOU, CAP.

HERE, DIANE, I BROUGHT LOBSTERS FOR DINNER!

OH, YUM!

THE AVENGERS ARE INTERESTED IN LEASING PART OF HYDROBASE TO STORE THEIR AIRCRAFT, NAMOR. I WAS JUST ABOUT TO GIVE THEM THE FIFTY-CENT TOUR... CARE TO TAG ALONG?

NO...I THINK NOT!

NAMOR, I'M SORRY! I SHOULDN'T HAVE ACCUSED YOU OF--!

I ACCEPT YOUR APOLOGY, WASP...

...I WON'T INTERRUPT YOUR BUSINESS ANY FURTHER!

SO THAT'S THE FAMOUS SUB-MARINER! HE'S EVERY BIT AS REGAL AS I'D HEARD, BUT I DIDN'T EXPECT HIM TO BE SO...SUBDUED.

HE SEEMED TO BE HOLDING BACK SOME TERRIBLE SORROW.

15

YOU'RE RIGHTER THAN YOU COULD IMAGINE, CAPTAIN. IT WAS JUST A FEW WEEKS AGO THAT THE HIGH COUNCIL OF ATLANTIS ASKED NAMOR TO *ABDICATE* HIS *THRONE.* *

HE'S NO LONGER PRINCE OF ATLANTIS. HE'S LOST HIS *PEOPLE* AND HIS *COUNTRY.*

WE HAD NO IDEA! THERE HADN'T BEEN ANY WORD FROM ATLANTIS SINCE THEY RECALLED THEIR MISSION TO THE *U.N.!*

BUT IF HE'S IN SOME SORT OF *EXILE,* WHERE'S HE BEEN LIVING?

*IT HAPPENED IN ISSUE #4 OF THE *SUB-MARINER* LIMITED SERIES.

*HERE,* PART OF THE TIME. MOSTLY, HE'S JUST BEEN WANDERING ABOUT THE NORTH ATLANTIC.

WELL...

...I, UH, SUPPOSE WE SHOULD GET ON WITH THE TOUR. FOLLOW ME PLEASE...

SOON, DEEP BELOW THE SURFACE...

AND BELOW THAT SECTION ARE THE MAGNO-WAVE POWER GENERATORS.

AMAZING! WHAT SORT OF R.F. FIELD FLUX IS THERE?

I REALLY COULDN'T TELL YOU, KNIGHT. A LOT OF THIS STUFF IS *BEYOND* ME. LUCKILY, THOUGH, IT'S BEEN EASY TO MAINTAIN.

THIS IS, OF COURSE, THE HEART OF HYDROBASE SECURITY... A COMPLETELY COMPUTERIZED VISUAL, RADAR, AND SONAR SURVEILLANCE OF THE BASE PERIMETER ABOVE AND BELOW THE SURFACE--

--AND ALL OF IT TIED IN TO AUTO-MATED *DEFENSES.* I'LL SHOW YOU SOME OF THOSE NEXT.

BUT AS THE GROUP MOVES ON, HERCULES HANGS BACK--

--HIS ATTENTION DRAWN TO ONE PARTI-CULAR MONITOR.

SHORTLY...

HO! PRINCE *NO-MORE!*

YES, YOU...YOU SON OF A SEA COW! I HEAR THAT YOUR BLUE-SKINNED TOADIES FINALLY THREW YOU OUT!

I DON'T KNOW WHAT YOUR *PROBLEM* IS, HERCULES, BUT WE HAVE NO REASON TO *FIGHT.*

??!??

NO REASON, EH?

THEN I SHALL GIVE YOU A REASON!

WHA--?!

KRAK

WHIZZZZZZ

WUULMPH

17

YOU... OLYMPIAN... DOLT!

BTOK

PRINCE OR NOT, NAMOR THE FIRST TAKES *THAT* FROM NO ONE!

HAH! WAS THAT FEEBLE *TAP* SUPPOSED TO FELL ME, NO-MORE?

RAK

DID YOU ABDICATE YOUR FABLED *MIGHT*, ALONG WITH YOUR *THRONE*? COME DOWN OUT OF THE SKIES, AND I'LL SHOW YOU TRUE MIGHT!

NAMOR? VERY WELL, IF YOU WON'T COME DOWN--

"--I'LL KNOCK YOU DOWN!"

SPRAK

KRUMPA

18

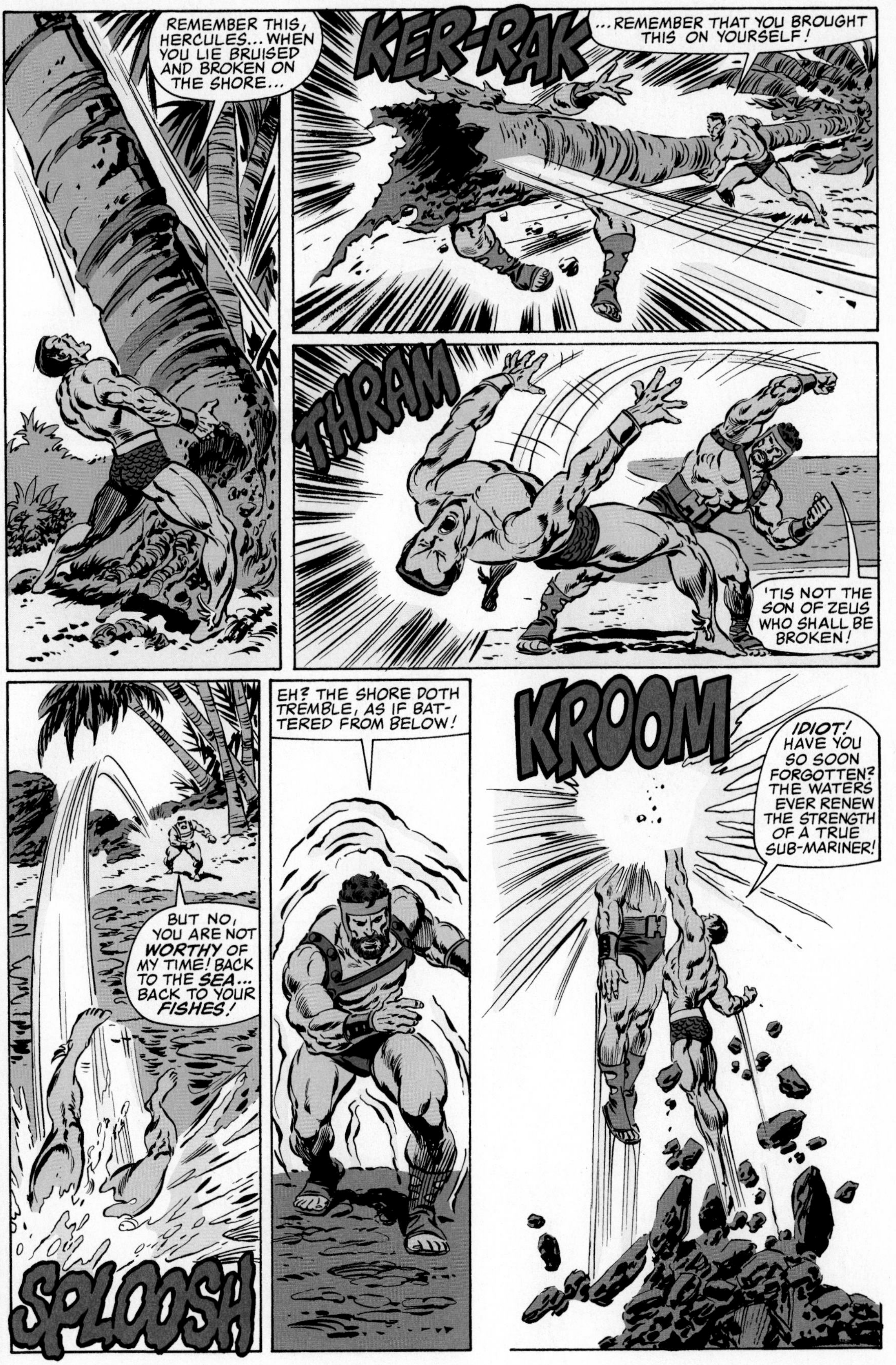
REMEMBER THIS, HERCULES... WHEN YOU LIE BRUISED AND BROKEN ON THE SHORE...
KER-RAK
...REMEMBER THAT YOU BROUGHT THIS ON YOURSELF!
THRAM
'TIS NOT THE SON OF ZEUS WHO SHALL BE BROKEN!
BUT NO, YOU ARE NOT WORTHY OF MY TIME! BACK TO THE SEA... BACK TO YOUR FISHES!
SPLOOSH
EH? THE SHORE DOTH TREMBLE, AS IF BATTERED FROM BELOW!
KROOM
IDIOT! HAVE YOU SO SOON FORGOTTEN? THE WATERS EVER RENEW THE STRENGTH OF A TRUE SUB-MARINER!

DEEP WITHIN THE BASE...

AA-OO-GAH AA-OO-GAH

WHAT ON EARTH--?!?

HEY, WHERE'S HERCULES?

WHILE, ABOVE...

THE PRINCE OF POWER SHALL *NEVER* YIELD!

NOR WILL I!

SUDDENLY...

STOP!!

≡WHUNGH!≡

I WON'T LET YOU WRECK THIS BASE!

THE *LIGHTNING* ...TAKES ON HUMAN FORM! WHAT KIND OF WOMAN WIELDS SUCH POWER?

AWAY WITH YOU, CAPTAIN MARVEL! I NEED NO *HELP* TO FIGHT NAMOR!

NOBODY'S FIGHTING ANYBODY UNTIL I GET SOME ANSWERS!

THERE'LL BE TIME ENOUGH FOR *ANSWERS* WHEN THE BATTLE'S WON!

AYE! SO BE IT!

HOLD IT! HEY!

THE LADY SAID, "HOLD IT!"

KLANG

CAPTAIN AMERICA! YOU DARE UPSET MY FOOTING WITH YOUR SHIELD?!

CONSIDER YOURSELF LUCKY, HERC. CAPTAIN MARVEL WOULD'VE DONE A LOT WORSE, IF SHE HADN'T CAUGHT SIGHT OF US!

EASY, NAMOR-- LET'S KEEP OUR COOL!

I THOUGHT YOU DIDN'T WANT ANY TROUBLE!

I DIDN'T! IT WAS YOUR FRIEND HERCULES WHO STARTED THIS!

OH, NO! HERCULES ...YOU DIDN'T!

HAH-HA-HA! AYE, WASP... I DID!

BUT...WHY?

I DID NOT LIKE THE DOLEFUL LOOK OF THIS SUB-MARINER. THE NAMOR I HAD FOUGHT IN TIMES PAST WAS A MIGHTY MAN... A SOUL TRULY WORTHY OF THE GIFT OF BATTLE.

I WANTED TO PROVE TO MYSELF THAT HE STILL WAS WORTHY...

...AYE, AND I WANTED TO PROVE IT TO HIM, AS WELL!

YOU MEAN, YOU DID THIS MERELY TO...

...HEH-HEH... HAH-HA...

HA-HAH-HAH-HA!

HERCULES, I BELIEVE I SEE THE LOGIC IN YOUR ACTIONS, MAD AS THEY WERE!

AH, I THOUGHT THE GIFT OF BATTLE WOULD TEAR YOUR MIND FROM YOUR SORROWS.

YES, YOUR "GIFT" WAS MOST... DISTRACT-ING! BUT NOW, IT'S ONLY FAIR THAT I GIVE YOU A GIFT, AS WELL!

UH-OH! NOW WHAT?

JUST A FEW HOURS LATER...

NAMOR, MY FRIEND, THIS GIFT OF YOURS RIVALS EVEN MINE OWN FOR SHEER PLEASURE!

I'LL SAY! I HAVEN'T BEEN TO A CLAM BAKE IN YEARS!

NAMOR ALWAYS FINDS THE BEST SEAFOOD!

EAT UP, EVERYONE! THERE'S STILL PLENTY OF STEAMERS... MORE LOBSTER, TOO!

REALLY? I DIDN'T KNOW YOU WERE FROM NEW ORLEANS.

22

**There you go, Wasp!**

**So tell me...do you think you're interested in using Hydrobase?**

**Well, honestly, I'm not sure. Your facilities are excellent... but there's still an accessibility problem. If we had some way of getting to and from the base easily--!**

**That may not be an insurmountable problem, Jan. I think I can come up with a way of transporting us between here and the mansion that will satisfy our needs... and the FAA!**

**Eh? What has become of Namor? Not off by himself brooding again, is he?**

**Don't worry about Namor, Hercules. He and Cap went off to have a private talk.**

**Yeah, they're probably trading old war stories or something.**

**...I've escaped the drudgery of the throne...gained a new freedom... but at considerable cost.**

**So, what do you intend to do with the rest of your life? You've gotten a lot of mileage since the war, but you look like you still have a good many years ahead of you.**

**Yes, my mother's people are a long-lived race. I don't know...**

**...two-thirds of this world are covered with water. That's a lot of territory to roam.**

**That's it? You're just going to wander?**

23

NAMOR, I'D HATE TO SEE YOU *SQUANDER* YOUR LIFE LIKE THAT. EVERYONE NEEDS A *PURPOSE* IN LIFE!

BUT I AM NOT "EVERYONE"! MY LINEAGE IS OF BOTH THE *LAND* AND THE *SEA*, BUT I AM ACCEPTED BY *NEITHER*. I NO LONGER HAVE A PLACE AMONG MY *MOTHER'S* PEOPLE--

--AND THE SURFACE WORLD, MY *FATHER'S* WORLD, HAS WANTED NO PART OF ME. WHAT ELSE IS THERE FOR ME TO DO, BUT WANDER?

YOU COULD BECOME AN *AVENGER*.

YOU'RE NOT SERIOUS!

I'M *VERY* SERIOUS! ALL RIGHT, GRANTED YOU'RE NO CHOIR BOY... BUT I HAPPEN TO KNOW THAT YOU'VE ALSO DONE A LOT OF *GOOD* FOR THIS WORLD, MORE THAN MOST OF ITS PEOPLE REALIZE!

I REMEMBER HOW WE FOUGHT OUR WAY ACROSS OCCUPIED EUROPE IN WORLD WAR II. YOU PUT ALL YOUR MIGHT INTO HELPING US TOPPLE THE NAZI MENACE.

WE COULD'VE BEATEN HITLER *WITHOUT* YOU... BUT IT WOULD'VE COST A LOT MORE LIVES.

YOUR MEMORY IS BETTER THAN MOST, CAP. THE WAR WAS A *LONG* TIME AGO. PEOPLE TEND TO REMEMBER WHAT THEY WANT...

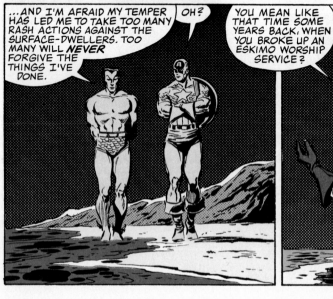

...AND I'M AFRAID MY TEMPER HAS LED ME TO TAKE TOO MANY RASH ACTIONS AGAINST THE SURFACE-DWELLERS. TOO MANY WILL *NEVER* FORGIVE THE THINGS I'VE DONE.

OH?

YOU MEAN LIKE THAT TIME SOME YEARS BACK, WHEN YOU BROKE UP AN ESKIMO WORSHIP SERVICE?

I VAGUELY RECALL DOING SOMETHING LIKE THAT. HOW DID *YOU* KNOW--?

ONE OF THE ESKIMOS TOLD THE STORY TO PERSONNEL AT A U.S. WEATHER STATION... I GOT ALL THE DETAILS A FEW MONTHS LATER. THAT'S HOW I KNOW YOU HURLED THEIR ICE-COVERED *TOTEM* OUT TO SEA.

"BUT THE STORY DOESN'T STOP THERE. YOU SEE, THE *OBJECT* IN THAT BLOCK OF ICE WAS A *MAN*... A MAN WHO'D ACCIDENTALLY BEEN THROWN INTO A STATE OF *SUSPENDED ANIMATION!*"

"AS THE TOTEM DRIFTED INTO THE WARM WATERS OF THE GULF STREAM, ITS ICY SHEATH SLOWLY MELTED."

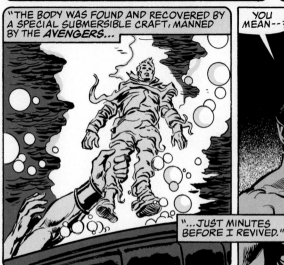

"THE BODY WAS FOUND AND RECOVERED BY A SPECIAL SUBMERSIBLE CRAFT, MANNED BY THE *AVENGERS*..."

"...JUST MINUTES BEFORE I REVIVED."

YOU MEAN--?

*YOU'RE* RESPONSIBLE FOR MY BEING HERE. I *OWE* YOU FOR THAT.

*NOW*, WILL YOU LET ME PUT YOUR NAME IN NOMINATION FOR AVENGERS MEMBERSHIP?

CAP... I...

...I WOULD BE *HONORED.*

NEXT ISSUE: THE SUB-MARINER'S FIRST MISSION AS AN *AVENGER*-- AND THE MOST UNEXPECTED RETURN OF ALL! WHATEVER YOU DO, DON'T MISS *AVENGERS #263* FOR THE STARTLING SECRET OF... *"WHAT LURKS BELOW!"*

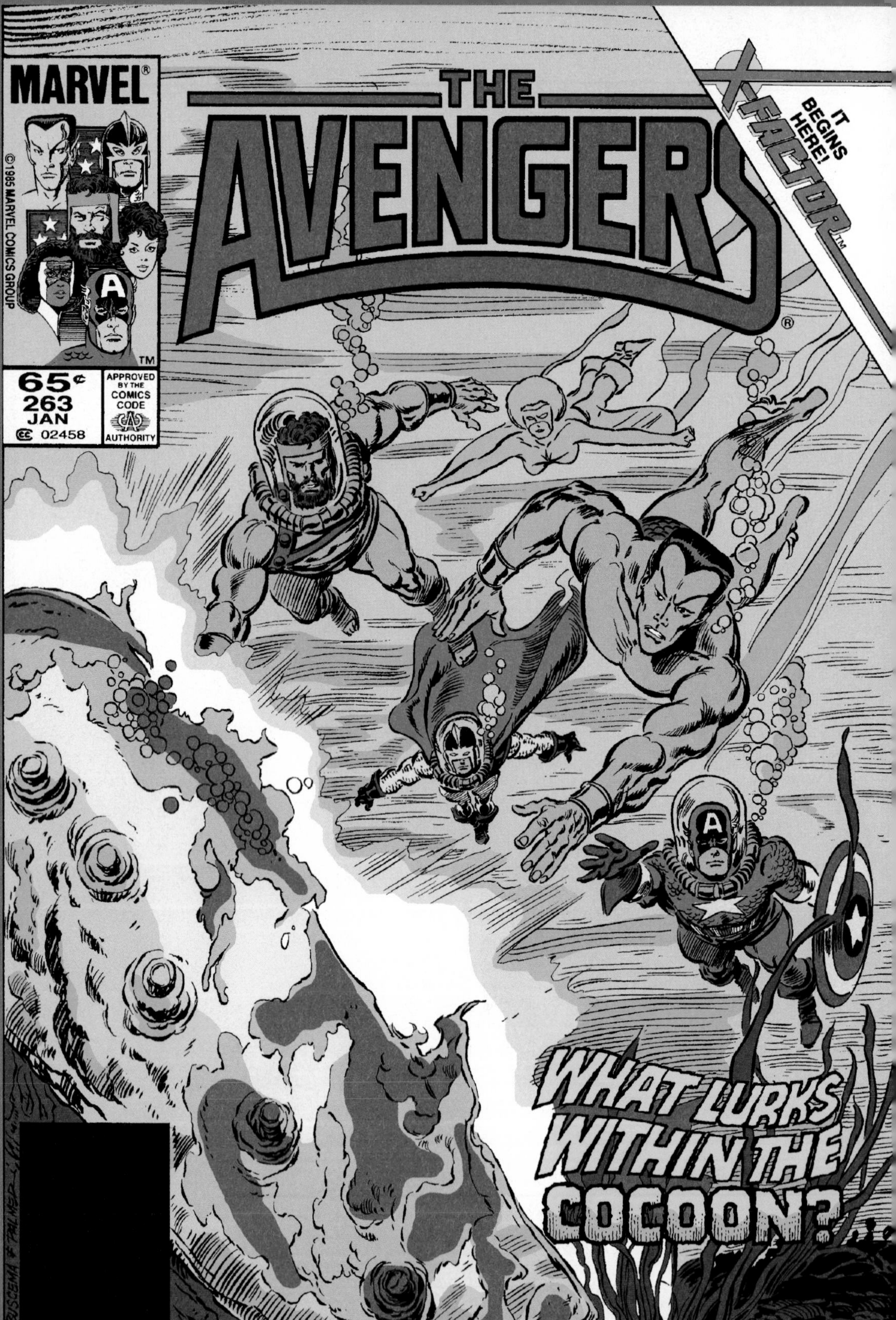

MARVEL®
©1985 MARVEL COMICS GROUP
THE AVENGERS®
IT BEGINS HERE!
X-FACTOR™
65¢
263
JAN
02458
APPROVED BY THE COMICS CODE AUTHORITY
WHAT LURKS WITHIN THE COCOON?...

JFK INTERNATIONAL AIRPORT...

TOWER, THIS IS CHARTER-AIR BETA-5-NINER... STILL WAITING CLEARANCE FOR *TAKEOFF.*

ROGER, BETA-5-NINER... JUST KEEP YOUR SHIRTS ON. WE'LL GET TO YOU.

"WE'LL GET TO YOU." I HATE BEING MADE TO *WAIT* LIKE COMMON RABBLE.

WILL YOU SHUT UP, *MORLAK?* ONCE OUR NEW PROJECT IS UNDERWAY, NO ONE WILL EVER BE ABLE TO MAKE YOU WAIT AGAIN!

IF WE CAN GET IT UNDERWAY, *ZOTA!*

DOUBTS FROM *YOU, SHINSKI?*

NOT ABOUT OUR ABILITY TO MAKE OUR PROJECT WORK... WE OF THE *ENCLAVE* POSSESS THE GREATEST *MINDS* ALIVE TODAY! THE CONTENTS OF THIS CRATE ALONE WILL MAKE US *MASTERS* OF THIS UNWORTHY WORLD!

NO, I AM AFRAID THAT WE WILL BE STOPPED BEFORE WE CAN REACH OUR *NEW RETREAT!*

YOUR FACES ARE ON *WANTED POSTERS* AROUND THE WORLD -- AND YOU WERE NONE TOO CAREFUL IN ACQUIRING THIS PLANE! WHAT IF YOU WERE *SPOTTED?*

WE HAVE BEEN KEPT WAITING HERE FAR LONGER THAN TRAFFIC WOULD REQUIRE. THE AUTHORITIES COULD BE CLOSING IN ON US EVEN NOW!

YOU'RE *PARANOID,* SHINSKI!

MAYBE NOT, ZOTA. *LOOK...*

"...POLICE VANS! AND THEY'RE HEADED THIS WAY!

"GET US OUT OF HERE, ZOTA! *NOW!*"

ROGER STERN
WRITER

JOHN BUSCEMA
BREAKDOWNS

TOM PALMER
FINISHER

JIM NOVAK
LETTERER

CHRISTIE SCHEELE
COLORIST

MARK GRUENWALD
EDITOR

JIM SHOOTER
EDITOR-IN-CHIEF

BETA-5-NINER--YOU ARE *NOT* CLEARED FOR TAKE OFF!

BETA-5-NINER, DO YOU *COPY?*

BETA-5--! FOR PETE'S SAKE, *STOP!*

YOU'RE HEADED RIGHT FOR A 747!!

DESPERATELY, ZOTA PULLS HIS JET INTO A SHARP, BANKING *TURN*, BUT...

KRRNNG

HOPELESSLY OUT OF CONTROL, THE PLANE SLAMS TO THE GROUND -- SKIDDING ACROSS THE RUNWAY AND OUT INTO JAMAICA BAY!

IN SECONDS, THREE QUARTERS OF ITS RUPTURED HULL HAS SUNK BENEATH THE MURKY WATERS.

THIS IS AGENT FREEMAN! I WANT *AMBULANCES* AND A DREDGING CREW -- AND I WANT 'EM NOW!

I'LL NEED *DIVERS*, TOO! THERE'S NO TELLING WHAT IS ABOARD THAT PLANE!

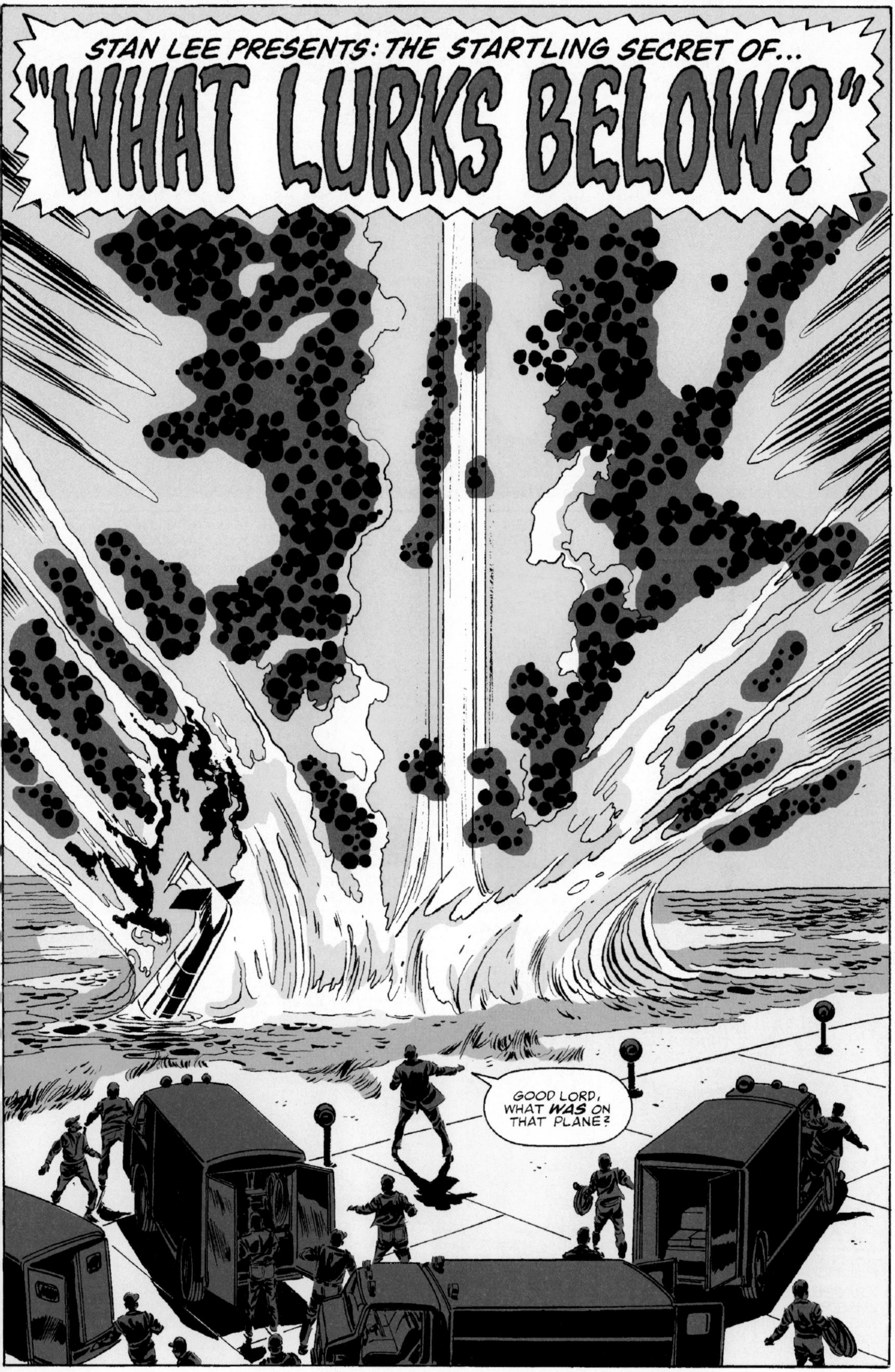
STAN LEE PRESENTS: THE STARTLING SECRET OF...
"WHAT LURKS BELOW?"
GOOD LORD, WHAT WAS ON THAT PLANE?

AT THAT MOMENT, IN THE FIFTH AVENUE HEAD-QUARTERS OF EARTH'S MIGHTIEST SUPER-TEAM...

TELL ME I HEARD YOU *WRONG!* TELL ME YOU DIDN'T JUST SAY THAT YOU INTEND TO MAKE THE *SUB-MARINER* AN AVENGER!

I DIDN'T *THINK* OUR GOVERNMENT LIASON WOULD TAKE THE NEWS TOO WELL!

I KNOW THAT NAMOR HASN'T ALWAYS BEEN ON THE *BEST OF TERMS* WITH THE SURFACE WORLD, MR. SIKORSKI... BUT HERE'S OUR CHANCE TO *CHANGE* THAT.

BUT, *CAP...*

THERE SHOULDN'T BE ANY PROBLEMS WITH *IMMIGRATION...* NAMOR'S FATHER WAS AN AMERICAN CITIZEN. AND HE *DID* DEFEND THESE SHORES DURING WORLD WAR II.

BUT...

MR. SIKORSKI, YOU KNOW THAT AS LONG AS OUR *SECURITY CLEARANCE* IS IN LIMBO, THE FEDERAL GOVERNMENT HASN'T ANY *SAY* IN WHAT WE DO! WE DIDN'T EVEN HAVE TO INFORM YOU OF OUR NEW MEMBER... BUT WE DID.

SCORE ONE FOR YOU, JAN!

THIS WON'T MAKE MY JOB ANY *EASIER,* WASP! I'VE BEEN WORKING FOR *WEEKS* TO FIND A WORKABLE FORMULA FOR RESTORING AVENGERS PRIORITY--!

WE APPRECIATE THAT, SIR. BUT I THINK NAMOR WILL WORK OUT.

FROM FIRM TO REASSURING IN LESS THAN A MINUTE...

...JANET VAN DYNE, YOU *ARE* A WONDER! I WONDER IF THERE'S ROOM ON YOUR CALENDER FOR DINNER WITH AN ADMIRING BLACK KNIGHT?

YOU SEE? *CAPTAIN AMERICA* VOUCHES FOR THE SUB-MARINER. I'M SURE YOU HAVE NOTHING TO *WORRY* ABOUT!

THREE LEVELS ABOVE...

AND *HERE*, NAMOR, BE THE PRIVATE QUARTERS OF AVENGERS-IN-RESIDENCE.

WHAT...OFF THIS COMMON HALL?

THE, UH, ROOMS ARE VERY *SPACIOUS*--

--AND CAN BE *DECO-RATED* TO YOUR LIKING!

WELL! SO I *SEE*!

THESE QUARTERS ARE INDEED NOTEWORTHY... SIMPLE, BUT WITH A CLASSIC ELEGANCE. YES, *THIS* WILL SUIT ME FINE, JUST AS IS!

NO DOUBT IT *WOULD*, WERE IT NOT ALREADY SPOKEN FOR NAMOR. 'TIS *MINE*!

AND I *LIKE* IT A GREAT DEAL, HERCULES. OF COURSE, YOU WOULDN'T MIND *SWITCHING* ROOMS!

YES, I *WOULD* MIND.

I'M SURE THAT--!

SEE *HERE*, HERCULES--!

NO, *YOU* SEE HERE--!

WITH A SHRUG OF RESIGNATION, *CAPTAIN MARVEL* TRANSFORMS HER PHYSICAL BODY INTO *PHOTONIC LIGHT*, AND...

I'VE ALREADY BROKEN UP *ONE* FIGHT BETWEEN THOSE TWO-- I DON'T FEEL LIKE MAKING A *CAREER* OUT OF IT!

31

I WONDER IF MAKING THE SUB-MARINER AN AVENGER WAS SUCH A GOOD IDEA. NAMOR CERTAINLY ISN'T GOING OUT OF HIS WAY TO *FIT IN.*

ATOP A HIGH TOWER, THE GOLDEN AVENGER WILLS HERSELF BACK TO HUMAN FORM...

MAYBE IT'S JUST *ME.*

NAMOR WAS *BORN* WITH THOSE INCREDIBLE AMPHIBIAN POWERS OF HIS, AND RAISED AS THE "AVENGING SON" OF ATLANTEAN ROYALTY. I SUPPOSE I CAN'T EXPECT HIM TO ACT LIKE THE *REST* OF US...

...BUT HE'D STILL BE A LITTLE EASIER TO TAKE IF HE DIDN'T ACT SO HIGH-AND-MIGHTY!

BACK HOME IN NEW ORLEANS, SUPER-BEINGS DON'T GET THE *MEDIA* COVERAGE THEY DO HERE IN NEW YORK--

--BUT EVEN SO, I'VE HEARD MORE THAN A FEW STORIES ABOUT THE SUB-MARINER... *NONE* OF THEM *FAVORABLE!*

OH, I'M PROBABLY WORRYING ABOUT NOTHING! AFTER ALL, *CAPTAIN AMERICA* NOMINATED NAMOR, AND I'VE NEVER HAD REASON TO DOUBT CAP'S JUDGMENT BEFORE, BUT...

...I DON'T KNOW THAT I FULLY *TRUST* THE SUB-MARINER.

JUST THEN...

WHAT ON EARTH--?!?

THAT PLUME OF ENERGY MUST HAVE SHOT A *MILE* OR MORE INTO THE SKY.

AND IT LOOKED TO BE COMING RIGHT FROM THE MIDDLE OF--

--JFK AIRPORT!

EXCUSE ME... I'M CAPTAIN MARVEL OF THE AVENGERS. ARE YOU IN CHARGE HERE? WHAT'S GOING ON?

UH...Y-YES. YES, I AM. AS TO WHAT'S GOING ON, I WISH I KNEW.

I'M *DEREK FREEMAN*, FBI. SOME FUGITIVES CRASHED INTO THE BAY DURING AN ATTEMPT TO AVOID CAPTURE... I BELIEVE YOU KNEW THEM AS THE *ENCLAVE*.

THE ENCLAVE?! YES, I WAS IN ON THEIR *FIRST* CAPTURE.* ARE THEY STILL ALIVE?

THEY'RE THE *LEAST* OF MY WORRIES NOW, THOUGH. I DON'T KNOW WHAT ALL CARGO THEY HAD IN THEIR PLANE, BUT AFTER IT SPILLED INTO THE BAY, THOSE ENERGY GEYSERS STARTED ERUPTING EVERY FEW MINUTES.

I SENT A COUPLE OF DIVERS DOWN JUST BEFORE THE LAST ONE. I HOPE THEY'RE ALL RIGHT.

AW, DON'T WORRY 'BOUT THOSE *TWO*, MR. FREEMAN! THEY'LL PROB'LY BE BREAKING THE SURFACE--

YES. THEY WERE IN PRETTY BAD SHAPE WHEN WE FISHED THEM OUT, BUT I THINK THEY'LL *LIVE*.

*AVENGERS ANNUAL #12.

FOOOSH

--ANY MINUTE NOW. I... HOLY GEEZ--!

NELSON, ARE YOU OKAY?

Y-YEAH, I THINK SO. HOW'S CARTER?

YOUR BUDDY HAD THE WIND KNOCKED OUT OF HIM, BUT HE'LL BE ALL RIGHT.

YOU TWO SHOT OUT OF THE WATER LIKE A COUPLE OF POLARIS MISSILES. WHAT HAPPENED DOWN THERE?

I'M NOT SURE. WE FOUND...SOMETHING. IT SEEMED TO BE THE SOURCE OF THAT CRAZY ENERGY. WHEN CARTER POKED IT WITH A PROBE, THERE WAS THIS VOICE...

...IT WASN'T LIKE ANY VOICE I'D EVER HEARD!

IT WARNED US TO KEEP AWAY. THEN, THE NEXT THING I KNEW, SOMETHING GRABBED US... AND THREW US OUT OF THE WATER!

I'D SAY THIS WAS OUT OF THE FBI'S LEAGUE, AGENT FREEMAN. I SUGGEST YOU CALL THE AVENGERS AT ONCE! TELL THEM I'M CHECKING THIS OUT!

WHEW!! THAT'S ONE TAKE-CHARGE LADY!

THIS BAY'S A LOT *DEEPER* THAN IT LOOKS. MURKY DOWN HERE... BUT STILL, I'D BETTER HOLD MY LIGHT BACK TO *"LOW BEAMS"*--

--IF I WANT TO SNEAK UP ON THIS *WHATEVER-IT-IS.*

WELL, NOW! WHAT HAVE WE HERE? A BIG OL', BUSTED-UP *CRATE*--

--WITH WHAT LOOKS LIKE THE SHATTERED REMAINS OF SOME SORT OF HEAVY *GLASS TANK* INSIDE. BUT WAS IT SHATTERED ON IMPACT, OR DID SOMETHING *BREAK OUT?*

EH? THAT LIGHT'S NOT COMING FROM ME! WHERE--?

AH-HAH, HERE'S THE *SOURCE* OF ALL THAT ENERGY!

BUT WHAT IS IT?

**WHATEVER** IT IS, IT'S CERTAINLY A MESS! IT ALMOST LOOKS LIKE A **COCOON** FOR A GIANT-SIZED BUTTERFLY!

THAT LITTLE ENERGY CRACKLE IT'S EMITTING SEEMS TO BE ON THE **WANE**. MAYBE IT'S GROWING **DORMANT**.

WELL, WHATEVER IT'S DOING, I'LL FEEL A LOT BETTER AFTER I SEE WHAT'S UNDER THAT **COVERING**.

WITH A SINGLE, PRACTICED THOUGHT, CAPTAIN MARVEL TRANSFORMS HER LIGHT ENERGY--

--INTO A STREAM OF **X-RAYS**. BUT, AS THE SENTIENT RAYS TRY TO PIERCE THE SURFACE OF THE "COCOON", THEY MEET UNEXPECTED **RESISTANCE**.

NO...**NO**!

KEEP AWAY!

WH-WHAT **IS** THIS THING?! IT NOT ONLY REPELLED MY X-RAY BOMBARDMENT, IT'S TURNED ME PHYSICAL!

LEAVE ME ALONE!

THIS FORCE...IS KEEPING ME FROM **CHANGING**! AND IT'S NOT LETTING GO!

LEAVE... ME... ALONE!

BLASTED VOICE IS DRIVING ME CRAZY! G-GOT TO BREAK FREE ...OR I'LL DROWN.

UHN? THE FORCE... IS WEAKENING.

CAN'T CONCENTRATE ENOUGH TO CHANGE. MUST... GET...

...**AWAY**! HOOWAAGH! ≡ KAUFF-KAUFF≡

ELSEWHERE...

HAH-HA-HA! THAT'S IT, AVENGERS! FLY AWAY WHILE YOU CAN!

IDIOTS! IT WAS SO EASY TO TRAIN A SURVEILLANCE CAMERA ON YOUR FAMOUS MANSION!

I STILL DON'T SEE WHAT GOOD THAT CAMERA DOES US, MELTER!

THAT'S WHY YOU'LL NEVER BE MORE THAN HIRED MUSCLE, KEEGAN! BUT I'LL EXPLAIN ONE MORE TIME! BY KEEPING WATCH LIKE THIS--

--I'LL BE ABLE TO TELL WHEN THE WHOLE TEAM HAS ASSEMBLED IN THE MANSION. WHEN I'M CERTAIN THAT THEY'RE ALL THERE, I'LL USE MY IMPROVED MELTING RAY TO DESTROY THEM-- MANSION AND ALL!

AFTER I'VE DESTROYED THE AVENGERS, NO ONE WILL EVER LAUGH AT THE MELTER AGAIN! ONCE I STRAP ON THE RAY PROJECTOR--

--I'LL BECOME TOTALLY... WHA--?

K-KEEGAN?!?

YES, MELTER...THAT'S THE REAL KEEGAN. I'VE GOT YOUR MELTING DEVICE RIGHT HERE!

BUT THAT'S NOT ALL I HAVE!

SPAK

PLM

NEEYAKK!

JUSTICE IS SERVED!

KRUNK

37

WHILE, AT JFK...

THE *AVENGERS!* AWRIGHT, NOW WE'LL GET SOME ACTION!

HEY, TED... DO *YOU* SEE WHAT I SEE?

YEAH... THE *SUB-MARINER!* WHAT'S THAT *CREEP* DOIN' WITH THE AVENGERS?!

SHORTLY...

...AND THEN, THE DIVERS WADED IN AND HELPED ME TO SHORE.

MARVEL, YOU SAID THIS THING LOOKED LIKE AN OLD *MATTRESS* COVERED WITH *BARNACLES?*

YES...YOUR SKETCH IS VERY CLOSE!

I WAS *AFRAID* OF THAT. THIS ISN'T THE *FIRST* TIME THE ENCLAVE HAS CREATED SUCH A THING.

THE ENCLAVE HAS TRIED ON AT LEAST *TWO* PREVIOUS OCCASIONS TO GENETICALLY ENGINEER A RACE OF *SUPER-BEINGS...* BOTH TIMES INVOLVED COCOONS MUCH LIKE THE ONE YOU DESCRIBED!

*MARVEL TWO-IN-ONE #61.

**FANTASTIC FOUR #66-67.

"ACCORDING TO INFORMATION COMPILED BY THE FANTASTIC FOUR, THE MOST RECENT ATTEMPT YIELDED A MYSTERIOUS WOMAN KNOWN ONLY AS *HER*\*--BUT THEIR FIRST EXPERIMENT\*\* CREATED THE MAN WHO BECAME *ADAM WARLOCK!*

"BOTH HER AND WARLOCK REJECTED THE ENCLAVE'S ATTEMPTS TO SUBVERT THEIR WILLS. BUT THERE'S NO WAY OF KNOWING HOW THIS NEW BEING IS DEVELOPING DOWN THERE!"

YOU'RE RIGHT, CAP! WE COULD HAVE OUR HANDS *FULL* WITH THIS CREATURE. WE'D BETTER--!

THERE'S NOTHING TO *WORRY* ABOUT, WASP! THIS IS AN UNDERWATER MENACE-- I'LL HANDLE IT!

I WISH IT WERE THAT *SIMPLE*, NAMOR... BUT FIRST--! NAMOR?

NAMOR! COME BACK HERE!

OF ALL THE *NERVE*--!

HE IGNORED A DIRECT ORDER! WHEN WE GET BACK TO THE MANSION, I SAY WE BRING HIM UP ON *CHARGES!*

EASY, KNIGHT! SURE, NAMOR'S OUT OF LINE, BUT IT *HAS* BEEN A LONG TIME SINCE HE'S BEEN PART OF A *REAL TEAM!* HE'LL GET USED TO FOLLOWING ORDERS!

I HOPE YOU'RE RIGHT, CAP. ON SOMETHING AS *SERIOUS* AS THIS, WE CAN'T AFFORD ANY SCREW--

--UPS!

FOOSH

WHAT THE --?!?

**Panel 1:**
WHY, MR. SUB-MARINER-- DON'T TELL ME YOU WERE THROWN OUT OF THE WATER BY THAT ITTY-BITTY *COCOON!*

I...

**Panel 2:**
LOOK, I'LL SAY THIS *ONCE*...YOU CAN BE PART OF THE *TEAM*, OR YOU CAN *LEAVE!*

NICE OF YOU TO REJOIN US, NAMOR!

SAVE YOUR SARCASM, CAP. I KNOW WHEN I HAVE BEEN *HUMBLED.*

**Panel 3:**
IN THE AVENGERS, WE WORK *TOGETHER*, NAMOR! REMEMBER THAT NEXT TIME, BEFORE YOU GO OFF HALF-COCKED!

MY ATOMIC STEED'S ALL READY TO GO! WHAT'S THE *PLAN?*

**Panel 4:**
WE WERE JUST DISCUSSING THAT, DANE. THE ENCLAVERS MIGHT BE CONSCIOUS BY NOW, AND WILLING TO TALK. I COULD FLY TO THE HOSPITAL AND CHECK.

GOOD IDEA, C.M. IT WOULD HELP IF WE KNEW MORE ABOUT WHAT WE'RE UP AGAINST...HOW IT WAS CREATED ...WHAT *WEAK SPOTS* IT MIGHT HAVE!

**Panel 5:**
AGREED. C.M., GO FIND OUT ALL YOU CAN, AS FAST AS YOU CAN!

AND WHAT OF THE *REST* OF US? ARE WE TO JUST STAND IDLY BY?

**Panel 6:**
HARDLY! AS LONG AS THAT CREATURE IS ACTIVE DOWN THERE, WE DON'T HAVE THE LUXURY OF *WAITING!*

MOMENTS LATER...

DOES EVERYBODY *READ* ME? LET'S HAVE A COMMUNICATIONS CHECK.

I READ YOU, WASP.

CHECK. LOUD AND CLEAR.

YES, MY RADIO *EAR-PLUG* ALLOWS ME TO HEAR YOU ALL QUITE WELL. I ASSUME MY *THROAT-MIKE* TRANSMITS AS CLEARLY.

AYE, NAMOR. BUT ENOUGH TALK... LEAD US TO THIS *BEAST!*

IT'S HARDLY A BEAST, HERCULES-- AT LEAST, NOT IN THE USUAL SENSE. THERE'S OUR QUARRY DEAD AHEAD.

ALL RIGHT, AVENGERS, YOU KNOW WHAT TO DO.

SLOWLY, CAUTIOUSLY, THE FIVE HEROES SURROUND THE EERIE COCOON...

THIS IS THE GREAT THREAT? IT'S LETTING US GET AWFULLY *CLOSE!*

ITS ENERGIES BUT *FLICKER* THROUGH A DOZEN RIPS AND TEARS. I CANNOT BELIEVE THAT THIS BESODDEN *LUMP* WAS RESPONSIBLE FOR--!

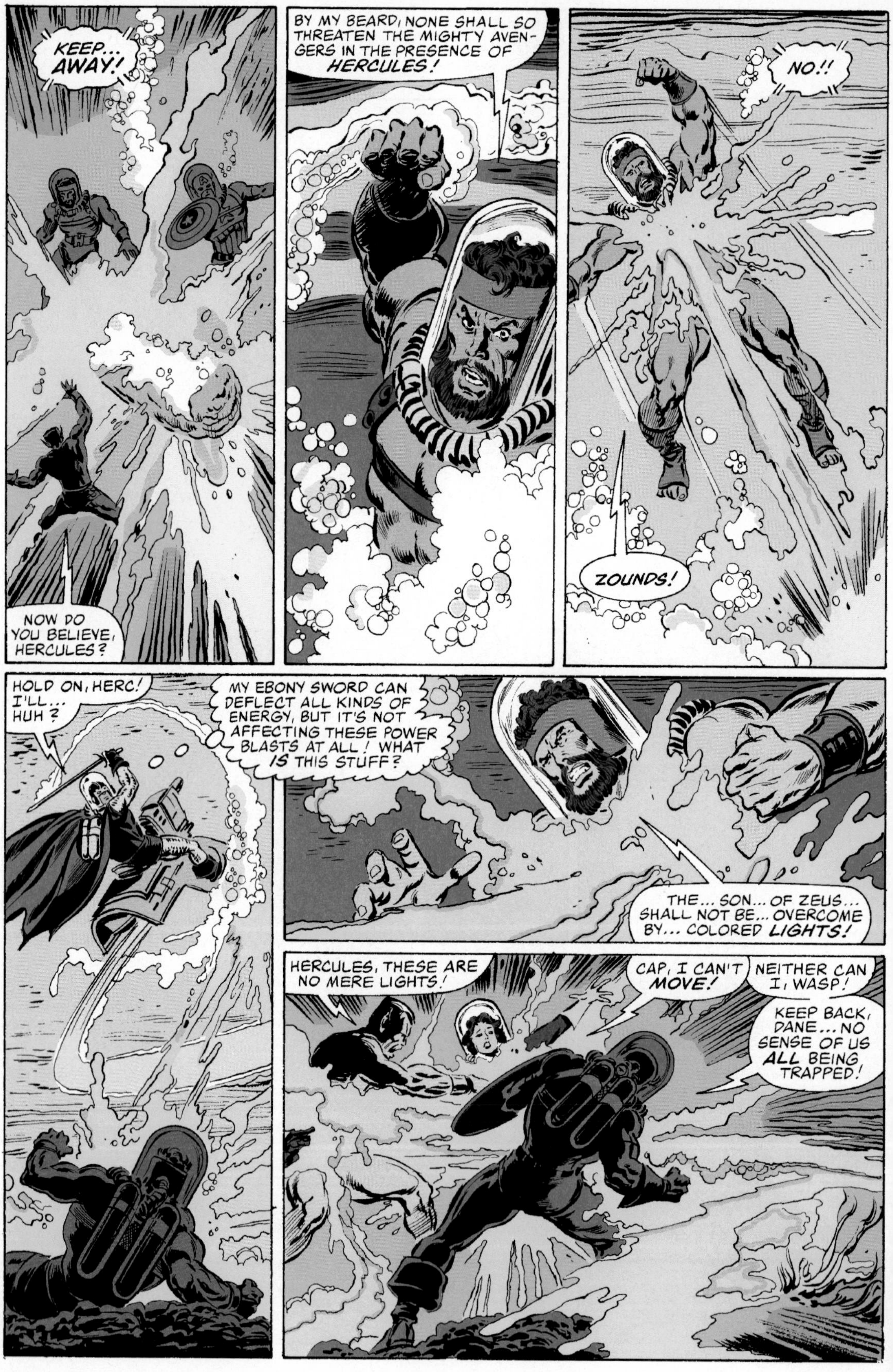
KEEP... AWAY!
NOW DO YOU BELIEVE, HERCULES?
BY MY BEARD, NONE SHALL SO THREATEN THE MIGHTY AVENGERS IN THE PRESENCE OF HERCULES!
NO!!
ZOUNDS!
HOLD ON, HERC! I'LL... HUH ?
MY EBONY SWORD CAN DEFLECT ALL KINDS OF ENERGY, BUT IT'S NOT AFFECTING THESE POWER BLASTS AT ALL! WHAT IS THIS STUFF?
THE... SON... OF ZEUS... SHALL NOT BE... OVERCOME BY... COLORED LIGHTS!
HERCULES, THESE ARE NO MERE LIGHTS!
CAP, I CAN'T MOVE!
NEITHER CAN I, WASP!
KEEP BACK, DANE... NO SENSE OF US ALL BEING TRAPPED!

AT THAT MOMENT, MILES AWAY...

PROFESSOR SHINSKI? CAN YOU HEAR ME?

UHNN... WHO...?

I'M CAPTAIN MARVEL. YOU MUST HELP ME.

YOUR PARTNERS ARE STILL UNCONSCIOUS... AND YOUR CREATION IS LOOSE AT THE BOTTOM OF JAMAICA BAY. I CAN'T PROMISE ANYTHING, BUT IF YOU'LL TELL ME ALL ABOUT IT, THE COURTS MIGHT GO EASIER ON YOU.

CREATION?

WHAT... CREATION?

IN THE COCOON. I FOUND THE SHATTERED CRATE IT ESCAPED FROM.

YOUNG LADY... THERE WAS NO COCOON IN ANY CRATE. MY ASSOCIATES AND I WERE NEARLY KILLED BY PREVIOUS COCOON CREATURES... WE KNEW BETTER THAN TO TRY SUCH A THING AGAIN.

THERE WAS ONE CRATE... IT HELD MY NEW DISCOVERY IN A SPECIAL GLASS TANK. EVEN IF THE CRATE AND TANK WERE SHATTERED... THERE'D BE NO THREAT.

IN THOSE WATERS, THE NEW COMPOUNDS WOULD BE RENDERED INERT... HARMLESS...

HE'S LOST CONSCIOUSNESS AGAIN. I'M SURE HE WAS TELLING THE TRUTH-- HE WAS TOO OUT-OF-IT TO HAVE LIED.

BUT IF THE ENCLAVERS DIDN'T MAKE THAT THING, WHERE DID IT COME FROM?!

WHILE...

BAH! 'MIDST ALL THIS MUCK AND MIRE, 'TIS A *BATTLE* JUST TO GET *FOOTING*! BUT YET SHALL I OVERPOWER THIS FORCE!

HE'S DOING IT! THE OLYMPIAN IS ACTUALLY MAKING HEADWAY AGAINST THIS CRUSHING FORCE, WHILE I STAND *HELPLESS* IN ITS POWER!

HOW MUCH MORE MUST I BE HUMBLED?!

LISTEN UP, AVENGERS-- THIS FORCE BOLT SEEMS TO STOP ONLY MY *FORWARD* MOVEMENTS! AS I FALL BACK, ITS POWER *FADES OUT*!

SAME HERE, CAP! BACK OFF, EVERYBODY!

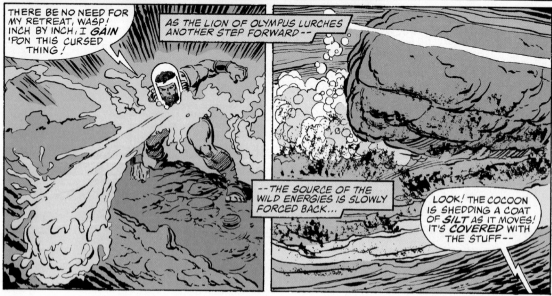

THERE BE NO NEED FOR MY RETREAT, WASP! INCH BY INCH, I *GAIN* 'PON THIS CURSED THING!

AS THE LION OF OLYMPUS LURCHES ANOTHER STEP FORWARD--

--THE SOURCE OF THE WILD ENERGIES IS SLOWLY FORCED BACK...

LOOK! THE COCOON IS SHEDDING A COAT OF *SILT* AS IT MOVES! IT'S *COVERED* WITH THE STUFF--

44

--BUT THE DEBRIS FROM THE *PLANE* IS STILL *CLEAN!*

OF COURSE, I SHOULD HAVE NOTICED SOONER! IT TAKES TIME FOR *THAT* MUCH SILT TO SETTLE ON AN OBJECT!

THEN THE COCOON COULDN'T HAVE COME FROM THE PLANE!

THAT *CONFIRMS* WHAT I'VE LEARNED. PROFESSOR SHINSKI CLAIMS THAT THE ENCLAVE HAD *NOTHING* TO DO WITH IT!

THEN WE'RE BACK TO SQUARE ONE. WHAT *IS* THIS THING?

*WHAT* IT IS MATTERS NOT! HERCULES SHALL O'ER-COME IT!

BUT, AS THE MAN-GOD CLOSES IN ON HIS TARGET...

NO...NO, *PLEASE!* GET BACK...STAY AWAY!

HAH! 'TIS *WEAKENING!*

HERCULES, YOU BIG LUNK, CAN'T YOU HEAR? IT'S *AFRAID!*

BACK OFF!

AND AS HERCULES HALF-TURNS TOWARD HIS GROUP'S LEADER, HE LOSES HIS FOOTING AND...

ZEUS--!!

CAP, COULD THIS THING HAVE JUST BEEN REACTING TO BEING *JOSTLED* AND *PROBED*--?

AND BEEN ACTING IN *SELF-DEFENSE?* THAT'S A DISTINCT POSSIBILITY, YES!

THEN WE HAVE TO CONVINCE IT THAT WE MEAN NO HARM. EVERYBODY STAY BACK.

THAT WEIRD VOICE WAS SOME SORT OF MENTAL PROJECTION ...CAN IT "HEAR" ME AS WELL? MAYBE IF I *CONCENTRATE*--!

HELLO? WE WON'T HURT YOU...WE WANT TO HELP!

HELP?

JAN, *NO!*

HOLD IT, DANE--

--I THINK SHE'S *ONTO* SOMETHING!

YES. WE'LL DO ALL WE CAN.

H-HELP... HELP... ME...

AVENGERS, COME HERE--BUT *SLOWLY!*

HELLO, CAN YOU HEAR ME?

NO USE...THE VOICE FADED AWAY AS THAT CRACKLING ENERGY DISAPPEARED. THIS OUTER COVER PEELS OFF LIKE OLD ROTTED *FABRIC.* I WONDER...

WHAT IN THE WORLD IS *THIS?!*

SO, ONE MYSTERY UNLOCKS TO SHOW YET *ANOTHER.* YOU'VE FOUND US A CHINESE PUZZLE!

LET'S HOPE IT'S *SOLVABLE,* NAMOR!

SHORTLY, BACK AT AVENGERS MANSION...

SO, SIR KNIGHT, WHAT MANNER OF BEAST *IS* THIS?

I WISH I HAD AN *ANSWER,* HERCULES. THE OUTER COVERING WAS JUST PART OF SOME OLD MATTRESS. THE THINGS THAT GET DUMPED IN THAT BAY--!

ANYWAY, THE CAPSULE ITSELF IS SOMETHING LIKE A *STASIS FIELD,* BUT IT DOESN'T *BEHAVE* LIKE ANY I'VE EVER ENCOUNTERED.

AND YOU HAVEN'T HEARD ANY MORE OF THAT *VOICE?*

NOT A PEEP. THERE HASN'T BEEN A SINGLE *LIFE-SIGN.* IT'S AS IF IT SWITCHED ITSELF *OFF.* IF ONLY WE KNEW WHERE IT CAME FROM!

I'VE CHECKED WITH SEVERAL SOURCES IN THE *INTELLIGENCE COMMUNITY,* BUT NONE WERE ABLE TO SHED MUCH LIGHT ON THAT. I KNOW THAT A *SPACE SHUTTLE* CRASHED INTO JAMAICA BAY A FEW YEARS BACK.

PERHAPS THE SHUTTLE PICKED THIS THING UP IN *SPACE.* CAPTAIN MARVEL'S CALLING NASA NOW, TO SEE IF THEY CAN TELL US MORE.

SUDDENLY, OVER THE INTER-COM...

NASA DOESN'T KNOW ANYTHING ABOUT OUR MYSTERY CAPSULE, CAP--

--BUT THE AIRPORT ADMINISTRATORS ARE ON THE LINE! THEY WANT US TO COORDINATE MOP-UP OPERATIONS WITH AGENT FREEMAN...JUST IN CASE THERE ARE ANY MORE SURPRISES!

THAT SHOULDN'T TAKE *ALL* OF US! OH, WELL...

TRANSFER THE CALL TO THE *MAIN ASSEMBLY,* C.M.

WILL DO!

47

THE LABORATORY DOOR WHISPERS *SHUT* BEHIND THE AVENGERS, LOCKING THE MYSTERIOUS CAPSULE AWAY FROM SIGHT.

THERE IS NO ONE TO OBSERVE THE *POWER* THAT SURGES FROM DEEP WITHIN THE OPAQUE CAPSULE, TURNING IT FIRST TRANSLUCENT--

--AND THEN NEARLY *TRANSPARENT.* NO ONE SEES THE BEAUTIFUL FORM WHICH LIES BENEATH ITS SURFACE ...NO ONE "HEARS" THE LAST VESTIGE OF A MENTAL CRY.

*SCOTT--!*

IN SECONDS, THE POWER FADES. THE CAPSULE AGAIN GROWS OPAQUE...AND *SILENT.*

AND THE YOUNG WOMAN THE WORLD ONCE KNEW AS *JEAN GREY* IS ONCE MORE HIDDEN FROM THE WORLD.

OUR STORY CONTINUES IN FANTASTIC FOUR #286 ...ON SALE ONE WEEK FROM NOW! WHATEVER YOU DO, DON'T MISS...

# "...LIKE A PHOENIX!"

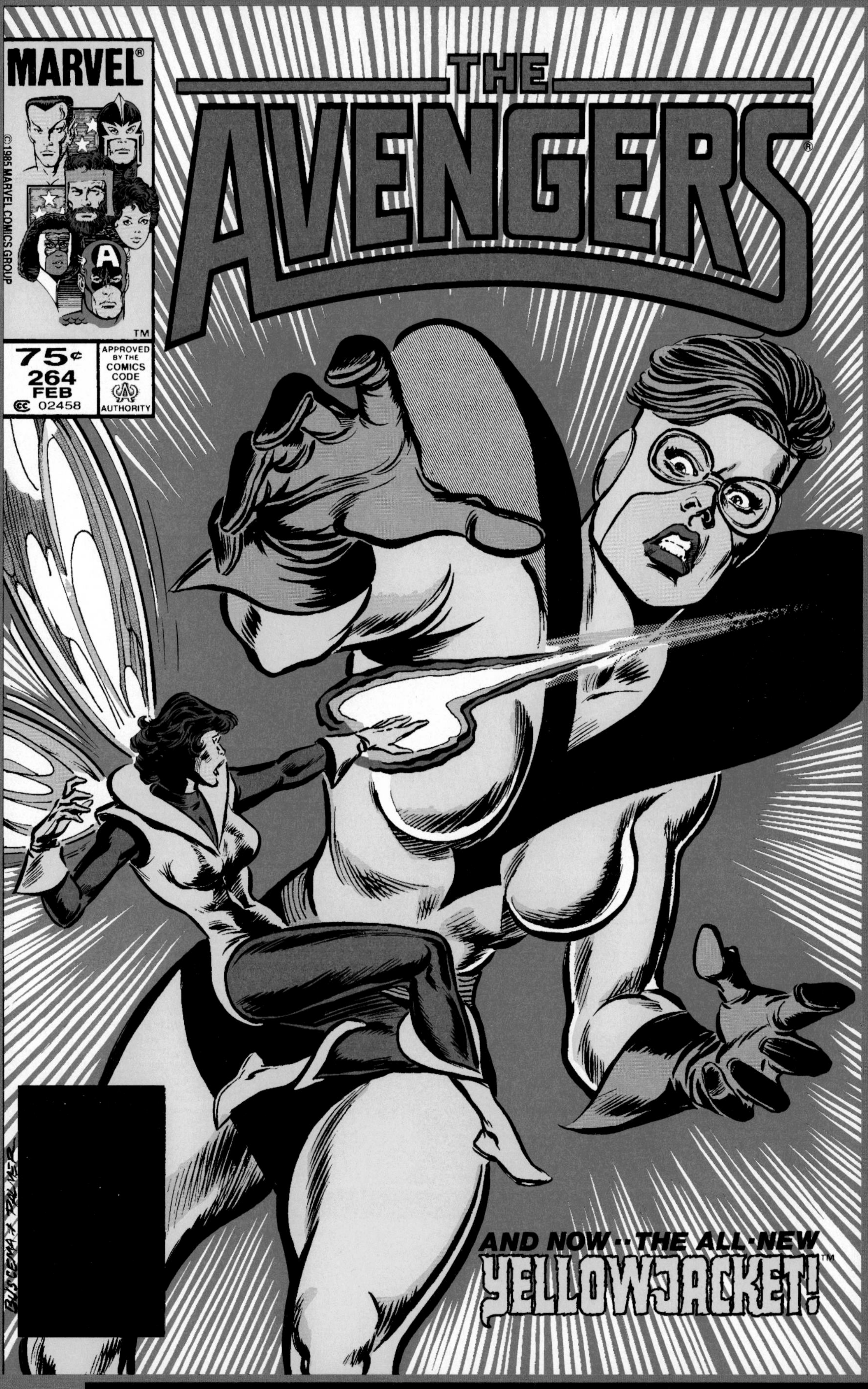
MARVEL®
© 1985 MARVEL COMICS GROUP
THE
AVENGERS®
TM
75¢
264
FEB
02458
APPROVED BY THE COMICS CODE AUTHORITY
AND NOW -- THE ALL-NEW
YELLOWJACKET!™

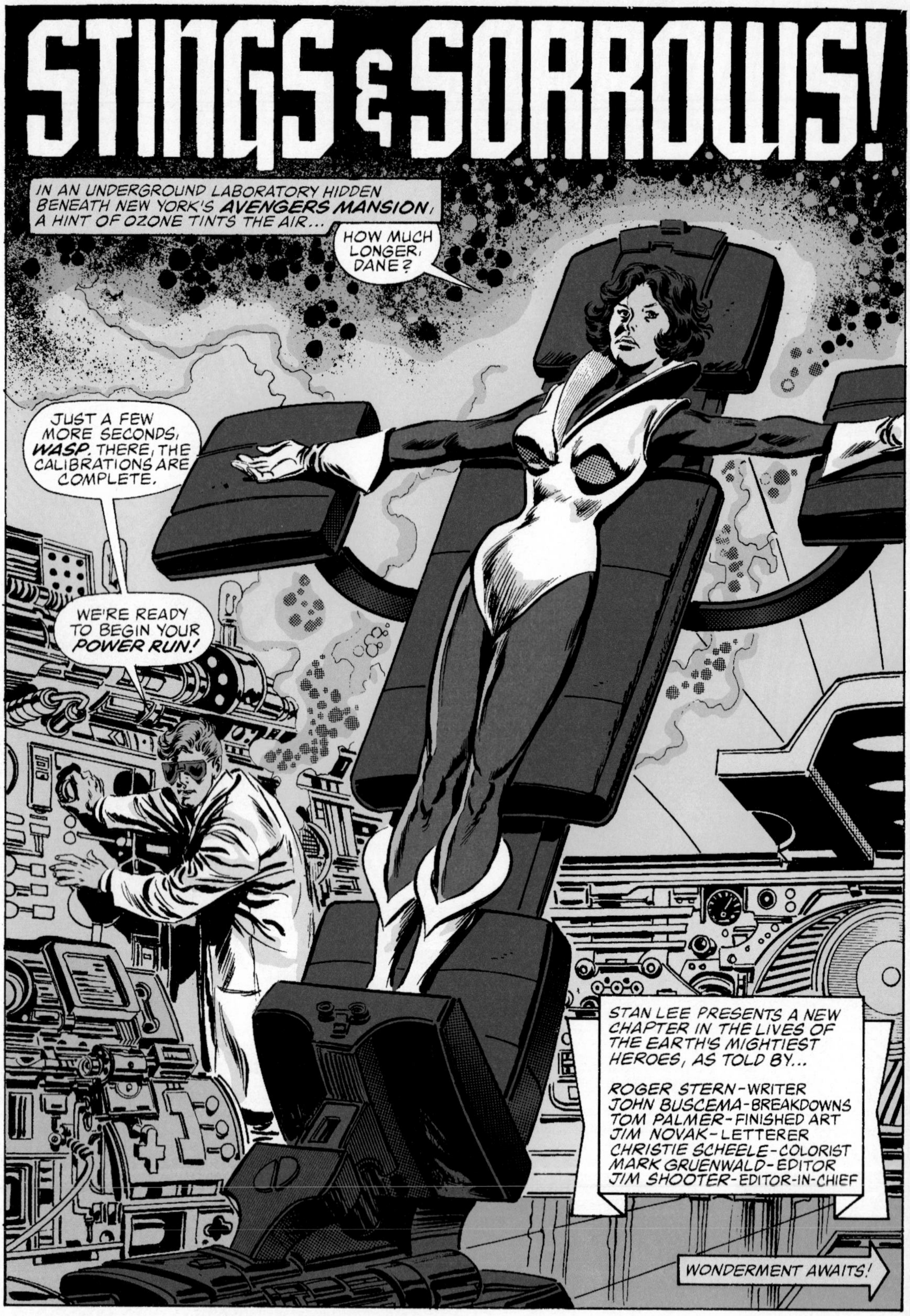
STINGS & SORROWS!
IN AN UNDERGROUND LABORATORY HIDDEN BENEATH NEW YORK'S AVENGERS MANSION, A HINT OF OZONE TINTS THE AIR...
HOW MUCH LONGER, DANE?
JUST A FEW MORE SECONDS, WASP. THERE, THE CALIBRATIONS ARE COMPLETE.
WE'RE READY TO BEGIN YOUR POWER RUN!
STAN LEE PRESENTS A NEW CHAPTER IN THE LIVES OF THE EARTH'S MIGHTIEST HEROES, AS TOLD BY...
ROGER STERN-WRITER
JOHN BUSCEMA-BREAKDOWNS
TOM PALMER-FINISHED ART
JIM NOVAK-LETTERER
CHRISTIE SCHEELE-COLORIST
MARK GRUENWALD-EDITOR
JIM SHOOTER-EDITOR-IN-CHIEF
WONDERMENT AWAITS!

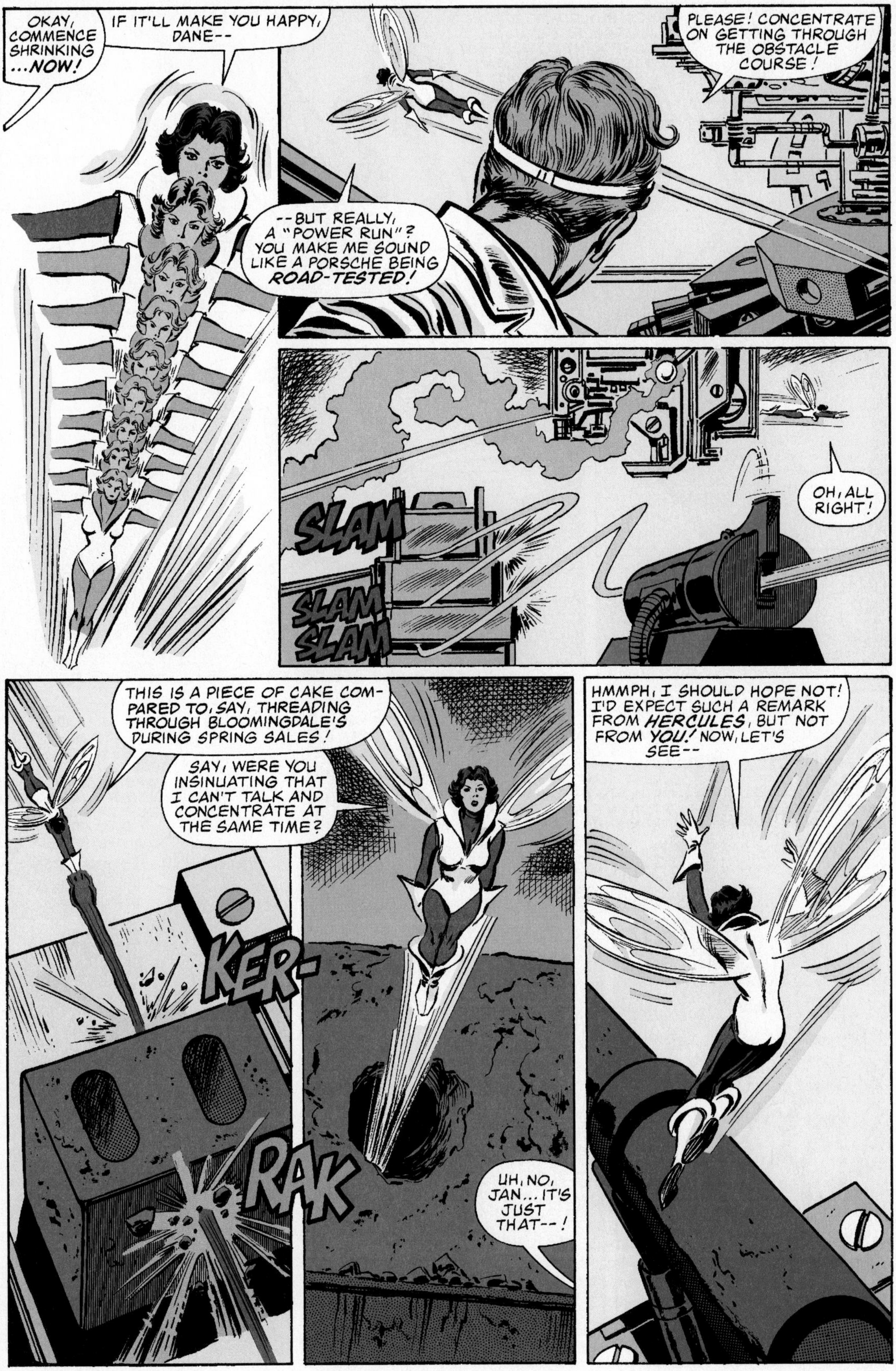
OKAY, COMMENCE SHRINKING ...NOW!
IF IT'LL MAKE YOU HAPPY, DANE--
--BUT REALLY, A "POWER RUN"? YOU MAKE ME SOUND LIKE A PORSCHE BEING ROAD-TESTED!
PLEASE! CONCENTRATE ON GETTING THROUGH THE OBSTACLE COURSE!
SLAM
SLAM
SLAM
OH, ALL RIGHT!
THIS IS A PIECE OF CAKE COMPARED TO, SAY, THREADING THROUGH BLOOMINGDALE'S DURING SPRING SALES!
SAY, WERE YOU INSINUATING THAT I CAN'T TALK AND CONCENTRATE AT THE SAME TIME?
KER-
RAK
UH, NO, JAN... IT'S JUST THAT--!
HMMPH, I SHOULD HOPE NOT! I'D EXPECT SUCH A REMARK FROM HERCULES, BUT NOT FROM YOU! NOW, LET'S SEE--

--NEXT, YOU WANT ME TO PIT MY STRENGTH AGAINST THIS *TEST ROD*, RIGHT?

YES, BUT DON'T STRAIN YOURSELF TOO MUCH. I JUST WANT TO SEE HOW MUCH FORCE YOU CAN EASILY EXERT AT... THAT...

...SIZE.

IS THIS GOOD ENOUGH?

IS THAT *GOOD* ENOUGH? I'LL SAY IT IS! YOU JUST BENT A 2-INCH DIAMETER *STEEL BAR* NEARLY DOUBLE! I HAD NO IDEA YOU COULD DO THAT!

WELL, I COULDN'T ALWAYS. BUT A COUPLE OF YEARS AGO, MY... EX-HUSBAND, *HANK PYM*, MODIFIED MY POWERS SO THAT MY STRENGTH IS BOOSTED AS I SHRINK.*

I JUST DON'T SHOW IT OFF SO MUCH. IT'S MORE EFFICIENT TO ZAP AN OPPONENT WITH MY *STING* THAN TO RIP HIS ARM OFF...LESS MESSY, TOO!

UH... YEAH.

*CIRCA MARVEL TEAM-UP #59-60.*

INTERESTING PRINT-OUT?

YES. IT LOOKS LIKE YOUR BODY CHEMISTRY'S ADAPTED TO YOUR WASP POWERS BETTER THAN EVEN YOUR... UH... THAN *DR. PYM* ANTICIPATED.

HOW SO?

"THERE'S BEEN A SUBTLE MOLECULAR CHANGE IN SOME OF THE BIOENGINEERED CELLS THAT PYM FIRST IMPLANTED TO GIVE YOU WINGS AND ANTENNAE WHEN YOU SHRANK TO THE SIZE OF AN INSECT.

...BUT LOOK AT YOURSELF! YOU'RE FULLY WINGED...AT ONE FOOT TALL!

"THE ANTENNAE CELLS EVENTUALLY FAILED, BUT THE WING CELLS HAVE MULTIPLIED. THE GROWTH'S BEEN SO GRADUAL, YOU HAVEN'T NOTICED IT..."

OH, MY!

BET THAT EVER SINCE I BECAME AVENGERS CHAIRWOMAN, I'VE BEEN SUBCONSCIOUSLY MAKING MYSELF A LITTLE BIGGER--

--SO I COULD BE BETTER SEEN AND HEARD!

IF MY FIGURES ARE CORRECT, YOU SHOULD BE ABLE TO KEEP YOUR WINGS AND FLY AT EVEN LARGER SIZES!

I CAN? HOW LARGE?

IF YOU'LL LAND ON THAT SENSOR GRID, WE'LL SEE IF WE CAN FIND OUT!

WHILE I MONITOR YOUR VITAL SIGNS, I WANT YOU TO SLOWLY WILL YOUR- SELF TO GROW...

...THAT'S IT... SLOWLY... S-L-O-W-L-Y...

HOLD IT! THAT'S YOUR MAXIMUM WING-SIZE!

THIS IS NEARLY MY FULL HEIGHT!

A FOOT SHORTER, TO BE EXACT. BUT CAN YOU FLY?

I...I CAN!

THIS IS **WONDERFUL**!

CAREFUL, JAN--

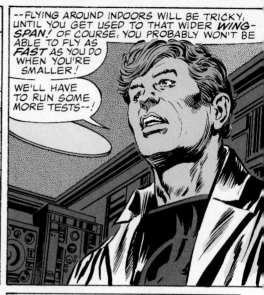

--FLYING AROUND INDOORS WILL BE TRICKY, UNTIL YOU GET USED TO THAT WIDER **WING-SPAN**! OF COURSE, YOU PROBABLY WON'T BE ABLE TO FLY AS **FAST** AS YOU DO WHEN YOU'RE SMALLER!

WE'LL HAVE TO RUN SOME MORE TESTS--!

NO, YOU DON'T! IT'S A PERFECTLY BEAUTIFUL DAY, AND I WON'T SPEND ONE MORE MINUTE **COOPED UP** IN HERE!

DID I SAY "NOW"?

I CAN TEST YOU LATER. GO ON...HAVE **FUN**!

WELL, I NEVER--! A SCIENTIST WHO ISN'T STUFFY? YOU'RE ONE-OF-A-KIND, **DANE WHITMAN**! THANKS!

UH, JAN...HOW ABOUT WE... CELEBRATE YOUR "NEW POWER" OVER **DINNER**?

SOUNDS LOVELY! WHY DON'T WE MEET AT TRADER VIC'S... AROUND EIGHT?

SURE, I'LL MAKE THE RESERVATIONS.

YOU'RE A **DOLL**! CIAO!

SO, I'M A DOLL, HUH? AND "ONE-OF-A-KIND". THOSE'RE THE NICEST THINGS ANY WOMAN'S SAID ABOUT ME IN A LONG TIME...

...A LONG, **LONG** TIME.

SECONDS LATER...

OH, THIS IS *ECSTASY!* NO MORE FLITTING THROUGH A GIANT WORLD... AND NO MORE DODGING BIRDS! FROM NOW ON, THEY'LL HAVE TO GET OUT OF *MY* WAY!

WHEEEEEEEE

BUT, WHILE JANET VAN DYNE GLEEFULLY BUZZES CENTRAL PARK...

...A NONDESCRIPT VAN IDLES AT CURBSIDE ON A SIDESTREET NEXT TO THE AVENGERS' FIFTH AVENUE MANSION...

THIS IS IT...

...HERE'S WHERE I FIND OUT WHETHER OR NOT MY LAST THREE MONTHS' *WORK* HAS BEEN A *WASTE.*

THERE'S A BRIEF ELECTROMAGNETIC DISCHARGE FROM THE HELMET THE DRIVER DONS--

--A DISCHARGE MIMICKED INSTANTLY BY ANOTHER HELMET LOCKED AWAY DEEP WITHIN THE MANSION... THE CYBERNETIC HELMET WORN BY *DR. HENRY PYM* WHEN HE WAS THE AVENGER KNOWN AS *YELLOWJACKET!*

THE DISCHARGE CRACKLES THROUGHOUT THE TINY STORAGE *LOCKER,* PROBING EVERY INCH... ITS POWER LINGERING OVER THE BOLTS OF THREE SPECIALLY ENCODED ELECTROMAGNETIC LOCKS...

...UNTIL THOSE BOLTS *POP OPEN!*

WILD ENERGIES PLAY ACROSS THE PROUD UNIFORM WHICH HANGS ALONGSIDE THE HELMET, SWITCHING ON HIDDEN *POWER-PACKS*, ACTIVATING SCORES OF *MICROCIRCUITS* WOVEN THROUGHOUT THE FABRIC!

*EPAULET-WINGS* VIBRATE, GIVING THE CLOTHING AN EERIE SEMBLANCE OF *LIFE!*

THE TWITCHING UNIFORM FLOPS FROM ITS HOOK--FALLING ACROSS THE HELMET, WHICH ELECTRONICALLY LOCKS ITSELF INTO PLACE.

AND THEN, LIKE SOME *MACABRE MARIONETTE*, YELLOWJACKET'S UNIFORM REALLY BEGINS TO MOVE!

THE HELMET'S PERIPHERAL-VISION GOGGLES GLOW, AS THE THRUMMING ARTIFICIAL WINGS PROPEL THE UNIFORM OUT OF THE STORAGE ROOM.

WHILE, ONE FLOOR AWAY...

I'D BETTER GET IN A LITTLE *SWORD* PRACTICE THIS AFTERNOON.

MY SCIENTIFIC EXPERTISE MAY HELP THE AVENGERS--

--BUT WHEN WE'RE CALLED TO BATTLE, THEY NEED MY GOOD RIGHT ARM...AND THE ENCHANTED EBONY BLADE OF THE *BLACK KNIGHT!*

I WONDER WHAT MY OLD PHYSICS PROF WOULD SAY--

--IF HE KNEW THAT HIS "PROBLEM PUPIL" HAD ACQUIRED A *MAGIC SWORD?*

IT'S HARD FOR ME TO *BELIEVE* SOMETIMES. CERTAINLY, THERE WERE PLENTY OF TIMES I WISH I'D NEVER LAID EYES ON MY SWORD...

...NEVER BECOME LINKED TO ITS ENCHANTMENT ... OR ITS CURSE!

"THAT CURSE LED ME TO THE *12TH CENTURY*, WHERE I WASTED FIVE YEARS OF MY LIFE, FIGHTING IN THE BLOODY CRUSADES.

"AND AFTER I FINALLY RETURNED TO THE PRESENT--

"--THE SWORD DROVE ME TO BATTLE MY OLD ALLY, *DR. STRANGE*... UNTIL DOC HELPED ME BREAK THE CURSE AND REGAIN MY SANITY!"*

*IN DOCTOR STRANGE #68.

BUT TO THINK THAT, AFTER TWENTY YEARS OF SCIENTIFIC STUDY, I WOULD WIND UP WITH A CRAZY *MYSTICAL BOND* TO AN ANCIENT ANCESTOR'S SWORD. *WEIRD!*

LOST IN THOUGHT--

--THE BLACK KNIGHT DOES NOT NOTICE THE ODDLY FLOPPING FORM WHICH PASSES BY HIS LAB...

...AND OTHERS.

THAT'S IT, *HERCULES*--

--HOLD IT RIGHT THERE! THAT'S PERFECT.

I APPRECIATE THIS. I DON'T KNOW HOW I'LL EVER REPAY YOU AND THE OTHER AVENGERS FOR ALL THE *HELP* AND *HOSPITALITY* YOU'VE EXTENDED TO MY FAMILY.

'TIS OUR HONOR TO AID THE FANTASTIC FOUR, *REED RICHARDS.* I MUST CONFESS, THOUGH, THESE DEVICES YOU DESIGN *MYSTIFY* ME!

57

WELL, THIS PARTICULAR MODULE IS AN AMPLIFYING COMPONENT FOR THE COSMIC-EMISSION DETECTION WEB WHICH THE BLACK KNIGHT DEVISED TO TRACE THE *BEYONDER.*

WE'LL ALL SLEEP A LOT EASIER IF WE CAN KEEP TRACK OF *HIS* ESCAPADES!

'PON THAT I CAN AGREE...

...THERE BE ALL TOO MANY STRANGE COMINGS AND GOINGS 'ROUND HERE FOR THE SON OF ZEUS!

SHORTLY, IN THE MANSION'S KITCHEN...

AH! A PICTURE-PERFECT BATCH OF TOLLHOUSE COOKIES, IF I DO SAY SO MYSELF!

OF COURSE, THE *TRUE WORTH* OF SUCH MORSELS CAN BE JUDGED ONLY IN THE *TASTING,* SO...

AND WHAT ARE WE UP TO THIS FINE AFTERNOON, MASTER *FRANKLIN?*

I'M DRAWING, UNCA JARVIS.

WELL, DO YOU THINK YOU COULD BE INTERRUPTED LONG ENOUGH TO TRY A COOKIE OR TWO?

OBOY! YEAH!

MIND YOU, NOT A WORD OF THIS TO YOUR MOTHER!

UNNOTICED BY THE AVENGERS' *BUTLER* AND YOUNG *FRANKLIN RICHARDS*, THE EERIE SHAPE STREAKS OVER THE WALL AND INTO THE WAITING VAN...

I DID IT! I *DID IT!*

POM!

I ACTUALLY BOOSTED HENRY PYM'S OLD YELLOWJACKET OUT-FIT FROM AVENGERS MANSION, RIGHT UNDER THE NOSES OF THOSE SUPER BOY-SCOUTS!

OH, BABY, AND IF I CAN GET AWAY WITH THIS, THERE WON'T BE *NOTHIN'* I CAN'T DO!

JUST ONE MORE STOP NOW, AND I'LL HAVE IT ALL!

MEANWHILE, IN THE MANSION'S *SECOND-FLOOR STUDY...*

SO THIS IS WHAT HAS BECOME OF THE MIGHTY *SUB-MARINER...*

...FORCED TO GIVE UP THE *THRONE* OF ATLANTIS... DWELLING HERE IN THE LAND OF MY FATHER, AMONG BEINGS WHO ONCE WERE MY MIGHT-IEST *FOES.* I HAVE BECOME AN AVENGER ...AN HONOR TO BE CERTAIN...

...BUT WILL THAT HONOR BE *ENOUGH?* WHAT WILL BE THE WORLD'S REAC-TION, WHEN MY PRESENCE HERE BECOMES COMMON KNOWLEDGE?

OH, EXCUSE ME, I DIDN'T KNOW ANY-ONE WAS IN HERE!

EH? THAT'S QUITE ALL RIGHT PLEASE--

--COME IN, SUSAN. TRUTH TO TELL, EVER SINCE THE WASP TOLD ME YOU WERE RESIDING HERE, I HAD BEEN HOPING OUR PATHS WOULD CROSS.

SHE'S MORE BEAUTIFUL EACH TIME WE MEET...

"...I STILL RECALL THE DAY I FIRST LAID EYES ON HER."

WELL! HERE IS A PRIZE WORTH CATCHING!

YOU'RE THE LOVELIEST HUMAN I'VE EVER SEEN! IF YOU WILL BE MY BRIDE--!

"AS THE INVISIBLE GIRL, SHE WAS WELL NAMED. HERS WAS A GIRLISH BEAUTY THEN--"

-- IT HAS SINCE BLOSSOMED INTO SOMETHING SO MUCH GREATER!

NAMOR?

MY PARDON, SUSAN. I WAS LOST IN THOUGHT.

MOMMY! MOMMY, LOOK!

WHAT IS IT, FRANKLIN?

I DREW A PICTURE OF YOU AN' ME AN' DADDY... GOIN' TO RUMPY-MYERS FOR ICE CREAM! SEE?

THAT'S VERY GOOD, DEAR! I THINK WE SHOULD SHOW THIS TO YOUR FATHER!

AN' GO TO RUMPY-MYERS?

WE'LL SEE.

I... AH... SHOULD BE GOING, SUSAN. PERHAPS WE'LL TALK ANOTHER TIME...

...PERHAPS.

NEW ORLEANS...

GET THOSE OTHER *HOSES* UP HERE! COME ON-- *MOVE IT!*

WE'RE COMING TO YOU LIVE FROM THE SCENE OF THE *WORST FIRE* TO HIT THE WAREHOUSE DISTRICT IN OVER A DECADE! CITY FIREFIGHTERS ARE VALIANTLY BATTLING TO SAVE THE BLOCK, BUT WE'VE JUST RECEIVED WORD--

"--THAT A *FIREMAN* IS DOWN, TRAPPED SOME-WHERE IN THAT BLAZING INFERNO!"

≶KAFF-KAFF≶ F-FORGET IT, FRANK...YOU'RE NEVER GONNA BUDGE THAT *BEAM!* YOU AND HUEY GET YER TAILS OUTTA HERE!

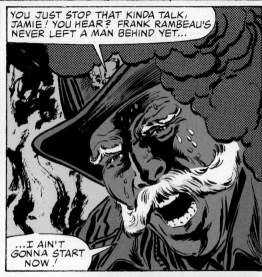

YOU JUST STOP THAT KINDA TALK, JAMIE! YOU HEAR? FRANK RAMBEAU'S NEVER LEFT A MAN BEHIND YET...

...I AIN'T GONNA START NOW!

AT THAT MOMENT, UNSEEN BY THE CROWD BELOW, CAPTAIN MARVEL STREAKS ACROSS THE LOUISIANA SKIES...

IT'S EVEN *WORSE* THAN IT LOOKED ON TV...

...AND IF I KNOW *DADDY*, HE'S RIGHT IN THE *THICK* OF IT!

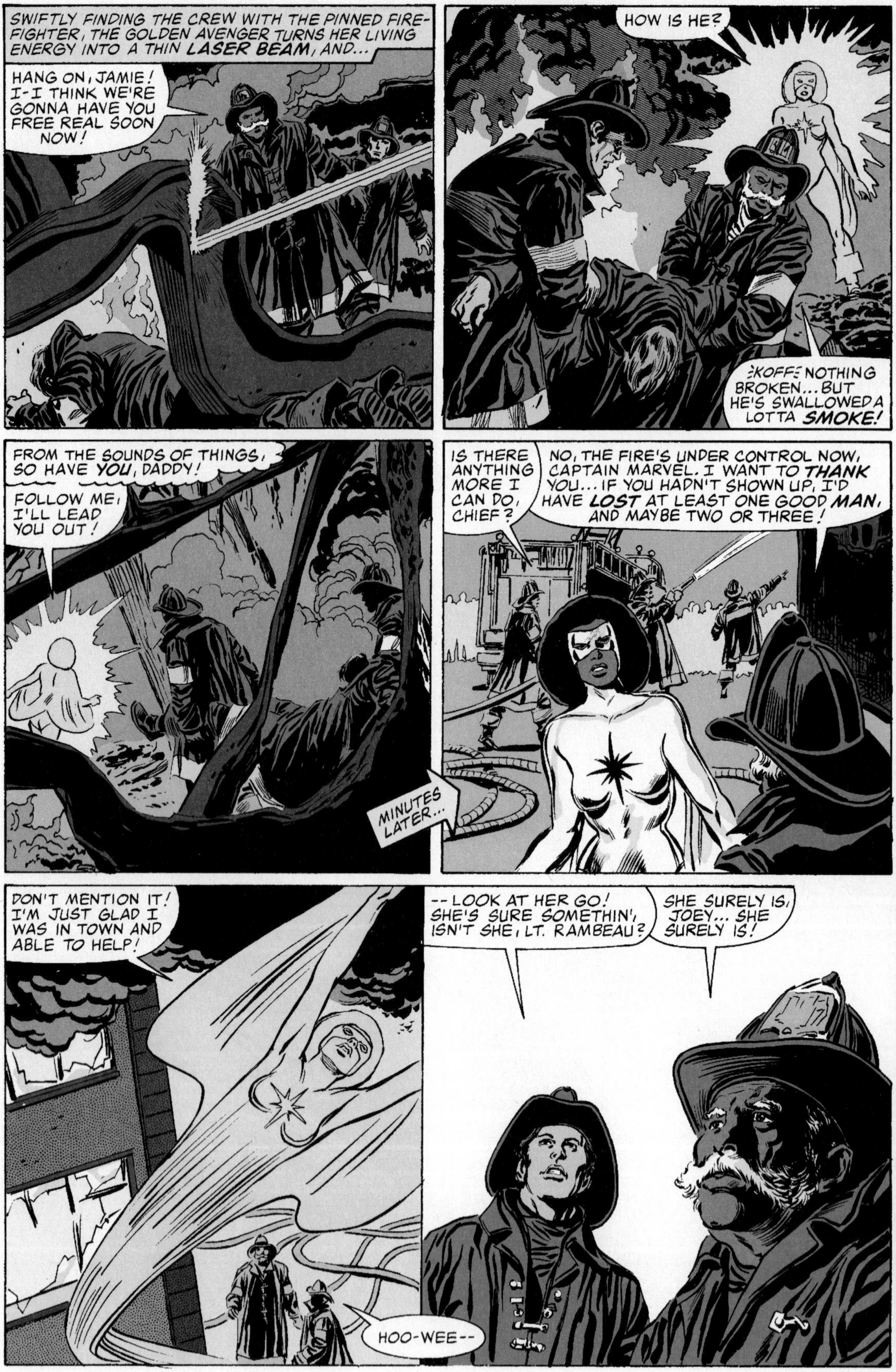
SWIFTLY FINDING THE CREW WITH THE PINNED FIRE-FIGHTER, THE GOLDEN AVENGER TURNS HER LIVING ENERGY INTO A THIN LASER BEAM, AND...
HANG ON, JAMIE! I-I THINK WE'RE GONNA HAVE YOU FREE REAL SOON NOW!
HOW IS HE?
KOFF NOTHING BROKEN... BUT HE'S SWALLOWED A LOTTA SMOKE!
FROM THE SOUNDS OF THINGS, SO HAVE YOU, DADDY!
FOLLOW ME, I'LL LEAD YOU OUT!
MINUTES LATER...
IS THERE ANYTHING MORE I CAN DO, CHIEF?
NO, THE FIRE'S UNDER CONTROL NOW, CAPTAIN MARVEL. I WANT TO THANK YOU... IF YOU HADN'T SHOWN UP, I'D HAVE LOST AT LEAST ONE GOOD MAN, AND MAYBE TWO OR THREE!
DON'T MENTION IT! I'M JUST GLAD I WAS IN TOWN AND ABLE TO HELP!
HOO-WEE--
--LOOK AT HER GO! SHE'S SURE SOMETHIN', ISN'T SHE, LT. RAMBEAU?
SHE SURELY IS, JOEY... SHE SURELY IS!

MOMENTS LATER, IN THE BACK ROOM OF A CERTAIN FRENCH QUARTER SEAMSTRESS SHOP...

Marias

...AND THE BLAZE HAS AT LAST BEEN CONTAINED--

--FOLLOWING THE SUCCESSFUL RESCUE OF A TRAPPED SMOKE-EATER, AIDED BY THE TIMELY APPEARANCE OF THE FAMED NEW YORK AVENGER, *CAPTAIN MARVEL.*

THANK HEAVENS, SHE GOT THERE IN TIME!

WELL, I *AM* AS FAST AS LIGHT, MOMMA!

MHHMPH? MONICA! YOUR *FATHER*... HOW'S--?

DADDY'S FINE, MOMMA-- HE WASN'T THE ONE WHO WAS TRAPPED. HE WAS JUST WORKING TO FREE THAT MAN. YOU SHOULDN'T *WORRY* SO.

BABY, I TRY NOT TO, BUT EVER SINCE THE TIME FRANK WAS TRAPPED IN THAT AWFUL CHURCH FIRE--! WELL, I'M JUST GLAD YOU WERE ABLE TO HELP HIM TODAY!

I'M GLAD, TOO, MOMMA.

BUT HOW THE DICKENS DID YOU GET IN HERE? I DIDN'T SEE YOU COME IN!

I ENTERED INVISIBLY... AS INFRA-RED ENERGY! AFTER ALL, WE DON'T WANT PEOPLE TO KNOW THAT AN AVENGER IS YOUR FAVORITE CUSTOMER.

THAT REMINDS ME, YOUR NEW *DRESS* IS READY. GO TRY IT ON!

MOMMA? I UNDERSTAND HOW YOU FEEL. I WORRY ABOUT DADDY, TOO... AND ABOUT MY TEAMMATES IN THE AVENGERS. BUT WE CAN'T LET *WORRIES* RUN OUR LIVES.

YOU'RE RIGHT, DEAR-- BUT THAT'S NOT EASY WITH A *FIREMAN* AND A *SUPER HERO* IN THE FAMILY!

SO MUCH CAN HAPPEN.

YES, THAT'S TRUE...

...SO MUCH *DOES* HAPPEN, AND SO QUICKLY! I'VE ALREADY SEEN A LOT OF *TRANSITION* IN THE AVENGERS. CAPTAIN AMERICA, THE WASP, AND I HAVE REALLY BEEN THE CONSTANTS IN A CHANGING TEAM.

CAP AND JAN HAVE BEEN SUCH GOOD *FRIENDS* TO ME. I THINK I COULD TRUST THEM WITH ANYTHING. THE BLACK KNIGHT, TOO.

JUST A FEW DAYS AGO, I WAS ON THE VERGE OF SHARING MY *CIVILIAN IDENTITY* WITH THE AVENGERS, BUT NOW-- SINCE THE SUB-MARINER JOINED US-- I'M NOT SURE I SHOULD.

COME TO THINK OF IT, COULD HERCULES BE TRUSTED TO KEEP MY IDENTITY A SECRET? I SUPPOSE I COULD TELL JUST CAP AND JAN AND DANE, BUT--!

MONICA? YOU'RE AWFULLY QUIET BACK THERE. WHAT'S WRONG?

NOTHING, MOMMA...THE DRESS FITS PERFECTLY!

HOW ABOUT WE COLLECT DADDY, AND TAKE HIM OUT TO *DINNER?* MY TREAT!

YOU SURE? HE GETS AWFULLY HUNGRY AFTER A FIRE!

SO DO I. MUST RUN IN THE BLOOD!

WHILE, IN NEW YORK...

DRAT, THE AFTERNOON'S FADING ALREADY! I'D BETTER HURRY HOME AND **CHANGE**, OR I'LL NEVER MAKE DINNER AT EIGHT!

AND SO, THE WASP SHOOTS WESTWARD--

-- LITTLE REALIZING THAT HER TURN HAS CARRIED HER AWAY FROM A CHANCE ENCOUNTER WITH ANOTHER AVENGER...CAPTAIN AMERICA!

I'VE RECEIVED SOME **STRANGE** CALLS --

-- SINCE I SET UP A NATIONWIDE TOLL-FREE NUMBER FOR PEOPLE TO REACH ME,* BUT THIS AFTERNOON'S CALL TOPS THEM ALL!

*IN **CAPTAIN AMERICA** #312.

IT WAS JUST A MATTER OF TIME BEFORE AN **OLD ENEMY** USED MY PHONE SERVICE...

... STILL, I NEVER EXPECTED TO GET AN OFFER LIKE THIS! IT COULD BE A **TRAP** --BUT IT'S SO BIZARRE, I JUST HAVE TO CHECK IT OUT! *

*HOW BIZARRE IS IT? FIND OUT IN **CAPTAIN AMERICA** #315--ON SALE IN THREE WEEKS!

SOON, OVER NEW JERSEY'S PALISADES PARKWAY...

MAYBE I AM A LITTLE **SLOWER** AT THIS SIZE, BUT THIS STILL BEATS PLAYING BUMPER-TO-BUMPER IN THAT TRAFFIC!

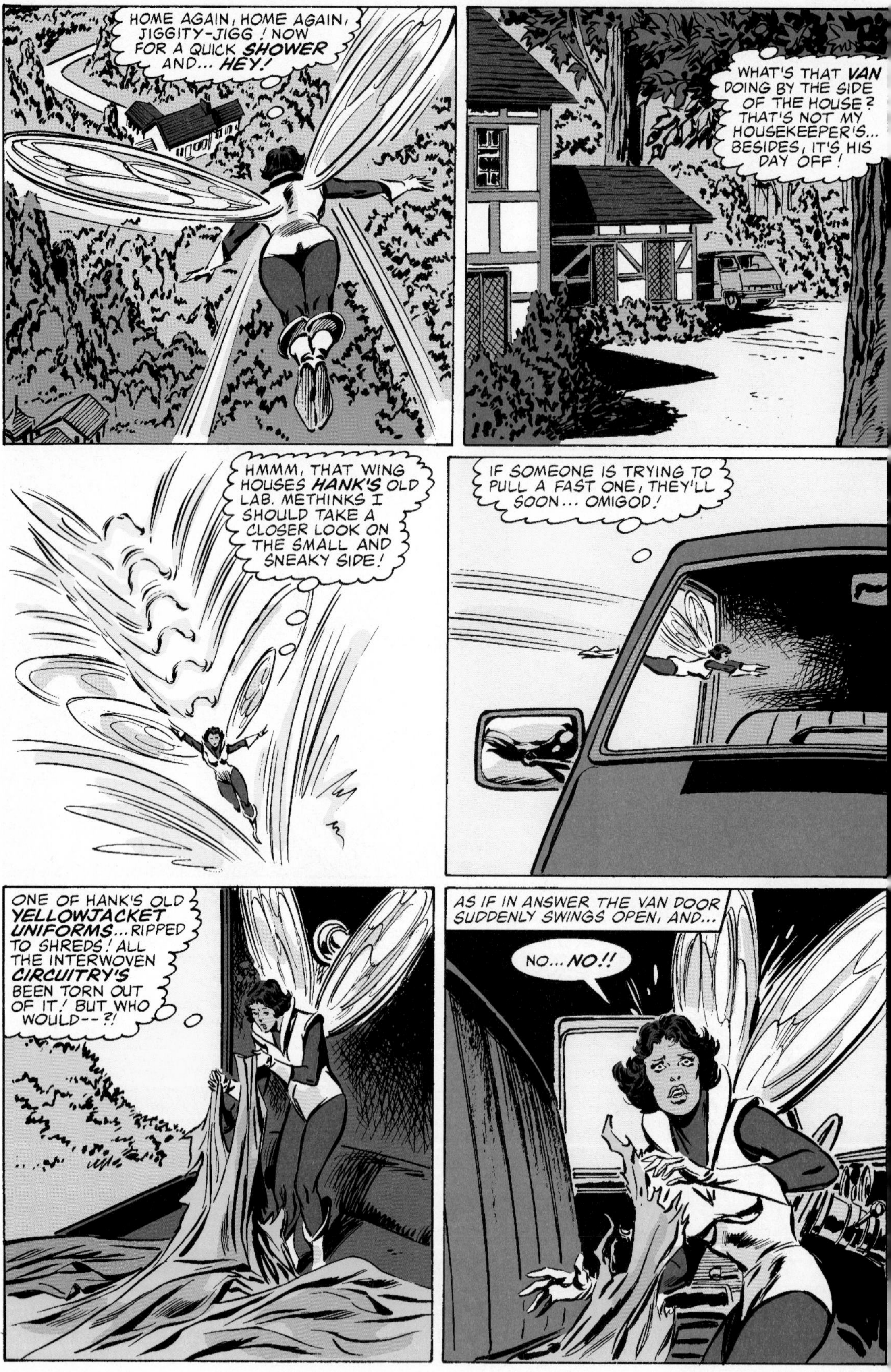
HOME AGAIN, HOME AGAIN, JIGGITY-JIGG! NOW FOR A QUICK SHOWER AND... HEY!
WHAT'S THAT VAN DOING BY THE SIDE OF THE HOUSE? THAT'S NOT MY HOUSEKEEPER'S... BESIDES, IT'S HIS DAY OFF!
HMMM, THAT WING HOUSES HANK'S OLD LAB. METHINKS I SHOULD TAKE A CLOSER LOOK ON THE SMALL AND SNEAKY SIDE!
IF SOMEONE IS TRYING TO PULL A FAST ONE, THEY'LL SOON... OMIGOD!
ONE OF HANK'S OLD YELLOWJACKET UNIFORMS... RIPPED TO SHREDS! ALL THE INTERWOVEN CIRCUITRY'S BEEN TORN OUT OF IT! BUT WHO WOULD--?!
AS IF IN ANSWER THE VAN DOOR SUDDENLY SWINGS OPEN, AND...
NO... NO!!

UH-OH.

HOW *DARE* YOU BREAK INTO MY HOME?

AND HOW *DARE* YOU DRESS *THAT WAY?!?*

WHAM

YOU'VE BEEN RAID- ING MY FORMER HUS- BAND'S *LAB,* HAVEN'T YOU? HOW DID YOU EVADE MY SECURITY SYSTEMS? AND WHERE'D YOU GET THAT OUTFIT? I WANT STRAIGHT *ANSWERS* OR I'LL...

...I'LL...

OOHHH... FLYING AROUND MANHATTAN ALL AFTERNOON...MUST'VE TAKEN MORE OUT OF ME THAN I'D REALIZED. AFTER USING ALL THAT ENERGY, MY BODY WASN'T READY FOR *RAPID GROWTH!*

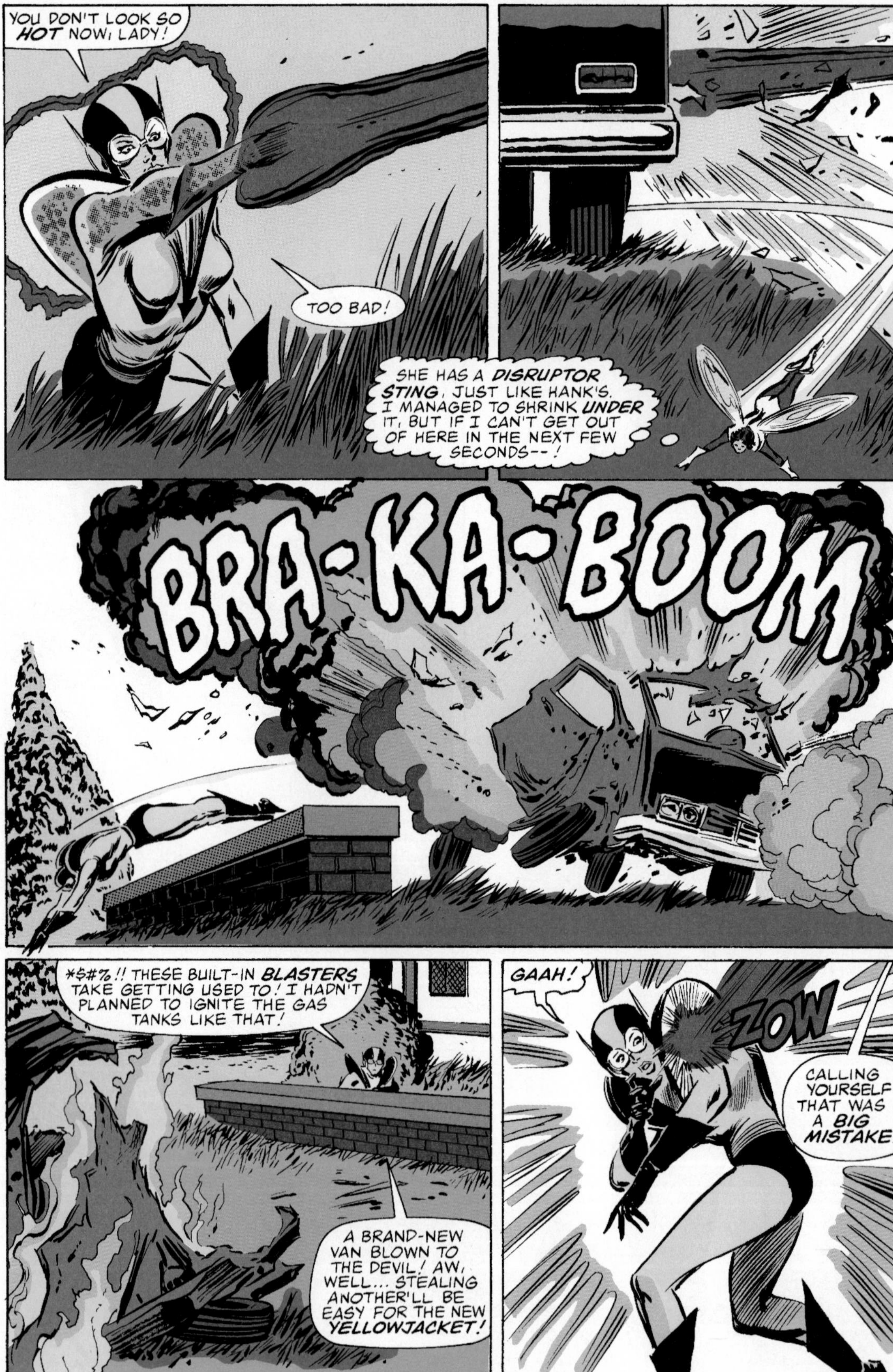

YOU DON'T LOOK SO *HOT* NOW, LADY!
TOO BAD!
SHE HAS A *DISRUPTOR STING*, JUST LIKE HANK'S. I MANAGED TO SHRINK *UNDER* IT, BUT IF I CAN'T GET OUT OF HERE IN THE NEXT FEW SECONDS--!
BRA-KA-BOOM
*$#%!! THESE BUILT-IN *BLASTERS* TAKE GETTING USED TO! I HADN'T PLANNED TO IGNITE THE GAS TANKS LIKE THAT!
A BRAND-NEW VAN BLOWN TO THE DEVIL! AW, WELL... STEALING ANOTHER'LL BE EASY FOR THE NEW *YELLOWJACKET*!
GAAH!
ZOW
CALLING YOURSELF THAT WAS A *BIG MISTAKE!*

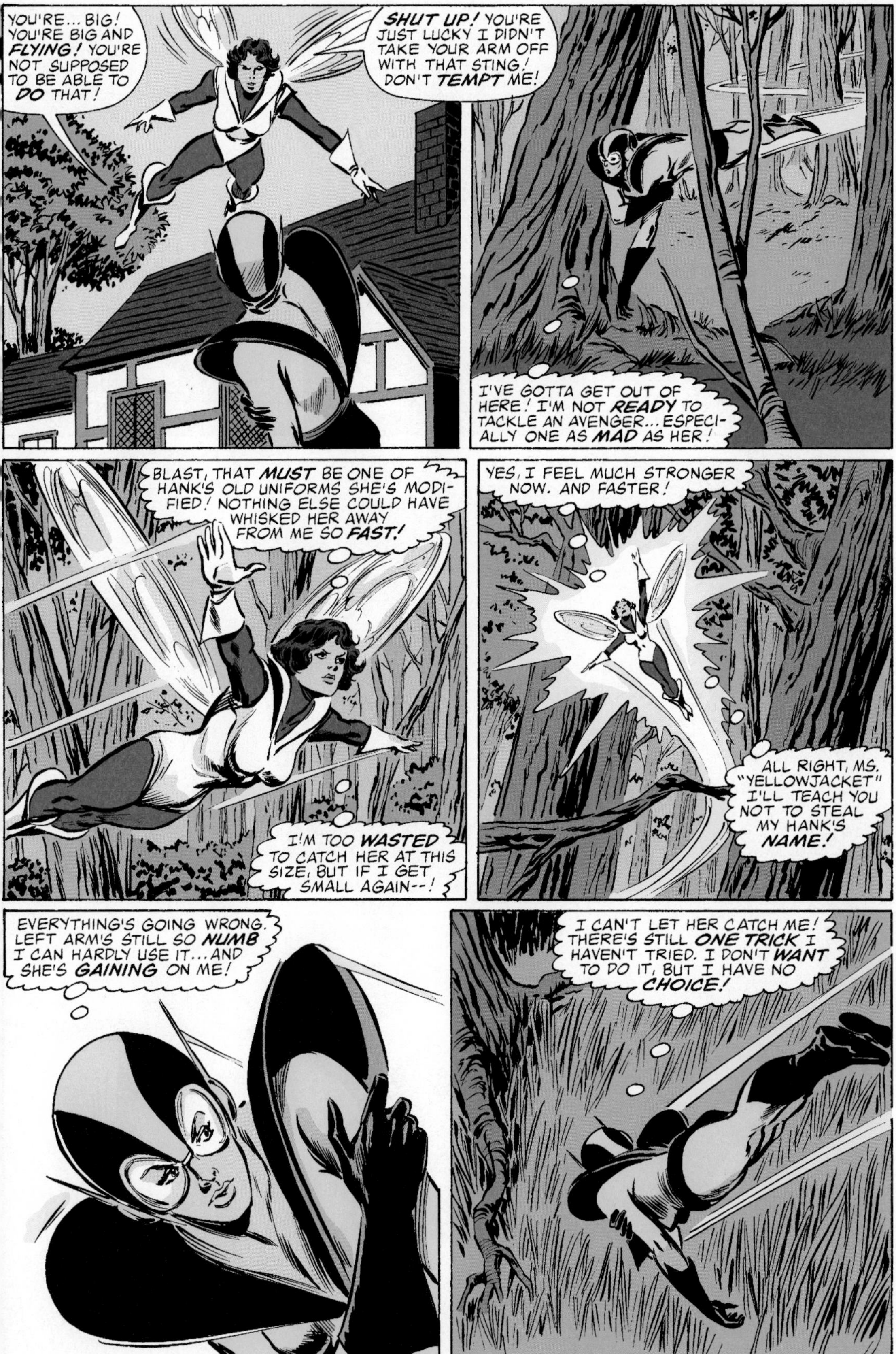
YOU'RE... BIG! YOU'RE BIG AND FLYING! YOU'RE NOT SUPPOSED TO BE ABLE TO DO THAT!
SHUT UP! YOU'RE JUST LUCKY I DIDN'T TAKE YOUR ARM OFF WITH THAT STING! DON'T TEMPT ME!
I'VE GOTTA GET OUT OF HERE! I'M NOT READY TO TACKLE AN AVENGER... ESPECIALLY ONE AS MAD AS HER!
BLAST, THAT MUST BE ONE OF HANK'S OLD UNIFORMS SHE'S MODIFIED! NOTHING ELSE COULD HAVE WHISKED HER AWAY FROM ME SO FAST!
I'M TOO WASTED TO CATCH HER AT THIS SIZE, BUT IF I GET SMALL AGAIN--!
YES, I FEEL MUCH STRONGER NOW. AND FASTER!
ALL RIGHT, MS. "YELLOWJACKET" I'LL TEACH YOU NOT TO STEAL MY HANK'S NAME!
EVERYTHING'S GOING WRONG. LEFT ARM'S STILL SO NUMB I CAN HARDLY USE IT... AND SHE'S GAINING ON ME!
I CAN'T LET HER CATCH ME! THERE'S STILL ONE TRICK I HAVEN'T TRIED. I DON'T WANT TO DO IT, BUT I HAVE NO CHOICE!

WHERE'D SHE GO?

THAT HELMET OF HERS... HANK WORE ONE LIKE IT WHEN HE WAS *GIANT-MAN!* I'LL BET IT HAS SIZE-CONTROL CYBERNETICS!

GREAT! IF SHE'S SHRUNK, I MAY NEVER FIND HER IN THESE TALL GRASSES!

EEEEEE!

?!?!?

GOOD GRIEF, SHE'S *HYSTERICAL!*

NO-NO-NO-NO-NO...

...NO-NO-N₃

SMEK

FOR PITY'S SAKE, GET *HOLD* OF YOURSELF!

FIRST TIME YOU'VE EVER *SHRUNK?*

BIG... EVERYTHING ...SO BIG...

IT'S HANK'S OLD DESIGN, ALL RIGHT! HERE'S THE MANUAL OVERRIDE CONTROL!

THERE, BACK TO *NORMAL!* CARE TO TRY ANYTHING NOW?

N-N-NO... I G-GIVE UP!

70

THAT'S THE FIRST SMART THING YOU'VE DONE! WHO ARE YOU AND WHERE'D YOU GET THE *GEAR* YOU'RE WEARING?

I DON'T HAVE TO SAY ANYTHING. I WANT A *LAWYER.*

SHORTLY...

I'M BETTING WE TURN UP A NAME AND A RECORD FOR OUR "JANE DOE" WITHIN 24 HOURS. WE'LL KEEP YOU INFORMED, MS. VAN DYNE.

THANK YOU, SERGEANT.

SHE LOOKS PRETTY HARD-BOILED NOW... WHAT MADE HER *FREAK OUT?*

SHE JUST COULDN'T ADJUST TO BEING *SMALL*... NOT EVERYONE CAN. THAT'S THE ADVANTAGE I HAVE.

ADVANTAGE?

FIVE-FOOT-FOUR IS THE *BIGGEST* I GET... I'VE BEEN SMALL ALL MY LIFE!

BUT YOU MUST EXCUSE ME, SERGEANT ...I HAVE TO DRESS FOR *DINNER!*

NEXT: IT BEGINS IN SECRET WARS II #8 ...IT CONTINUES IN AVENGERS #265 BATTLE WITH THE BEYONDER!

THE FATE OF YOUR WORLD HANGS IN THE BALANCE!

# WHO IS THE BEYONDER?

YEARS AGO, SCIENTIST OWEN REECE'S EQUIPMENT MALFUNCTIONED, BATHING HIM IN POWER AND TRANSFORMING HIM INTO THE VILLAINOUS, NEAR-OMNIPOTENT MOLECULE MAN. UNBEKNOWNST TO ANYONE, THIS EVENT ALSO PUNCTURED A PINHOLE INTO AN ADJACENT REALITY — A POCKET DIMENSION CONSISTING ENTIRELY OF ONE INFINITE, SEMISENTIENT, NONCORPOREAL ENTITY. PEERING THROUGH THE PINHOLE, THIS ENTITY REALIZED IT WAS NOT ALONE IN THE MULTIVERSE. IT BECAME FASCINATED WITH SUPERHUMANS, BUT WITHOUT A HUMAN PERSPECTIVE, WAS UNABLE TO UNDERSTAND CONCEPTS LIKE DESIRE, MORTALITY, GOOD AND EVIL.

AFTER YEARS OF OBSERVING, THE ENTITY TRAVELED INTO THE MARVEL UNIVERSE, WHERE IT CREATED A PATCHWORK ALIEN PLANET AND TRANSPORTED MANY OF EARTH'S HEROES AND VILLAINS THERE — INCLUDING THE MOLECULE MAN AND THE MIGHTY AVENGERS. THE "ONE FROM BEYOND" ORDERED THE TWO SIDES TO FIGHT ONE ANOTHER SO IT COULD STUDY MORTALS IN DETAIL. AFTER SEVERAL BATTLES, DOCTOR DOOM BRIEFLY ABSORBED THE ENTITY'S NEAR-INFINITE COSMIC POWER, ENDING THE SKIRMISHES — BUT THE "ONE FROM BEYOND" SOON REGAINED ITS POWER AND DEPARTED, ITS CURIOSITY ONLY PARTLY SATED.

THE SUPERHUMANS RETURNED TO EARTH, BUT MONTHS LATER THE ENTITY ARRIVED THERE AS WELL. TAKING A HUMANOID FORM BASED ON CAPTAIN AMERICA'S BODY AND BECOMING KNOWN AS "THE BEYONDER," THE ENTITY BEFRIENDED THE REFORMED MOLECULE MAN AND HIS GIRLFRIEND VOLCANA, AND TRIED TO UNDERSTAND THE NATURE OF MORTAL LIFE. HOWEVER, THE BEYONDER'S ALMOST INFINITE REALITY-CONTROLLING POWER MADE IT IMPOSSIBLE FOR HIM TO EXPERIENCE LIFE AS MORTALS DO. ABLE TO CREATE, ALTER OR DESTROY ANYTHING WITH MERELY A THOUGHT, THE BEYONDER WAS UNABLE TO EXPERIENCE THE STRUGGLE TO ACHIEVE A GOAL, THE THRILL OF A RISK, THE FEAR OF FAILURE, THE JOY OF ACCOMPLISHMENT... OR TO APPRECIATE THE PRECIOUS, FLEETING NATURE OF LIFE ITSELF.

GROWING MORE AND MORE FRUSTRATED WITH HIS INABILITY TO UNDERSTAND OR COEXIST WITH THE MORTAL WORLD, THE BEYONDER SOON BECAME ENRAGED. HE DECIDED TO DESTROY THE ENTIRE MULTIVERSE — HOPING THAT IF NOTHING ELSE EXISTED EXCEPT HIMSELF, HE COULD GO BACK TO HIS ORIGINAL EXISTENCE AS THE SUM TOTAL OF REALITY AND FIND THE CONTENTMENT FOR WHICH HE LONGED.

USING THE BLACK KNIGHT'S DETECTION GRID, THE AVENGERS TRACKED THE MADDENED BEYONDER TO THE AMERICAN MIDWEST. HOWEVER, WHEN THEY TRIED TO CALM HIM, THE BEYONDER CAPTURED CAPTAIN AMERICA AND CREATED A POWERFUL CYCLONE THAT SWEPT THE REST OF THE TEAM AWAY...

MARVEL®

© 1985 MARVEL COMICS GROUP

THE

AVENGERS®

75¢
265
MAR
02458

APPROVED
BY THE
COMICS
CODE
AUTHORITY

SECRET WARS II
CONTINUES IN THIS ISSUE!

THE RAGE
OF THE
BEYONDER!

BUSCEMA & PALMER

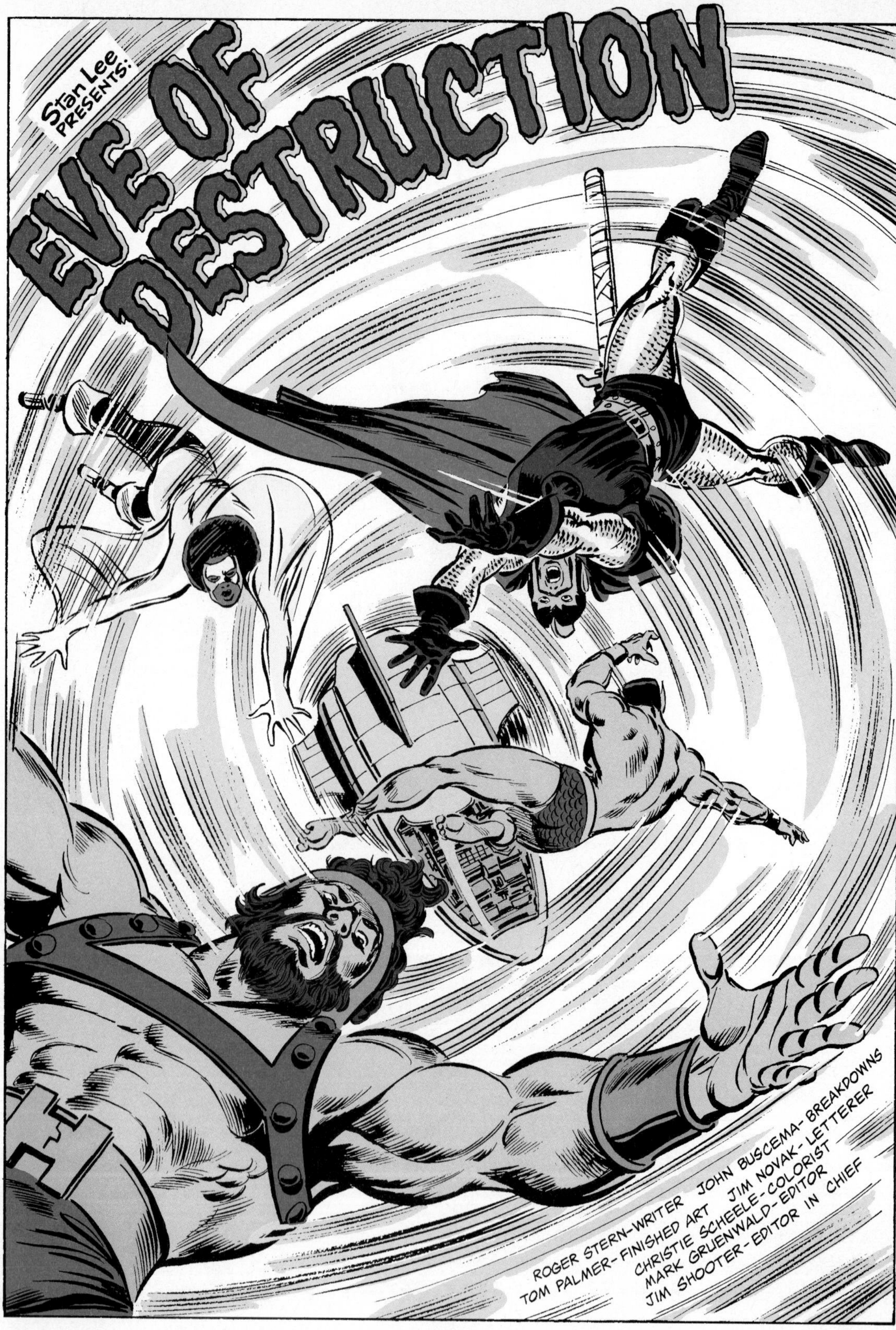
Stan Lee PRESENTS:
EVE OF DESTRUCTION
ROGER STERN-WRITER JOHN BUSCEMA-BREAKDOWNS
TOM PALMER-FINISHED ART JIM NOVAK-LETTERER
CHRISTIE SCHEELE-COLORIST
MARK GRUENWALD-EDITOR
JIM SHOOTER-EDITOR IN CHIEF

SECONDS AGO, THE DAY WAS BRIGHT AND SUNNY, HERE IN THE HEARTLAND OF AMERICA...

GOOD GAWD A'MIGHTY! A *TWISTER!*

B-BUT THAT CAN'T BE! THERE'S NO WIND, NO STORM...I-IT AIN'T *NATURAL!*

THEN, THE HEAVENS TURNED INSIDE OUT.

INDEED, INSIDE THE SWIRLING VORTEX...

THE POWER...HIT US SO FAST...SENT US SPINNING BEFORE WE KNEW WHAT WAS HAPPENING!

STILL SPINNING...THIS MUST BE SOME SORT OF ENERGY CYCLONE!

SO DIZZY!...BUT I... MUST...CONCENTRATE! MUST... *CHANGE...*

THROUGH DINT OF WILL, THE ASTOUNDING CAPTAIN MARVEL TRANSFORMS HER PHYSICAL BEING INTO PURE *ELECTRICAL ENERGY...*

I'M SLOWING THE CYCLONE SOME, NOT NEARLY ENOUGH! I COULD PROBABLY BLOW THIS "ENERGY WIND" OUT-- BUT IF I REALLY CUT LOOSE HERE, I MIGHT ELECTROCUTE THE OTHERS!

AND, AS FOR THOSE OTHER AVENGERS...

NO!! THE AVENGING SON WILL NOT BE HUMBLED THIS WAY!

I HAVE RESISTED THE POWER OF MIGHTY HURRICANES... FOUGHT MY WAY THROUGH SURGING WATERSPOUTS...

...AND I SHALL BE FREE OF THIS ALIEN TRAP! SO SPEAKS THE TRUE SUB-MARINER!

ZZARK

NAMOR'S PUTTING UP A GOOD FIGHT, BUT HE DOESN'T SEEM TO BE MAKING MUCH HEADWAY... NOT THAT I'M DOING ANY BETTER!

MY SWORD'S DIFFUSING SOME OF THE ENERGY, BUT MY ARM'LL GIVE OUT LONG BEFORE THE VORTEX DOES!

CAPTAIN MARVEL, CAN YOU HEAR ME? WE NEED A SUDDEN CONCUSSIVE SHOCK TO BLOW THIS THING APART... A BIG ONE!

IF A BLOW IS NEEDED, THEN 'TIS HERCULES YOU SHOULD CALL UPON, SIR KNIGHT!

FOR E'ER HAVE I BEEN THE PRINCE OF POWER!

SLAM

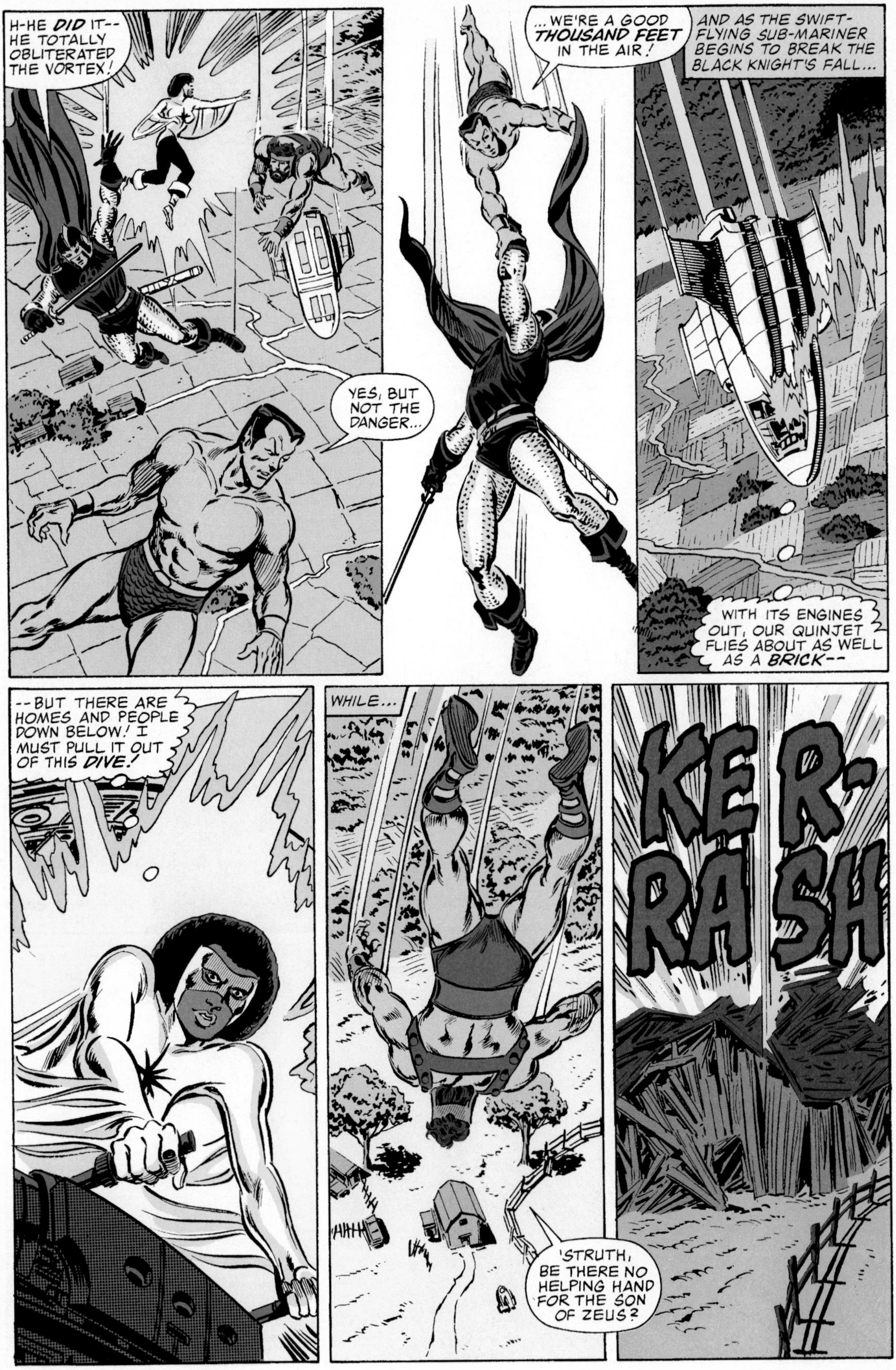

H-HE DID IT--
HE TOTALLY OBLITERATED THE VORTEX!
YES, BUT NOT THE DANGER...
...WE'RE A GOOD THOUSAND FEET IN THE AIR!
AND AS THE SWIFT-FLYING SUB-MARINER BEGINS TO BREAK THE BLACK KNIGHT'S FALL...
WITH ITS ENGINES OUT, OUR QUINJET FLIES ABOUT AS WELL AS A BRICK--
--BUT THERE ARE HOMES AND PEOPLE DOWN BELOW! I MUST PULL IT OUT OF THIS DIVE!
WHILE...
'STRUTH, BE THERE NO HELPING HAND FOR THE SON OF ZEUS?
KER-RASH

SECONDS LATER, CAPTAIN MARVEL MANAGES TO BRING THE QUINJET IN FOR A GENTLER, IF NOT MORE GRACEFUL LANDING...

PLOOOSH

MOOO!

AND...

THANKS FOR THE *SAVE*, NAMOR!

TORNADOS OUTTA A CLEAR, BLUE SKY... SPACESHIPS AN' FLYIN' MEN... WHAT IN THUNDER'S GOIN' ON HERE?

AND WHAT'D THEY DROP ON MY BARN?!

WHERE IS HE? WHERE IS THE MISCREANT WHO LET ME FALL?

WHERE IS THE *SUB-MARINER?*

I...EEE... UH...

78

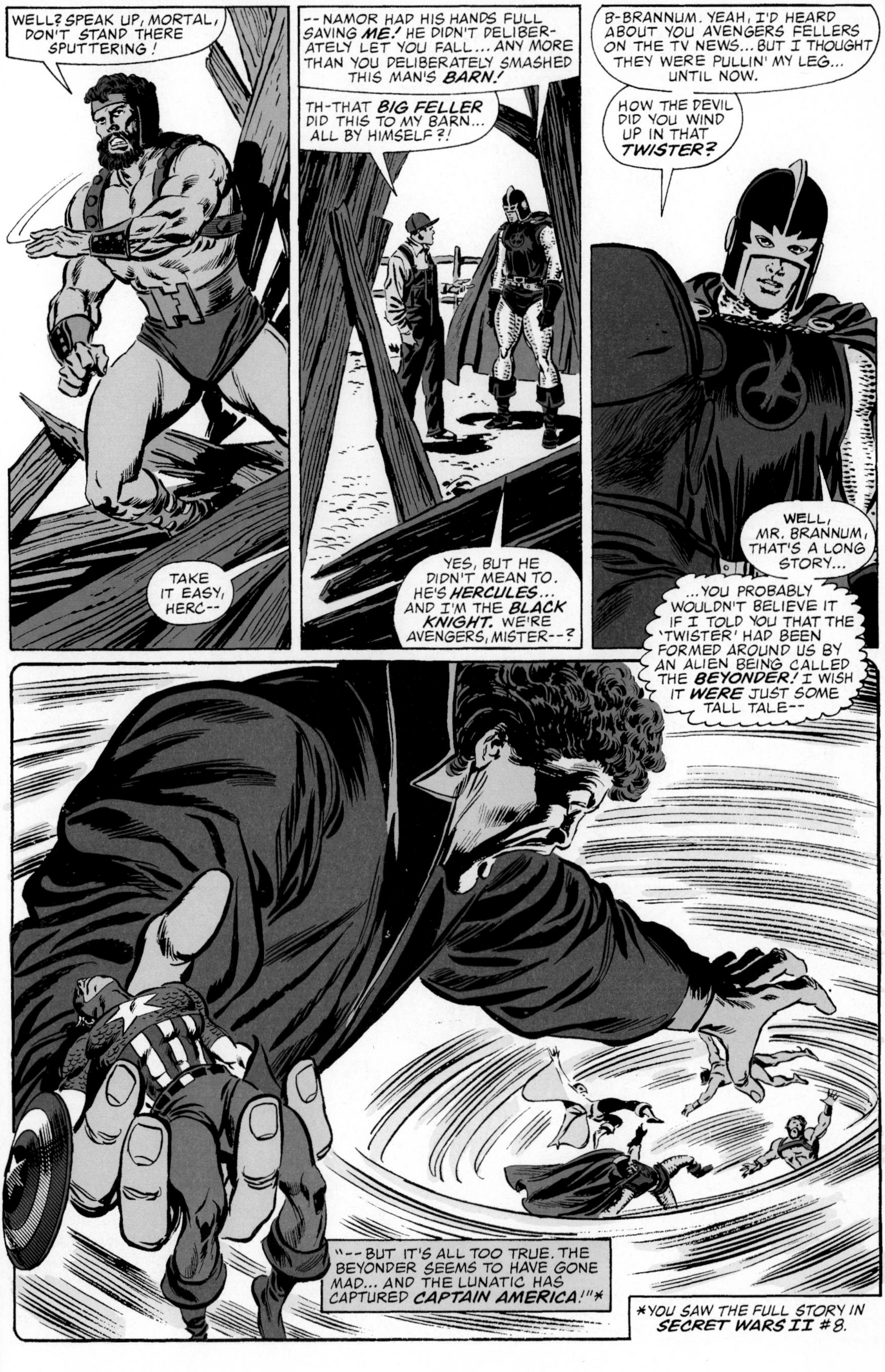
WELL? SPEAK UP, MORTAL, DON'T STAND THERE SPUTTERING!
TAKE IT EASY, HERC--
--NAMOR HAD HIS HANDS FULL SAVING ME! HE DIDN'T DELIBERATELY LET YOU FALL... ANY MORE THAN YOU DELIBERATELY SMASHED THIS MAN'S BARN!
TH-THAT BIG FELLER DID THIS TO MY BARN... ALL BY HIMSELF?!
YES, BUT HE DIDN'T MEAN TO. HE'S HERCULES... AND I'M THE BLACK KNIGHT. WE'RE AVENGERS, MISTER--?
B-BRANNUM. YEAH, I'D HEARD ABOUT YOU AVENGERS FELLERS ON THE TV NEWS... BUT I THOUGHT THEY WERE PULLIN' MY LEG... UNTIL NOW.
HOW THE DEVIL DID YOU WIND UP IN THAT TWISTER?
WELL, MR. BRANNUM, THAT'S A LONG STORY...
...YOU PROBABLY WOULDN'T BELIEVE IT IF I TOLD YOU THAT THE 'TWISTER' HAD BEEN FORMED AROUND US BY AN ALIEN BEING CALLED THE BEYONDER! I WISH IT WERE JUST SOME TALL TALE--
"--BUT IT'S ALL TOO TRUE. THE BEYONDER SEEMS TO HAVE GONE MAD... AND THE LUNATIC HAS CAPTURED CAPTAIN AMERICA!"*
*YOU SAW THE FULL STORY IN SECRET WARS II #8.

WE REALLY CAN'T DISCUSS OUR MISSION, SIR--

--BUT I CAN ASSURE YOU THAT YOU'LL BE REIMBURSED FOR ANY DAMAGES TO YOUR PROPERTY. OH, I'M *CAPTAIN MARVEL.*

*GULP* I'LL SAY!

THOSE TRIVIALITIES CAN BE SETTLED LATER, CAPTAIN. OUR MISSION HAS *CHANGED*, BUT IT'S BECOME NO LESS URGENT! I WANT YOU TO SCOUT AROUND OUR FOE'S LAST KNOWN LOCATION AND--!

WHAT GIVES *YOU* THE RIGHT TO ISSUE ORDERS, NAMOR?

IN THE ABSENCE OF THE WASP, AND WITH CAPTAIN AMERICA MISSING, *I* AM THE OBVIOUS LEADER. DID I NOT RULE *ATLANTIS?*

AYE, UNTIL THE ATLANTEANS *THREW YOU OUT!*

NO ONE "THREW" ME ANYWHERE, OLYMPIAN! BUT IF YOU WISH TO TRY--!

PLEASE, THERE'S NO NEED TO--!

ONE SIDE, MARVEL! THE SON OF ZEUS SHALL PUT THIS POINTY-EARED UPSTART IN HIS PLACE!

THAT'S ENOUGH-- OUT OF BOTH OF YOU!!

CHO OOM

WE DO **NOT** HAVE TIME FOR ANY MORE OF YOUR SQUABBLING! YOU'RE STILL A PROBATIONAL AVENGER, NAMOR--IF YOU WANT TO STAY A PART OF THIS TEAM, YOU'D BETTER STRAIGHTEN UP AND FLY RIGHT... AND *I MEAN IT!*

YOU... SHAME ME, MARVEL.

YOU SHAME YOURSELF, NAMOR...BUT YOU CAN WORK IT OFF BY SEEING TO OUR *QUINJET.*

VERY WELL, CAPTAIN...

...I ONLY WISH YOU WEREN'T SO... RIGHT.

AND YOU, HERCULES...DOES YOUR TEMPER **HAVE** TO BE AS LEGENDARY AS YOUR STRENGTH? I'D THINK THAT AFTER THOUSANDS OF YEARS, YOU'D BE **ABOVE** BICKERING WITH MORTALS.

NAMOR IS NO MERE MORTAL... BUT I SEE YOUR POINT, MARVEL. I... REGRET MY BEHAVIOR.

OH, LORDY... LOOKIT HIM! THAT THING'S THE SIZE OF A *BUS,* AND HE'S HEFTIN' IT AS EASY AS I'D LIFT A BAG OF FEED!

AND THE SILT MUST BE A *FOOT DEEP* IN THE SHALLOWS OF THAT POND!

81

YES, NAMOR DOESN'T SEEM TO HAVE THE BEST FOOTING. GO GIVE HIM A HAND, HERCULES.

MUST I?

HERCULES!

AS YOU WISH.

ALLOW ME TO ASSIST YOU...

...SEA SLUG...

THANK YOU.

MAY YOUR BEARD GROW INWARD.

UH, I DON'T WANNA KEEP YOU FOLKS FROM IMPORTANT BUSINESS, BUT MY BARN--!

I UNDERSTAND, MR. BRANNUM. JUST CALL THIS NUMBER-- COLLECT--AND EVERYTHING WILL BE TAKEN CARE OF.

"THE MARIA STARK FOUNDATION"?! WHEW, THAT'S SUPPOSED TO HAVE MORE MONEY THAN FORD AND CARNEGIE COMBINED!

WELL, C.M., YOU'RE CERTAINLY BETTER ABLE TO KEEP HERC AND SUBBY IN LINE THAN I AM. UNTIL WE CAN CONTACT THE WASP, IT LOOKS TO ME LIKE YOU'RE IN COMMAND.

IS THAT A VOTE OF CONFIDENCE, DANE--OR ONE OF SYMPATHY?

BOTH! SO, WHERE DO WE GO FROM HERE?

I HAVE A COUPLE OF IDEAS, BUT THEY ALL DEPEND ON GETTING THAT QUINJET BACK IN THE AIR!

LET'S HOPE IT'LL STILL FLY!

AT THAT MOMENT, IN A CHAMBER DEEP WITHIN A LOFTY PEAK OF THE COLORADO ROCKIES...

ΞUNNGHΞ WHERE AM I? MY WRISTS--!

YOU'LL FIND THEY'RE HELD QUITE SECURELY, CAP--

--IN A GOOD THREE INCHES OF SOLID GRANITE... MORE THAN YOU'RE CAPABLE OF BREAKING WITH YOUR BARE HANDS.

YOU SEEM AWFULLY SURE OF MY *LIMITS*, BEYONDER.

OH, I KNOW THEM VERY WELL CAP. YOU SEE, I SPENT SIX HOURS OF MY FIRST DAY ON EARTH *FOLLOWING* YOU. I OBSERVED YOUR EVERY MOVE AND ANALYZED YOU--

--RIGHT DOWN TO YOUR SUBATOMIC STRUCTURE. THEN I MADE A COPY OF YOUR BODY*. IT'S THE ONE I WEAR NOW... WITH A FEW *ALTERATIONS*.

*IN *CAPTAIN AMERICA* #308.

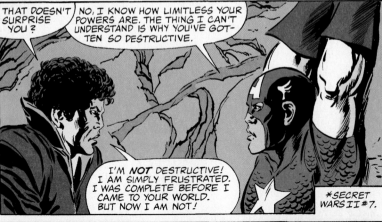

THAT DOESN'T SURPRISE YOU?

NO, I KNOW HOW LIMITLESS YOUR POWERS ARE. THE THING I CAN'T UNDERSTAND IS WHY YOU'VE GOTTEN SO DESTRUCTIVE.

I'M *NOT* DESTRUCTIVE! I AM SIMPLY FRUSTRATED. I WAS COMPLETE BEFORE I CAME TO YOUR WORLD. BUT NOW I AM NOT!

*SECRET WARS II #7.

I CANNOT GET BACK THE PEACE I KNEW BEFORE I LEARNED OF YOUR UNIVERSE

I'M AFRAID I WILL HAVE TO ERASE ALL OF EXISTENCE BEFORE I AM CONTENT AGAIN.

A SHORT TIME LATER, A SILVERY DART OF TITANIUM STEEL THUNDERS WEST OVER THE GREAT PLAINS AT TWICE THE SPEED OF SOUND!

NORTHWEST OF WICHITA, KANSAS, THE JET IS OVERTAKEN BY A HIGH-FREQUENCY *RADIO WAVE* WHICH SUDDENLY SHIFTS INTO A PENCIL-THIN BEAM OF *LIGHT*--

--BEFORE PASSING THROUGH THE CRAFT'S BULLETPROOF CANOPY...

...AND RESUMING HUMAN FORM!

WHAT'S THE WORD, C.M.?

NOT GREAT. I WASN'T ABLE TO LOCATE THE *WASP*... OR ANYONE ELSE.

HOW'S YOUR LUCK BEEN?

A LITTLE BETTER. I THINK I'VE FOUND OUR TARGET. I'VE JUST HOOKED THE AUTOPILOT INTO THIS NAVIGATIONAL COMPUTER...

...WHICH IN TURN IS LINKED TO THE SATELLITE DETECTION WEB I DEVISED. ALL THIS GEAR SAYS THAT THE BEYONDER IS RIGHT *HERE*... ABOUT 30 MILES OUTSIDE OF DENVER.

WE SHOULD BE THERE IN A MATTER OF *MINUTES.*

HMMM... I LEFT MESSAGES FOR THE WEST COAST AVENGERS, THE FANTASTIC FOUR, ALPHA FLIGHT, AND EVEN THE X-MEN, BUT--!

THE *X-MEN?!* THOSE MUTANTS HARBOR THE ARCH-FIEND *MAGNETO!*

I'M AS APPALLED BY THAT AS ANYONE, HERCULES. BUT THE BEYONDER'S BECOME SO CRAZED, WE'LL EVENTUALLY NEED ALL THE HELP WE CAN MUSTER.

IT'S A MOOT POINT ANYWAY... WE CAN'T WAIT FOR THAT HELP TO ARRIVE!

IT'S GOING TO BE JUST THE **FOUR** OF US...AGAINST THE BEYONDER? I'M NOT SURE WHAT WE CAN DO ONCE WE **FIND** HIM!

THAT IS SIMPLE. THE BEYONDER IS **MAD**--A DANGER TO ALL THAT LIVE. WE MUST SLAY HIM-- E'EN AS I, IN MY YOUTH, HAD TO SLAY THE MAD GIANT **ANTAEUS**.

"ANTAEUS WAS ROOFING A TEMPLE WITH THE SKULLS OF HIS MANY VICTIMS.

I STILL RECALL THAT DAY...

"THE GIANT FORCED ALL HE MET TO PERSONAL COMBAT...TO THE **DEATH.** INDEED, HE MIGHT HAVE SLAIN **ME**--

"--FOR HE WAS INVINCIBLE AS LONG AS HE TOUCHED THE EARTH.

"BUT FINALLY, I HELD HIM ALOFT AND SLEW HIM 'FORE HE COULD AGAIN TOUCH GROUND."

THIS IS HARDLY THE SAME SITUATION, HERC. AS FAR AS WE KNOW, THE BEYONDER DOESN'T **HAVE** ANY WEAK-NESSES WE CAN EXPLOIT.

STILL, WE MUST SLAY THE BEYONDER, OR ELSE HE WILL INEVITABLY SLAY US!

I'M NOT CONVINCED WE FACE A KILL-OR-BE-KILLED SITUATION...YET. **RESCUING** CAPTAIN AMERICA IS OUR FIRST PRIORITY. CAP MIGHT KNOW SOME WAY TO REASON WITH THE BEYONDER.

WHAT FOOLISHNESS! YOU CAN'T **REASON** WITH A BEING WHO CAN SHATTER GALAXIES! YOU CAN ONLY **SURRENDER**, AND THAT IS UNTHINKABLE...

...OR IS IT?

WHILE...

IT LOOKS LIKE THE BEYONDER'S COPY OF MY BODY REQUIRES *SLEEP* AS MUCH AS ANY MERE MORTAL.

THAT'S A BREAK FOR ME.

HE WASN'T KIDDING ABOUT THE STRENGTH OF THESE BONDS... THEY GRIP LIKE A *VISE!* BUT... IF I CAN... LOOSEN UP MY HANDS... WITHIN MY GAUNTLETS--!

THE GREAT MUSCLES OF HIS ARMS DRAW TIGHTER AND TIGHTER UNTIL IT SEEMS THAT HIS *BONES* WILL SNAP!

HIS HANDS GROW FIERY HOT... THEN, NUMB!

BUT CAPTAIN AMERICA DOES NOT GIVE UP!

PEELED A LOT OF SKIN OFF MY HANDS, BUT AT LEAST I'M *FREE!*

NOW WHAT DO I DO ABOUT THE BEYONDER? HE COULD WAKE AT ANY MOMENT, AND THEN I'D BE RIGHT BACK WHERE I STARTED... AT BEST!

THERE ARE A COUPLE OF *PRESSURE POINTS* IN THE NECK THAT I COULD HIT, THAT WOULD KEEP HIM OUT COLD FOR AT LEAST AN HOUR. BUT IS THAT ENOUGH TIME TO--?

GOOD LORD, I JUST REALIZED... WHAT IF HE *DREAMS?!*

WHEN DOCTOR DOOM BRIEFLY POSSESSED THE BEYONDER'S POWER,* HE HAD TO CONSTANTLY BE ON HIS GUARD TO KEEP THE POWER UNDER *CONTROL.* IF THE BEYONDER REACTS AS SUBCONSCIOUSLY AS AN ORDINARY MAN--

-- WITH HIS POWER... A *DREAM* MIGHT ERASE ALL OF *REALITY!*

*ISSUES #10-12 OF THE FIRST *SECRET WARS* LIMITED SERIES.

THERE'S NO TIME TO LOSE!

I HAVE TO KNOCK THE BEYONDER INTO DREAMLESS UNCONSCIOUSNESS AT *ONCE!*

WITH ALL THE POWER AT HIS CONTROL, THE LIVING LEGEND SPRINGS ACROSS THE CHAMBER AT HIS QUARRY.

BUT, A SPLIT-SECOND BEFORE CONTACT...

*GOOD,* CAP... VERY *GOOD!*

YOU ARE STILL THE MOST *RESOURCEFUL* MAN I'VE OBSERVED. KNOWING HOW RESOURCEFUL YOU CAN BE, I ASSUMED A SLEEP-LIKE STATE TO SEE HOW LONG IT WOULD TAKE YOU TO FREE YOURSELF.

YOUR ESCAPE WAS MOST *IMPRESSIVE* --BUT YOU'LL NOT FREE YOURSELF FROM THAT SUSPENSION FIELD!

THE FIELD WOULD HOLD YOU THERE FOR ETERNITY, IF I SO WILL IT. AND I JUST *MIGHT!*

YOU ARE CONSIDERED THE *IDEAL MAN* -- THE SOUND MIND IN THE SOUND BODY, THE PEAK OF HUMAN PERFECTION -- AND YET, THE FIRST THING YOU DID UPON GAINING FREEDOM WAS *ATTACK* ME!

*YOU* -- MY OWN MODEL FOR HUMANITY -- HAVE MADE ME YOUR *ENEMY,* JUST AS EVERYONE ELSE HAS! IS IT ANY WONDER THAT I...

...EH? WHAT'S THIS?

"...SOMEONE APPROACHES!"

THE BLACK KNIGHT'S APPARATUS INDICATED THAT THE BEYONDER WAS SOMEWHERE WITHIN THIS PEAK, YET THERE IS NOT A SINGLE *OPENING* ALONG ITS SURFACE.

THE BEYONDER HAS NO DOUBT *SEALED OFF* HIS LAIR. BUT I MUST GAIN ENTRY BEFORE THE OTHERS CATCH UP TO ME!

BEYONDER! IF YOU CAN HEAR ME, THE SUB-MARINER SEEKS AUDIENCE WITH YOU!

WOOM

IN ANSWER, A SMALL SECTION OF THE MOUNTAIN WALL MOMENTARILY BECOMES INTANGIBLE, AND...

NO NEED TO SHOUT, AVENGER. IF YOU HAVE COME TO MAKE DEMANDS--!

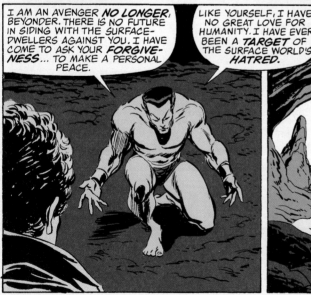

I AM AN AVENGER *NO LONGER,* BEYONDER. THERE IS NO FUTURE IN SIDING WITH THE SURFACE-DWELLERS AGAINST YOU. I HAVE COME TO ASK YOUR *FORGIVENESS...* TO MAKE A PERSONAL PEACE.

LIKE YOURSELF, I HAVE NO GREAT LOVE FOR HUMANITY. I HAVE EVER BEEN A *TARGET* OF THE SURFACE WORLD'S *HATRED.*

YES... I FIND THOSE IMAGES IN YOUR MIND ALL TOO CLEARLY.

ARISE, NAMOR...

... PERHAPS THERE IS A *ROLE* FOR YOU TO PLAY IN MY PLANS.

--REVEALING A NEWLY FORMED *PASSAGE.*

AS THE SUB-MARINER FALLS IN STEP ALONGSIDE THE BEYONDER, THE CAVERN WALL AHEAD OF THEM OPENS AT THEIR APPROACH--

COME, I SHALL SHOW YOU WHAT I INTEND TO DO TO THE WORLD!

NO SOONER HAVE THE TWO DISAPPEARED FROM SIGHT THAN THE CAVERN'S OTHER SIDE BEGINS TO *CRACK OPEN...*

?⁈?⁈ THAT SWORD--!

NOT SO LOUD, HERC!

ONE SIDE, DANE WHITMAN! I SHALL SHOW YOU HOW TO CLEAVE A *MOUNTAIN!*

C.M., WHERE ARE YOU?

OVER HERE, DANE, HURRY! WE HAVE TO BREAK CAP OUT OF THIS *FORCE-FIELD!*

SORRY IT TOOK SO LONG TO GET HERE, CAP! I SIGNALED NAMOR AND THE OTHERS AS SOON AS I'D SCOUTED OUT THIS PLACE AND KNEW YOU WERE OKAY.

WE'LL GET YOU OUT OF THERE, WHILE NAMOR HAS THE BEYONDER *DISTRACTED.*

WHAT KIND OF *FOOL* DO YOU TAKE ME FOR?!

WHA--? THE CAVE WALLS ARE... *MELTING AWAY!!*

BY ALL THE HOUNDS IN HADES--!

DID YOU THINK I WAS *UNAWARE* OF YOUR SCHEME? I SENSED CAPTAIN MARVEL'S ENERGIES THE MOMENT SHE PENETRATED THE MOUNTAIN--

--AND NAMOR'S MIND WAS AS AN *OPEN BOOK* TO ME! ALL THAT RIDICULOUS SUBTERFUGE... JUST TO *FREE* YOUR CAPTAIN AMERICA?

IF HE'S *THAT* IMPORTANT TO YOU, YOU CAN HAVE HIM!

THE BEYONDER'S GESTURE SENDS THE HELPLESS SUB-MARINER FLYING STRAIGHT AT THE CAPTIVE AVENGER--

--THE IMPACT *DISPERSING* BOTH OF THEIR PRISONS!

HEAR ME, BEYONDER! I AM AN *IMMORTAL*-- THE SON OF ZEUS --BUT NE'ER HAVE I TREATED MEN WITH SUCH CALLOUS DISREGARD!

YOU TOY WITH THE LIVES OF MORTALS, BUT YOU ARE ONLY A *PRETENDER* TO GODHOOD!

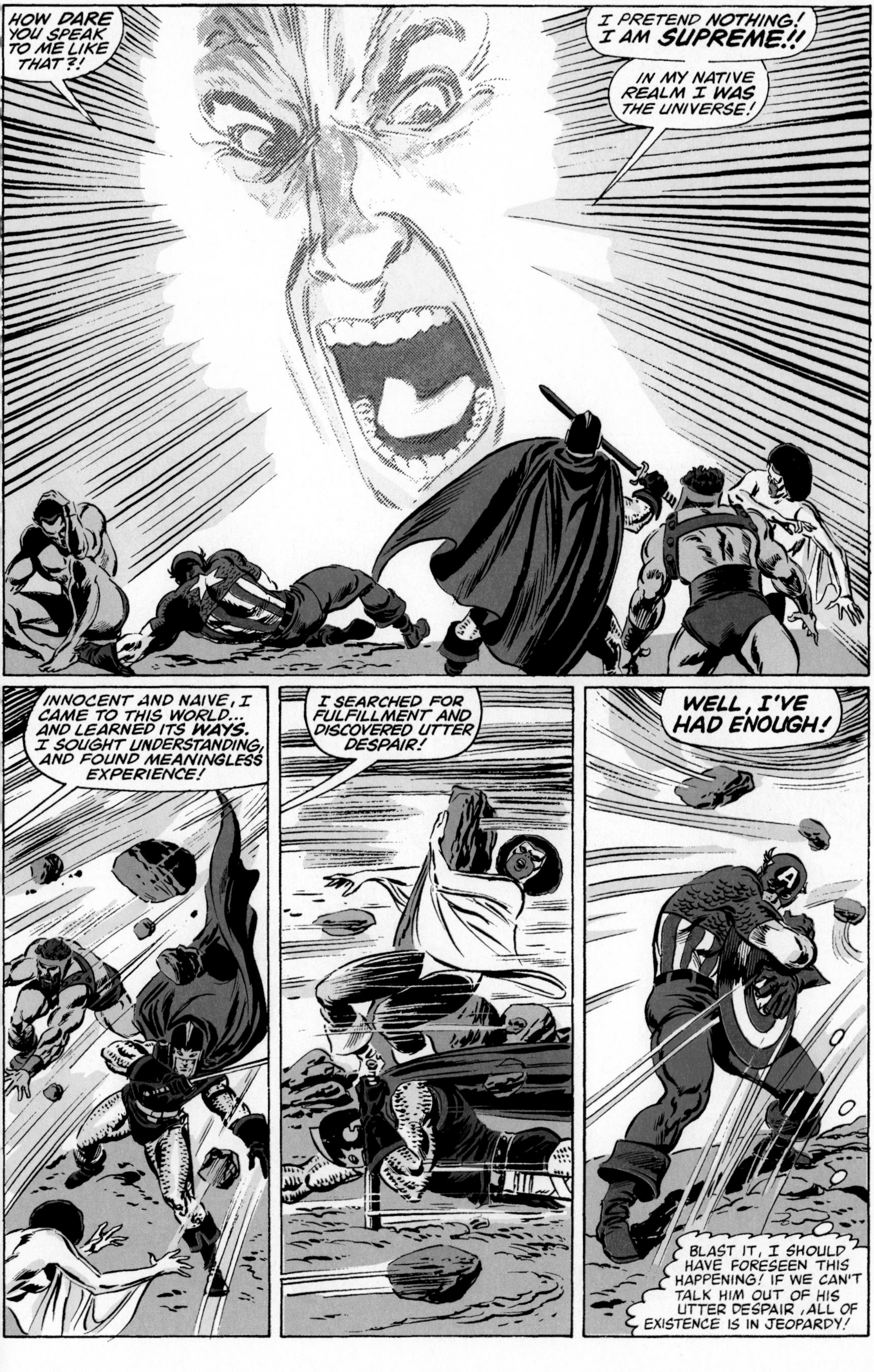

HOW DARE YOU SPEAK TO ME LIKE THAT?!
I PRETEND NOTHING! I AM SUPREME!!
IN MY NATIVE REALM I WAS THE UNIVERSE!
INNOCENT AND NAIVE, I CAME TO THIS WORLD... AND LEARNED ITS WAYS. I SOUGHT UNDERSTANDING, AND FOUND MEANINGLESS EXPERIENCE!
I SEARCHED FOR FULFILLMENT AND DISCOVERED UTTER DESPAIR!
WELL, I'VE HAD ENOUGH!
BLAST IT, I SHOULD HAVE FORESEEN THIS HAPPENING! IF WE CAN'T TALK HIM OUT OF HIS UTTER DESPAIR, ALL OF EXISTENCE IS IN JEOPARDY!

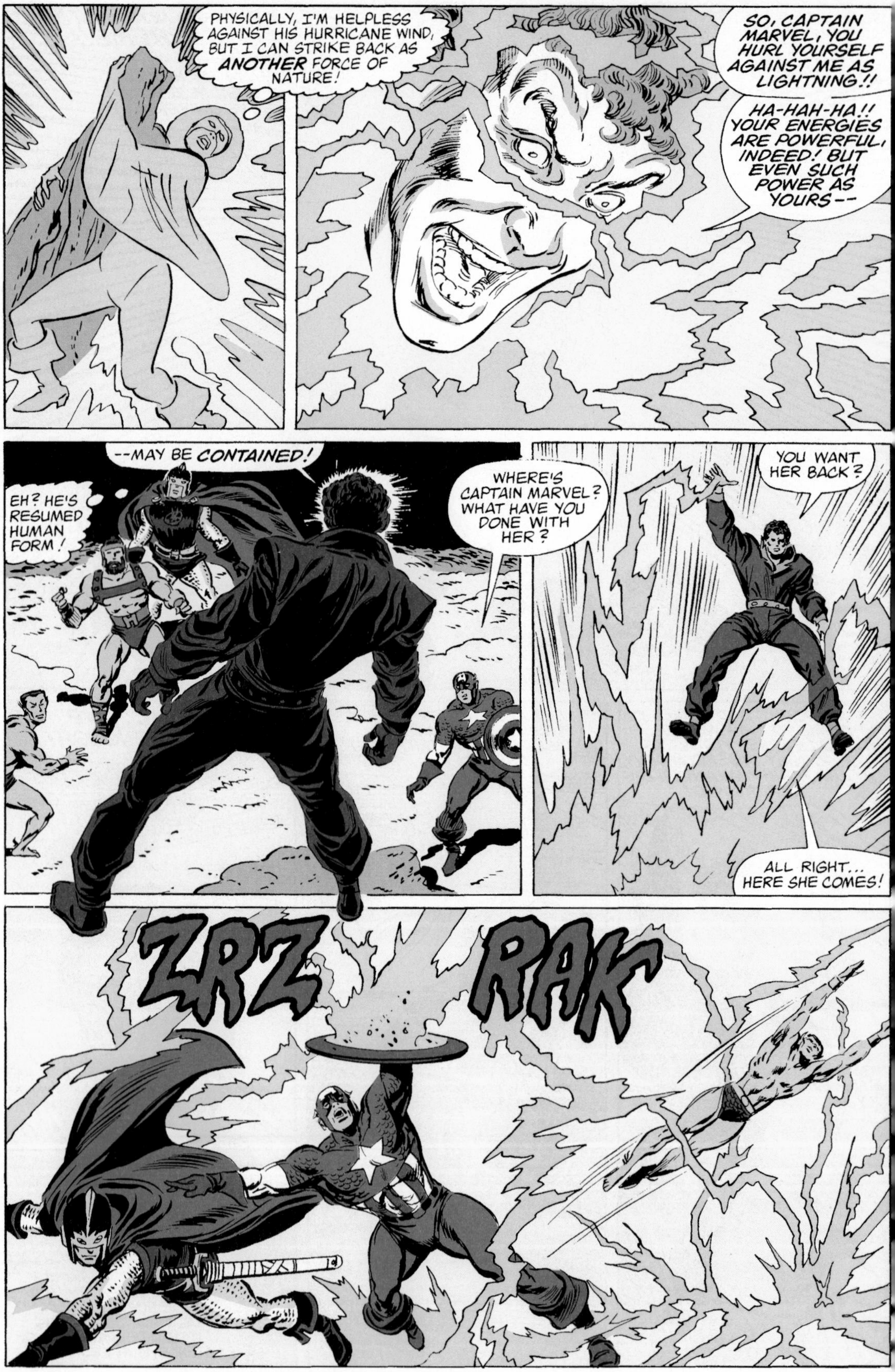
PHYSICALLY, I'M HELPLESS AGAINST HIS HURRICANE WIND, BUT I CAN STRIKE BACK AS ANOTHER FORCE OF NATURE!
SO, CAPTAIN MARVEL, YOU HURL YOURSELF AGAINST ME AS LIGHTNING!!
HA-HAH-HA!! YOUR ENERGIES ARE POWERFUL, INDEED! BUT EVEN SUCH POWER AS YOURS--
--MAY BE CONTAINED!
EH? HE'S RESUMED HUMAN FORM!
WHERE'S CAPTAIN MARVEL? WHAT HAVE YOU DONE WITH HER?
YOU WANT HER BACK?
ALL RIGHT... HERE SHE COMES!
ZRZ
RAK

BUT, WHILE THE MORTAL AVENGERS ARE PROTECTED BY CAPTAIN AMERICA'S MIGHTY SHIELD, ONE FIGURE DOES *NOT* ESCAPE THE LIGHTNING'S FURY!

FRAM

AND, AS THE DUST SETTLES...

KAFF-KAFF H-HERCULES? ARE YOU--?

I LIVE!

DO YOU HEAR, BEYONDER? HERCULES LIVES! AND AS LONG AS I LIVE, I WILL *OPPOSE* THY MADNESS!

THEN, YOU ARE A FOOL, GODLING!

I HAD HOPED TO FIND YOU SO-CALLED HEROES BETTER THAN THE COMMON HORDES OF HUMANITY--

--BUT YOU ARE EVERY BIT AS DEFIANT AS THE REST...PERHAPS MORE SO, BECAUSE OF YOUR *POWER!*

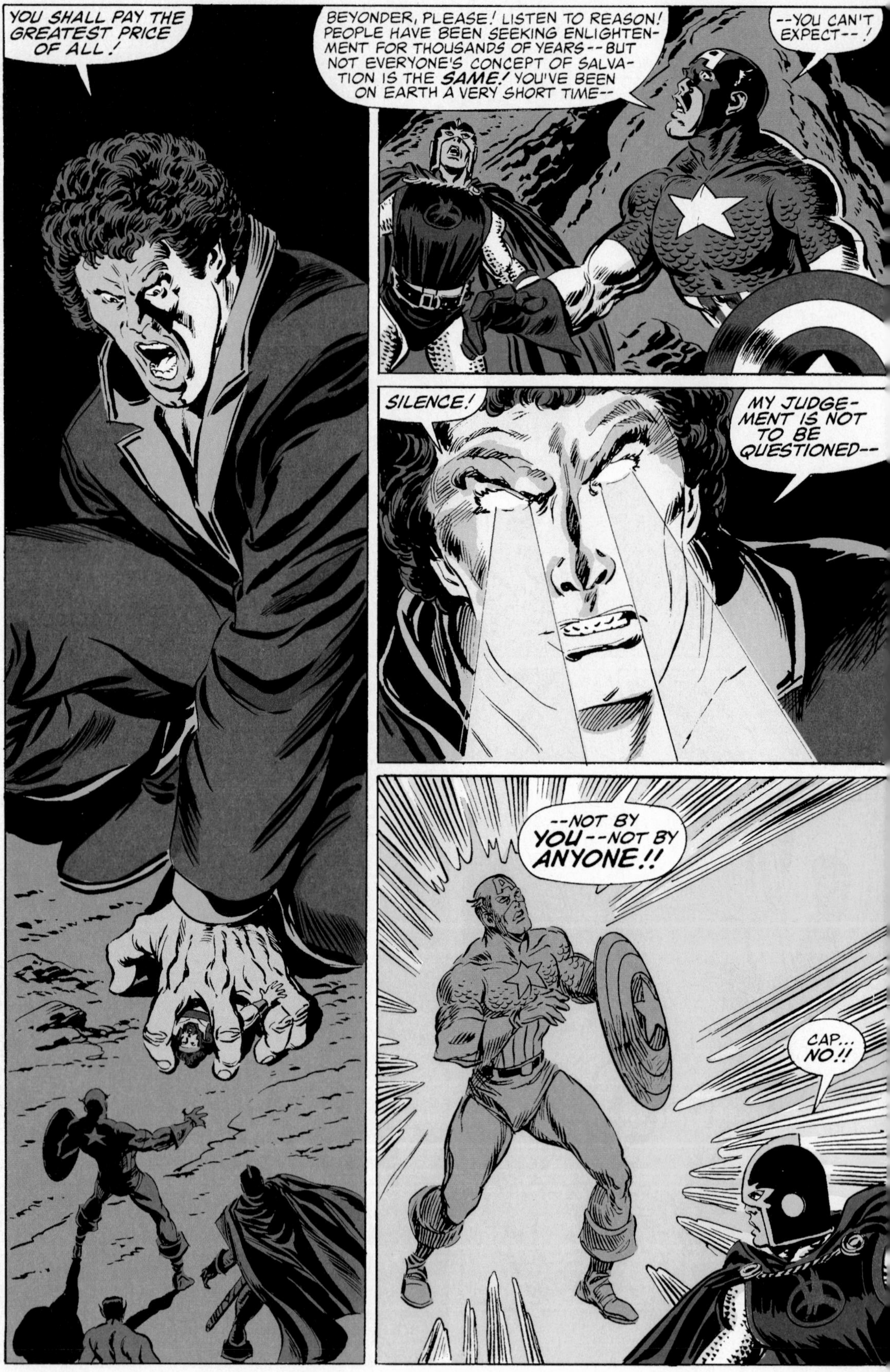
YOU SHALL PAY THE GREATEST PRICE OF ALL!
BEYONDER, PLEASE! LISTEN TO REASON! PEOPLE HAVE BEEN SEEKING ENLIGHTENMENT FOR THOUSANDS OF YEARS--BUT NOT EVERYONE'S CONCEPT OF SALVATION IS THE SAME! YOU'VE BEEN ON EARTH A VERY SHORT TIME--
--YOU CAN'T EXPECT--!
SILENCE!
MY JUDGEMENT IS NOT TO BE QUESTIONED--
--NOT BY YOU--NOT BY ANYONE!!
CAP... NO!!

TO BE CONCLUDED IN
**SECRET WARS II #9!**

AWARE OF THE BEYONDER'S PLAN, THE X-MEN GATHERED THE MARVEL UNIVERSE'S GREATEST HEROES AND BEGAN TO ORGANIZE A LAST-DITCH EFFORT TO STOP HIM. MEANWHILE, IN HIS PRIVATE COMPLEX BURIED DEEP WITHIN THE ROCKY MOUNTAINS, THE BEYONDER BEGAN TO WORRY THAT EVEN IF HE DESTROYED THE ENTIRE MULTIVERSE, THE MEMORY OF ITS EXISTENCE WOULD STILL HAUNT HIM, PREVENTING HIM FROM FINDING PEACE. THINKING MORE CALMLY, HE DECIDED TO TRY BECOMING MORTAL, IN HOPES OF BETTER INTERACTING WITH THE REST OF THE UNIVERSE.

THE BEYONDER CREATED A COMPLEX "BIRTHING MACHINE," REMOVED HIS COSMIC POWER AND STORED IT IN A LARGE CONTAINMENT VESSEL AND SENT HIS ESSENCE THROUGH THE MACHINE. HE RAPIDLY GREW FROM AN EMBRYO INTO A HUMAN ADULT — BUT FOUND THE SUDDEN ADJUSTMENT TO POWERLESS MORTALITY TO BE INCREDIBLY DISCONCERTING AND QUICKLY OPENED THE VESSEL AND RECLAIMED HIS POWER.

REASONING THAT HE NEEDED TO ATTAIN MORTALITY WHILE STILL KEEPING MUCH OF HIS POWER, THE BEYONDER CONNECTED THE CONTAINMENT VESSEL TO THE BIRTHING MACHINE. HOWEVER, AT THAT MOMENT, THE HEROES ATTACKED — JOINED BY THE MOLECULE MAN, WHO BATTLED THE BEYONDER ONE-ON-ONE. WEAKENED, FURIOUS AND UNABLE TO MAKE THE HEROES LISTEN TO HIS NEW PLAN, THE BEYONDER LASHED OUT WITH A DEATH-BOLT OF UNIMAGINABLE FORCE — VAPORIZING MOST OF THE ROCKY MOUNTAINS AND CARVING AN ENORMOUS GASH DEEP INTO THE PLANET'S CRUST.

THINKING THE HEROES DEAD, THE BEYONDER ONCE AGAIN PLACED HIS POWER IN THE CONTAINMENT VESSEL AND ENTERED THE BIRTHING MACHINE, WHICH THIS TIME BEGAN INTEGRATING HIS POWER INTO THE FORMING MORTAL EMBRYO. HOWEVER, THE HEROES HAD SURVIVED, SHIELDED BY THE MOLECULE MAN. REALIZING THAT THE BEYONDER WAS UNDERGOING A REBIRTH, SOME ADVOCATED KILLING HIM WHILE HE WAS HELPLESS, WHILE OTHERS ARGUED THAT THEY SHOULD TRY TO BEFRIEND THE NEW ENTITY THAT WOULD BE BORN. THE MOLECULE MAN, GRIEVOUSLY INJURED FROM HIS RECENT EXERTIONS, ENDED THE ARGUMENT BY BLASTING THE BIRTHING MACHINE — KILLING THE CHILD WITHIN — AND THRUSTING THE CONTAINMENT VESSEL'S BROKEN POWER CONDUIT THROUGH A PINHOLE PORTAL INTO AN EMPTY DIMENSION.

THE BEYONDER'S POWERS VENTED INTO THIS NEW REALM, FILLING IT WITH ENERGY AND RAW PROTOMATTER. OVER TIME, THE MATTER COOLED, COALESCING INTO STARS AND PLANETS... AND ON SOME OF THOSE PLANETS, LIFE EMERGED AND BEGAN TO EVOLVE. THE BEYONDER'S DREAM OF EXISTING AS ONE WITH THE MORTAL UNIVERSE HAD FINALLY BEEN REALIZED — BUT BACK ON THE DEEPLY DAMAGED EARTH, THE HEROES WERE FACING A GRAVE CRISIS...

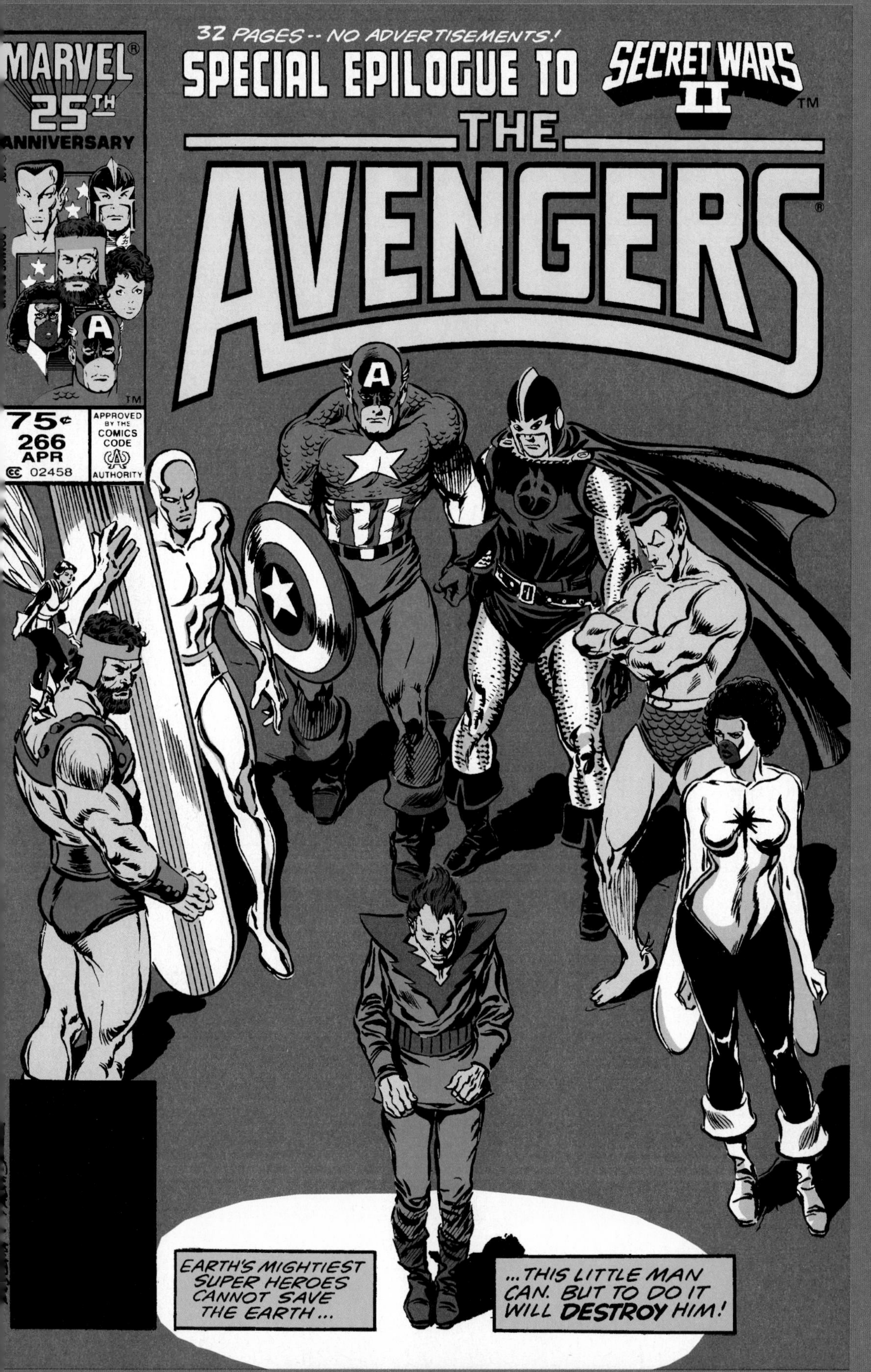
32 PAGES -- NO ADVERTISEMENTS!
SPECIAL EPILOGUE TO SECRET WARS II
THE AVENGERS
MARVEL 25TH ANNIVERSARY
75¢ 266 APR
02458
APPROVED BY THE COMICS CODE AUTHORITY
EARTH'S MIGHTIEST SUPER HEROES CANNOT SAVE THE EARTH...
...THIS LITTLE MAN CAN. BUT TO DO IT WILL DESTROY HIM!

STAN LEE PRESENTS: EARTH'S MIGHTIEST HEROES THE AVENGERS

# "...AND THE WAR'S DESOLATION!"

GUEST-STARRING THE FABULOUS FANTASTIC FOUR

BEHOLD THE *SILVER SURFER!* FOR UNTOLD AGES, HE SOARED AMONGST THE STARS, SEEKING OUT PLANETS TO SUSTAIN THE WORLD-DEVOURING *GALACTUS!* BUT THE DAY CAME WHEN HE DEFIED THE MASTER--

--AND ROSE UP IN DEFENSE OF OUR LITTLE WORLD. AS PUNISHMENT, GALACTUS CONDEMNED THE SURFER TO LIVE UPON THIS EARTH IN ETERNAL EXILE!

WHEN I PASSED THIS WAY MERE WEEKS AGO, THE *ROCKY MOUNTAINS* STOOD HERE, PROUD AND SERENE! NOW, IN THE WAKE OF THE FURY OF *THE ONE FROM BEYOND,* NOTHING REMAINS BUT A JAGGED *CHASM,* SCARRING THE EARTH!

ROGER STERN - WRITER
JOHN BUSCEMA - BREAKDOWNS
TOM PALMER - FINISHED ART
JIM NOVAK - LETTERER
CHRISTIE SCHEELE - COLORIST
MARK GRUENWALD - EDITOR
ADDITIONAL DIALOGUE BY
JIM SHOOTER - EDITOR IN CHIEF

AND BECAUSE OF IT, THE PLANET IS ENTERING THE EARLY STAGES OF ITS *DEATH THROES!*

IT IS AS THOUGH A GREAT HAND HAS RIPPED THE EARTH ASUNDER, TEARING AWAY A SECTION OF THIS MOUNTAIN RANGE--

--AND GOUGING OUT A CHASM WHICH REACHES DOWN TO THE FIERY MANTLE BENEATH THE EARTH'S CRUST.

IN RECENT WEEKS, I FELT A GREAT POWER MOVING ABOUT ON THIS EARTH... A BEING WHOSE MIGHT DWARFED THAT OF GALACTUS HIMSELF... BUT SOMEHOW, THIS ENTITY ELUDED ME.

UNTIL, FINALLY I WAS SUMMONED HERE, ALONG WITH MANY OF EARTH'S MIGHTIEST TO BATTLE HIM!

PHOENIX GATHERED US... AND TOGETHER WE ENDED THE THREAT OF THE BEYONDER FOREVER!

BUT NOT BEFORE THE EARTH ITSELF SUSTAINED THIS SEEMINGLY MORTAL WOUND!

EH? THAT BOLT OF ENERGY, IS IT--?!

CAPTAIN MARVEL!

HELLO, SURFER!

UH... MAY I CALL YOU THAT? WE REALLY HAVEN'T BEEN FORMALLY INTRODUCED!

YES.

99

I'VE COME TO ASK YOU TO HELP US STILL MORE! THE BEYONDER IS DEAD-- BUT, APPARENTLY THIS HUGE RIP IN THE EARTH'S CRUST HE MADE IS CAUSING PLANET-WIDE INSTABILITY! THE EARTH IS BEGINNING TO *WOBBLE* ON ITS AXIS-- AND SOON IT WILL *TEAR ITSELF APART!*

I KNOW. I WILL DO WHATEVER I CAN.

THANK HEAVENS! FOLLOW ME-- I'LL TAKE YOU TO THE OTHERS!

SHE TRANSFORMS HER PHYSICAL FORM INTO ENERGY! TRULY THERE BE NO END TO THE VARIETY OF HUMANKIND!

CAPTAIN MARVEL, HOW DID THIS ALL COME TO PASS? I KNOW LITTLE OF THE BEYONDER AND HIS SO-JOURN HERE!

WELL, IT'S A LITTLE HARD TO EXPLAIN. IT REALLY ALL STARTED A FEW MONTHS AGO...

"...WHEN A COUPLE DOZEN OF EARTH'S SUPER-BEINGS WERE TRANSPORTED ACROSS THE UNIVERSE BY THE INTELLIGENCE WE CAME TO CALL *THE BEYONDER!* HE DESTROYED AN ENTIRE GALAXY JUST TO *CLEAR SPACE* AROUND THE WORLD HE PUT US ON--

"--WHERE WE WERE EXPECTED TO BATTLE OUR ENEMIES IN A *GREAT COSMIC SECRET WAR.* WE SURVIVED THAT WAR AND RETURNED HOME, THINKING THAT WE WERE FREE OF THE BEYONDER! BOY, WERE WE *WRONG!*

" IT WASN'T ALL THAT LONG AFTERWARD THAT THE BEYONDER MADE HIS WAY TO EARTH. WE'VE SINCE DISCOVERED THAT HE FOLLOWED CAPTAIN AMERICA AROUND, OBSERVING HIM IN ACTION--

"--AND USING HIM AS A MODEL TO FORM A BODY OF HIS OWN." *

*IN *CAPTAIN AMERICA* #308.

"BUT THE BEYONDER DIDN'T EASILY ADJUST TO BEING HUMAN. HE MISUNDERSTOOD A LOT, AND CAUSED A LOT OF GRIEF IN HIS MANIA TO EXPERIENCE EVERYTHING.

"HIS POWER WAS SO GREAT--EVEN IN HUMAN FORM --THAT HE COULD LITERALLY DO ANYTHING...AND THAT MADE HIM THE MOST DANGEROUS MAN ALIVE. THE WASP ACTUALLY OFFERED HIM AVENGERS MEMBERSHIP--

"--HOPING THAT WE COULD KEEP AN EYE ON HIM--AND SOMEHOW TEACH HIM TO USE HIS POWER RESPONSIBLY. BUT HE DIDN'T GO FOR IT.

"WE LOST TRACK OF THE BEYONDER FOR A WHILE. FROM WHAT WE'VE PIECED TOGETHER, HE WENT OFF ON A MESSIANIC TRIP. WHEN THAT DIDN'T WORK OUT... HE WENT MAD!

"WE AVENGERS FINALLY CONFRONTED HIM HERE IN THE ROCKIES..."

THAT'S WHEN THE X-MEN, THE NEW MUTANTS, ALPHA FLIGHT, THE FANTASTIC FOUR, THE WEST COAST AVENGERS, THE VISION AND THE SCARLET WITCH, CLOAK AND DAGGER, POWER MAN AND IRON FIST, SPIDER-MAN, THE HULK AND YOU GOT INVOLVED!

AFTER IT WAS ALL OVER, THE AVENGERS AND THE F.F. STAYED TO MOP UP--THE OTHERS EITHER LEFT FOR THEIR OWN REASONS OR WE SENT THEM HOME! BUT THAT WAS BEFORE WE REALIZED THE MAGNITUDE OF THE CRISIS THAT STILL REMAINED!

*THE FULL STORY WAS IN SECRET WARS II #9... STILL ON SALE!

"IT WASN'T UNTIL AFTER THE BEYONDER HAD MET HIS END THAT THE EARTH BEGAN TO FALL APART!"

"SUDDENLY, THE GROUND SHOOK AND SEVERAL OF US WERE THROWN INTO THE CHASM! EVEN *CAPTAIN AMERICA* WAS CAUGHT OFF GUARD..."

EARTHQUAKE!

NESSUS' BLOOD, IS THERE NO END TO THESE TRIALS ?!?

THIS IS NO ORDINARY QUAKE! THIS... ≡YAARGH!≡

WHITMAN! HANG ON, AND I'LL--!

"BUT THE *BLACK KNIGHT* DIDN'T HEAR THE REST. THE SUDDEN PAIN OF A DISLOCATED SHOULDER MADE HIM LOSE CONSCIOUSNESS.

"AND BEFORE ANY OF US COULD GRAB HIM, HE WENT TUMBLING INTO THAT NIGHTMARE!"

"THE *SUB-MARINER* DOVE AFTER HIM WITHOUT A SECOND THOUGHT."

"NAMOR CAUGHT UP TO THE KNIGHT BEFORE HE COULD FALL MORE THAN A FEW HUNDRED FEET... BUT HE PUT HIMSELF IN MORTAL DANGER."

"MILE-HIGH GEYSERS OF MAGMA WERE ERUPTING BELOW THEM--"

"--AND THE INTENSE HEAT RAPIDLY DEHYDRATED THE SUB-MARINER. HE KNEW THAT HE'D NEVER BE ABLE TO FLY OUT OF THERE WITH THE KNIGHT."

"SO..."

HERCULES! *CATCH!!*

I HAVE HIM, NAMOR! NOW, GET OUT OF THERE, BEFORE THE FIRES CLAIM YOU!

NAMOR?

*NAMOR!*

DON'T WORRY, HERCULES -- I'LL GET HIM!

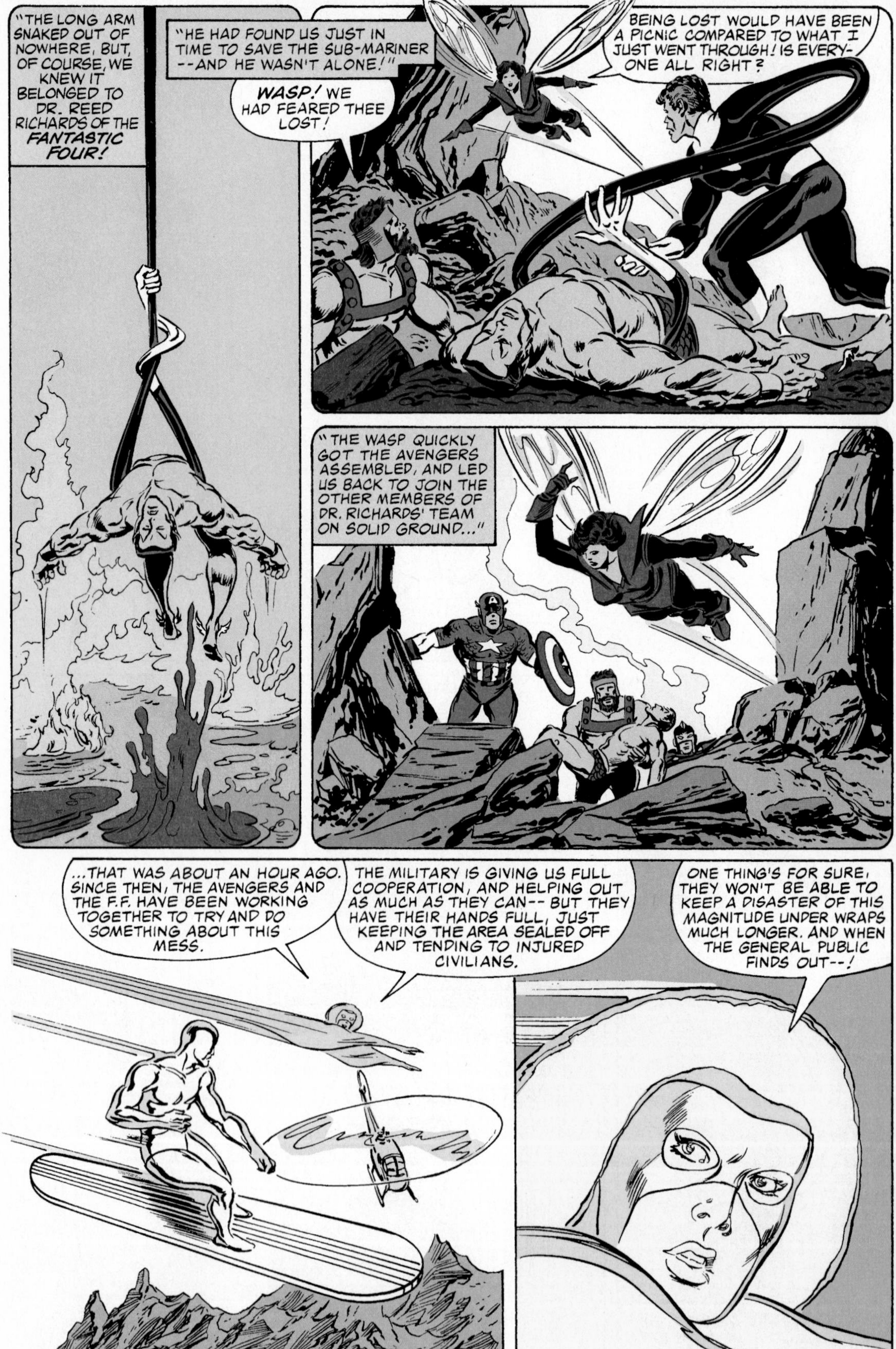
"THE LONG ARM SNAKED OUT OF NOWHERE, BUT, OF COURSE, WE KNEW IT BELONGED TO DR. REED RICHARDS OF THE FANTASTIC FOUR!
"HE HAD FOUND US JUST IN TIME TO SAVE THE SUB-MARINER --AND HE WASN'T ALONE!"
WASP! WE HAD FEARED THEE LOST!
BEING LOST WOULD HAVE BEEN A PICNIC COMPARED TO WHAT I JUST WENT THROUGH! IS EVERY-ONE ALL RIGHT?
"THE WASP QUICKLY GOT THE AVENGERS ASSEMBLED, AND LED US BACK TO JOIN THE OTHER MEMBERS OF DR. RICHARDS' TEAM ON SOLID GROUND..."
...THAT WAS ABOUT AN HOUR AGO. SINCE THEN, THE AVENGERS AND THE F.F. HAVE BEEN WORKING TOGETHER TO TRY AND DO SOMETHING ABOUT THIS MESS.
THE MILITARY IS GIVING US FULL COOPERATION, AND HELPING OUT AS MUCH AS THEY CAN-- BUT THEY HAVE THEIR HANDS FULL, JUST KEEPING THE AREA SEALED OFF AND TENDING TO INJURED CIVILIANS.
ONE THING'S FOR SURE, THEY WON'T BE ABLE TO KEEP A DISASTER OF THIS MAGNITUDE UNDER WRAPS MUCH LONGER. AND WHEN THE GENERAL PUBLIC FINDS OUT--!

IS SOMETHING WRONG? I MEAN, ASIDE FROM THE OBVIOUS?

FOR A MOMENT, I THOUGHT I SENSED A FAINT RELEASE OF ENERGY, SOMETHING ALMOST... FAMILIAR.

WRONG? I'M NOT CERTAIN.

BUT, NO... THERE'S NOTHING NOW. I MUST HAVE BEEN MISTAKEN.

AND SO, CAPTAIN MARVEL AND THE SILVER SURFER SOAR ON, UNAWARE OF EVENTS JUST BEYOND THE ROCKY RIDGE--

-- ON THE GROUNDS OF A HASTILY ERECTED MOBILE ARMY SURGICAL HOSPITAL.

HERE'S THAT ANTI-TETANUS VACCINE, DOC.

GOOD--

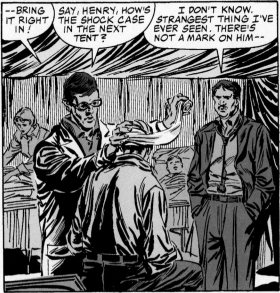

--BRING IT RIGHT IN!

SAY, HENRY, HOW'S THE SHOCK CASE IN THE NEXT TENT?

I DON'T KNOW. STRANGEST THING I'VE EVER SEEN. THERE'S NOT A MARK ON HIM--

"-- EXCEPT FOR THOSE WEIRD FACIAL SCARS, AND THEY'RE OLD. HE HAS NO SIGNS OF INJURY... NO FEVER... HE SHOULDN'T BE COMATOSE, BUT HE IS!"

OWEN... OH, BABY! GET WELL... PLEASE!

MILES TO THE NORTHWEST, A SQUAD OF ARMY ENGINEERS STANDS BY, AWED BY THE SPECTACLE BEFORE THEM...

NOR ARE THEY THE ONLY ONES...

ARMY ORDNANCE GOT ME THE COMPONENTS I NEEDED TO ASSEMBLE THIS *GEO-STRESS ANALYZER* IN RECORD TIME-- BUT I ALMOST WISH THEY *HADN'T!* ALL MY PRELIMINARY READINGS WERE *BAD NEWS!*

WATER

ZOUNDS! HOW DEEP IS THIS CHASM?

TWENTY MILES BELOW, THE F.F.'S *HUMAN TORCH* CIRCLES ABOUT THE STEAMING GEYSERS...

I TOLD REED I'D ABSORB SOME OF THE HEAT DOWN HERE TO STABILIZE THINGS WHILE HE TAKES HIS READINGS... BUT I DON'T KNOW HOW MUCH MORE OF THIS I CAN TAKE!

WHAT'S THE WORD, REED?

I'M NOT SURE, CAP. I'M AT A LOSS TO EXPLAIN WHY, BUT THE DETERIORATION OF EARTH'S CRUST AND MANTLE HAS SUDDENLY SLOWED--!

MY EARLIER READINGS INDICATED THAT EARTH WOULD BREAK UP INTO COSMIC RUBBLE WITHIN AN HOUR. NOW I'D SAY WE HAVE... ABOUT *SIX* HOURS!

THEN, AT LEAST WE HAVE *SOME* TIME! JUST TELL US WHAT TO *DO*, REED!

I WISH I KNEW. I DON'T KNOW HOW TO *BEGIN* TO SOLVE THIS ... SIX HOURS. ALL THE TIME IN THE WORLD MIGHT NOT BE ENOUGH!

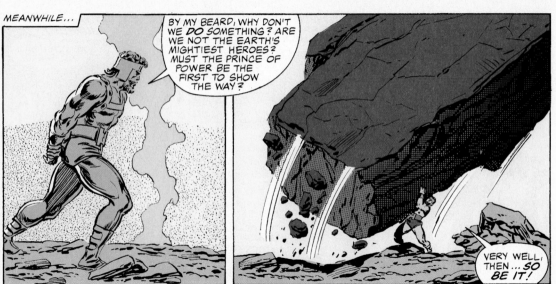

MEANWHILE...

BY MY BEARD, WHY DON'T WE *DO* SOMETHING? ARE WE NOT THE EARTH'S MIGHTIEST HEROES? MUST THE PRINCE OF POWER BE THE FIRST TO SHOW THE WAY?

VERY WELL, THEN... *SO BE IT!*

HOLD IT, MUSCLES! WHAT DO YOU THINK YOU'RE DOING?

REED RICHARDS SAYS THIS CHASM IS A DANGER, *SHE-HULK* --I INTEND TO FILL IT!

HERC, IT'S NOT THAT SIMPLE!

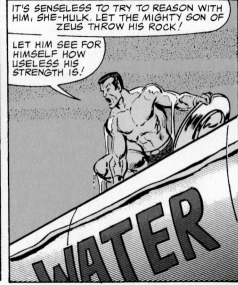

IT'S SENSELESS TO TRY TO REASON WITH HIM, SHE-HULK. LET THE MIGHTY SON OF ZEUS THROW HIS ROCK!

LET HIM SEE FOR HIMSELF HOW USELESS HIS STRENGTH IS!

WATER

BAH!!

KROOM

YOU ARE RIGHT, NAMOR! I *HATE* IT WHEN YOU ARE RIGHT!

BE THANKFUL YOU WERE NOT MY TARGET!

EVERYBODY, LOOK! I'VE FOUND US MORE HELP!

EH? *THE SILVER SURFER!*

WELCOME BACK, OLD FRIEND!

YOUR *POWER COSMIC* WILL ACCOMPLISH WHAT OUR MERE STRENGTH CANNOT!

MAY I EQUAL YOUR CONFIDENCE IN ME, NAMOR!

WHAT'S THE SITUATION, C.M.? WHAT DOES IT LOOK LIKE FROM HIGH UP?

IT--IT LOOKS LIKE THE END OF THE WORLD!

DON'T TALK THAT WAY, LADY! WE'VE BEEN IN TOUGH SITUATIONS BEFORE! WE'LL FIND A WAY TO LICK THIS!

GOOD OLD CAP--! SOMEHOW, HE ALWAYS MAKES YOU BELIEVE YOU'VE GOT A CHANCE! BOY, AM I GLAD HE'S HERE!

I'M NOT CERTAIN EVEN *YOUR* POWER WILL BE ENOUGH, SURFER. WHAT THE BEYONDER DID TO THIS REGION EXTENDS FAR BEYOND THE OBVIOUS GEOPHYSICAL INSTABILITY.

YOU ARE RIGHT, REED RICHARDS--

--MILLIONS OF CUBIC MILES OF CRUST HAVE SIMPLY DISSOLVED AWAY. IF THIS WOUND IN THE EARTH'S SURFACE IS TO BE *SEALED*--

--THE DISPERSED MATTER MUST BE DRAWN BACK AND REASSEMBLED. I DO NOT KNOW IF I AM *CAPABLE* OF SUCH A TASK, BUT I SHALL TRY.

THIS WILL BE DANGEROUS. I SUGGEST YOU HAVE THE SOLDIERS WITHDRAW FROM THE AREA.

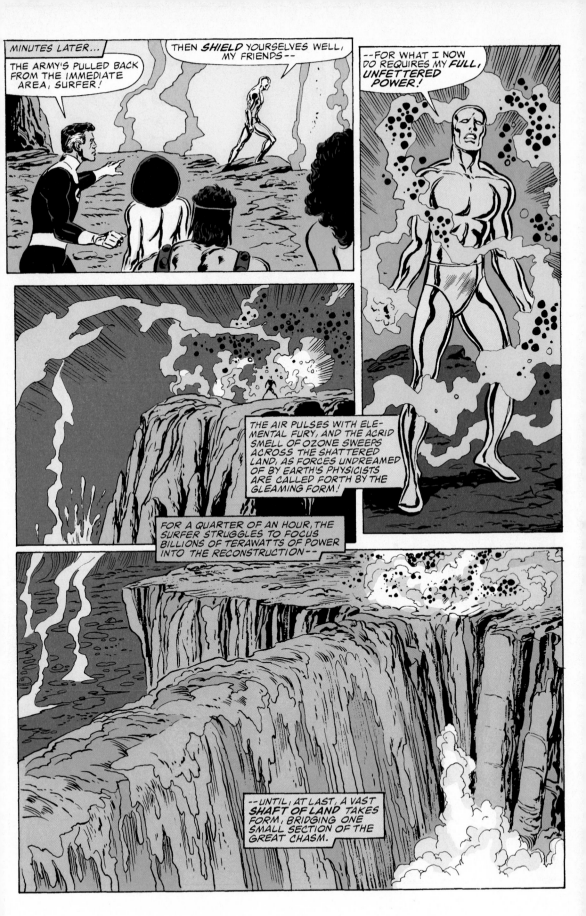

**MINUTES LATER...**

THE ARMY'S PULLED BACK FROM THE IMMEDIATE AREA, SURFER!

THEN *SHIELD* YOURSELVES WELL, MY FRIENDS--

--FOR WHAT I NOW DO REQUIRES MY *FULL, UNFETTERED POWER!*

THE AIR PULSES WITH ELEMENTAL FURY, AND THE ACRID SMELL OF OZONE SWEEPS ACROSS THE SHATTERED LAND, AS FORCES UNDREAMED OF BY EARTH'S PHYSICISTS ARE CALLED FORTH BY THE GLEAMING FORM!

FOR A QUARTER OF AN HOUR, THE SURFER STRUGGLES TO FOCUS BILLIONS OF TERAWATTS OF POWER INTO THE RECONSTRUCTION--

--UNTIL, AT LAST, A VAST *SHAFT OF LAND* TAKES FORM, BRIDGING ONE SMALL SECTION OF THE GREAT CHASM.

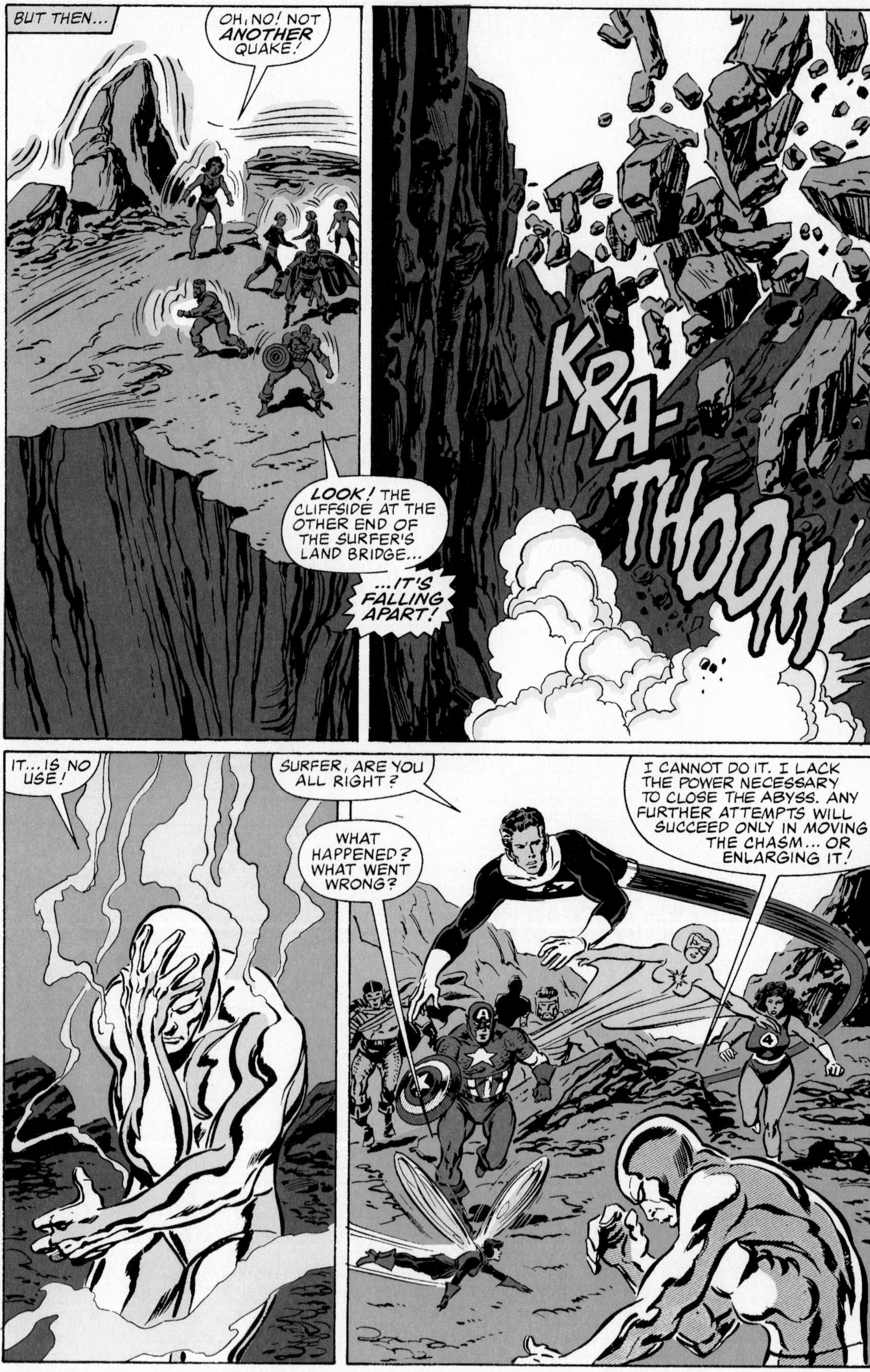

BUT THEN...
OH, NO! NOT ANOTHER QUAKE!
LOOK! THE CLIFFSIDE AT THE OTHER END OF THE SURFER'S LAND BRIDGE...
...IT'S FALLING APART!
KRA-THOOM
IT... IS NO USE!
SURFER, ARE YOU ALL RIGHT?
WHAT HAPPENED? WHAT WENT WRONG?
I CANNOT DO IT. I LACK THE POWER NECESSARY TO CLOSE THE ABYSS. ANY FURTHER ATTEMPTS WILL SUCCEED ONLY IN MOVING THE CHASM... OR ENLARGING IT!

THEN, THERE IS **NO HOPE** LEFT US? **NO ONE** WHO CAN RESTORE THESE SHATTERED LANDS?

THERE ARE NONE ON THIS WORLD WHO POSSESS THAT SUCH POWER

NO!

NO, YOU'RE WRONG, SURFER -- THERE **IS** ONE SUCH MAN! AND DURING OUR SHOWDOWN WITH THE BEYONDER, HE **PROVED** IT!

AT ONE POINT WHEN THE BEYONDER HAD BATTERED ALL OF US TO THE GROUND...

"--THE MOLECULE MAN TOOK HIM ON **ALONE!** EVEN THOUGH THE BEYONDER WAS NEAR-**OMNIPOTENT,** THE MOLECULE MAN **HELD HIS OWN** -- AT LEAST LONG ENOUGH FOR US TO GET TO OUR FEET!

"AND WHEN THE BEYONDER TRIED TO WIPE US ALL OUT WITH ONE DEVASTING DEATH BLAST -- THE SAME ONE THAT RIPPED OPEN THE EARTH'S CRUST--

" IT WAS THE **MOLECULE MAN'S** POWER **SHIELDING**-US THAT ALLOWED US TO PULL OURSELVES FROM THE RUBBLE ALIVE AND WHOLE!"

"I COULDN'T BELIEVE WE HAD SURVIVED! BUT EVEN MORE INCREDIBLE WERE THE MOLECULE MAN'S **WORDS**--"

IT'S A GOOD THING I'M NOT AS HEROIC AS YOU ALL ARE! MAYBE IF I WERE, I'D HAVE BURNED MYSELF OUT TOTALLY AGAINST THE BEYONDER--YOU KNOW, FIGHTING TO THE LAST BREATH AND ALL THAT.

THEN I WOULDN'T HAVE HAD THE STRENGTH LEFT TO SHIELD US... MOSTLY, ANYWAY!

BY THE WAY, I ALSO REMOVED *EVERY LIVING THING* FROM HIS *DEATHBLAST'S* PATH... THEY'RE ALL IN STASIS, IN SUB-SPACE! I'LL BRING 'EM BACK LATER, IF THERE *IS* A LATER!

HOW ARE SUCH THINGS *POSSIBLE*--? IT'S--IT'S BEYOND BELIEF!

BUT IF IT MAKES YOU FEEL ANY BETTER, ALL THIS HAS *COST* ME... *DEARLY!*

I'M HURT... BADLY!

I TRANSACT ON POWER LEVELS UNIMAGINABLE TO YOU, CAPTAIN AMERICA, AND THE BEYONDER, IT SEEMS, ON LEVELS UNIMAGINABLE TO *ME!*

CAN THIS BE TRUE?

WHO CAN SAY? BUT, AFTER ALL WE'VE SEEN... ANYTHING SEEMS POSSIBLE!

AT THIS POINT, I'D SAY WE CAN'T AFFORD TO OVERLOOK *ANY* POSSIBILITIES! THE MOLECULE MAN MAY BE UNABLE, BECAUSE OF HIS INJURIES, OR *UNWILLING* TO HELP US! BUT I THINK WE MUST FIND HIM... AND ASK FOR HIS AID!

WHAT?

I CAN'T BELIEVE I'M *HEARING* THIS! THE MOLECULE MAN'S A *BAD GUY!*

MAYBE... BUT IF THE WHOLE *WORLD'S* IN DANGER--WELL, HE LIVES HERE, TOO! WE'VE GOT TO ASK HIM--!

WHAT IS ALL THIS TALK OF APPEALS? IF YOU THINK THIS MOLECULE MAN CAN ACCOMPLISH WHAT NEEDS BE DONE, THEN WE MUST TRACK THE BRIGAND DOWN AND *FORCE* HIM TO RESTORE THE MISSING LAND.

THAT MAY NOT BE POSSIBLE, HERC--

THINK ABOUT IT--! IF THIS GUY CAN REALLY MANIPULATE MATTER ON THAT KIND OF SCALE, HOW COULD WE FORCE HIM TO DO *ANYTHING*?

WHAT? YOU THINK HIM MORE POWERFUL THAN I?

I'M AFRAID SO.

LET'S NOT FORGET THAT THE MOLECULE MAN ONCE DROPPED A MOUNTAIN ON SOME OF US!* BUT, HEY, LET'S SAY HE'S BECOME A GOODY TWO-SHOES AND HE'S WILLING TO HELP! SO *WHAT*? HE'S NEVER BEEN EXACTLY A ROLE MODEL OF MENTAL STABILITY!

WHAT IF HE FOLDS UNDER THE PRESSURE AND CAUSES AN EVEN GREATER CATASTROPHE?

WE *ALL* HAVE GRAVE RESERVATIONS ABOUT THIS, SHE-HULK. BUT MINE, AT LEAST, ARE SWIFTLY BEING OUT-WEIGHED BY OUR WORSENING SITUATION!

*IN ISSUE #4 OF THE FIRST *SECRET WARS* LIMITED SERIES.

I AGREE, REED. LIKE IT OR NOT, WE *NEED* THE MOLECULE MAN!

BUT HE *VANISHED* IN THE CONFUSION AFTER THE BATTLE WITH THE BEYOND-ER! WHO KNOWS WHERE HE IS NOW?

SURFER, CAN YOU *FIND* HIM FOR US?

I DO NOT KNOW. THE ENERGY I SENSED EARLIER WAS BUT A FADING REMNANT OF THAT WHICH I REMEMBERED FROM TIMES PAST. I... *WAIT!*

YES, I CAN FEEL HIS POWER ONCE MORE, BUT IT'S WEAK... VERY *WEAK!*

113

MILES AWAY, AT THE M.A.S.H. COMPOUND...

=UHHN= MAR-SHA?

IF OUR SHOCK CASE SHOWS ANY CHANGE, I WANT TO KNOW AT ONCE!

OWEN! OH, HONEY, YOU'VE HAD ME SO WORRIED! ARE YOU ALL RIGHT? WHAT'S WRONG?

IT'S JUST THAT... CONFRONTATION... WITH THE BEYONDER...TOOK A LOT OUT OF ME.

OWEN, I DON'T THINK YOU'RE SAFE HERE. THERE ARE DOCTORS AND SOLDIERS ALL AROUND--ASKING QUESTIONS! WE HAVE TO GET YOU OUT OF HERE!

I THINK I CAN... DIVERT ENOUGH POWER TO DO... SOMETHING ABOUT THAT... IF YOU'LL FIRE UP FOR ME!

BABY, YOU'VE GOT IT!

WITH A THOUGHT, THE YOUNG WOMAN TRANSFORMS HER BODY INTO THE SEETHING, IONIZED PLASMA OF VOLCANA!

AND THEN...

DOC, THE TENT THE SHOCK CASE WAS IN... IT'S TURNED INTO A... A...

...A BALLOON?

FILLING WITH AIR HEATED BY VOLCANA'S THERMAL ENERGY, THE MOLECULARLY-ALTERED TENT SWIFTLY WHISKS THEM HUNDREDS OF FEET INTO THE AIR.

JUST... MAINTAIN US AT THIS HEIGHT, MARSHA, AND THE WINDS...WILL CARRY US AWAY!

BUT...

DON'T BE ALARMED! I'M NOT HERE TO *HARM* YOU. THERE'S A MATTER OF GRAVE IMPORTANCE--!

VOLCANA RECOGNIZES THE NEW VOICE AT ONCE...

NOT YOU... *NOT HERE!*

SHE REMEMBERS THEIR LAST ENCOUNTER WITH CAPTAIN MARVEL, ON THE BEYONDER'S WONDERWORLD.* THE MOLECULE MAN HAD BEEN RECOVERING FROM INJURIES THEN, TOO--WHEN *THIS* AVENGER ATTACKED.

NOT AGAIN.!! NO!!!

*SECRET WARS #8.*

GONE...THE WITCH IS *GONE!*

M-MARSHA?

OH, BABY! DON'T WORRY! I WOULDN'T LET HER *HURT* YOU AGAIN!

I WON'T LET *ANYONE* HURT YOU... *EVER!*

REVERTING TO NORMAL, MARSHA RUSHES TO COMFORT THE MAN SHE LOVES.

WHILE, HIGH OVERHEAD...

I WISH I KNEW WHAT THAT SUDDEN FLARE WAS ALL ABOUT, SURFER. MAYBE I SHOULDN'T HAVE LET CAPTAIN MARVEL CONFRONT THE MOLECULE MAN ON HER OWN.

FROM WHAT I HAVE SEEN OF CAPTAIN MARVEL, SHE IS FULLY CAPABLE OF INITIATING CONTACT.

NO KIDDING! SHE'S THE MOST CAPABLE AVENGER I HAVE-- NEXT TO CAPTAIN AMERICA. BUT THE MOLECULE MAN IS SUCH AN *UNKNOWN QUANTITY.*

I HOPE C.M. HASN'T GOTTEN IN OVER HER HEAD.

ALL OF US, IT WOULD SEEM, ARE "IN OVER OUR HEADS"! CAPTAIN MARVEL WILL SPEAK OUR CASE AS WELL AS ANY! THERE IS NO PURPOSE IN DOUBTFUL RE-FLECTION UPON YOUR DECISION!

ON THE OTHER HAND, A LITTLE SECOND GUESSING *MAY* BE IN ORDER, SURFER!

I BLEW IT, JAN!

AFTER A QUICK BRIEFING...

I'M GLAD I TOOK THE PRECAUTION OF ASSUMING A *HOLOGRAPHIC IMAGE* OF MYSELF. VOLCANA IS ACTING LIKE A MOTHER BEAR PROTECTING HER CUB.

IF WE CAN'T CALM *HER* DOWN, WE MAY NEVER GET THROUGH TO *HIM.*

TIME IS FLEETING.

IF AN APPEAL IS TO BE MADE TO THE MOLECULE MAN, IT MUST BE SWIFT. MIGHT *I* SUGGEST A NEW TACK--?

MOMENTS LATER...

DON'T HOLD BACK ON MY ACCOUNT, C.M. GO ON AHEAD AND ALERT THE OTHERS. WE MUST BE *PREPARED* FOR THIS!

WILL DO!

MEANWHILE, THE SURFER SOARS INTO THE UPPER REACHES OF THE ATMOSPHERE, NOW USING HIS ASTOUNDING COSMIC POWER TO TWIST AND CHANNEL THE CURRENTS OF THE JET STREAM--

--INTO GALE FORCE WINDS!

OWEN! OWEN, WE'RE OUT OF *CONTROL!*

WE'LL *CRASH!*

NO, I DON'T THINK SO. THERE'S SOMETHING UNUSUAL ABOUT THESE WINDS. I CAN FEEL THEM EASING ALREADY.

WITHIN MINUTES, THE GALE HAS DIED DOWN TO A GENTLE BREEZE, WAFTING THE DESCENDING BALLOON DOWN TO A LANDING ON A PRECIPICE HIGH ABOVE THE INFERNO OF THE CHASM FLOOR.

117

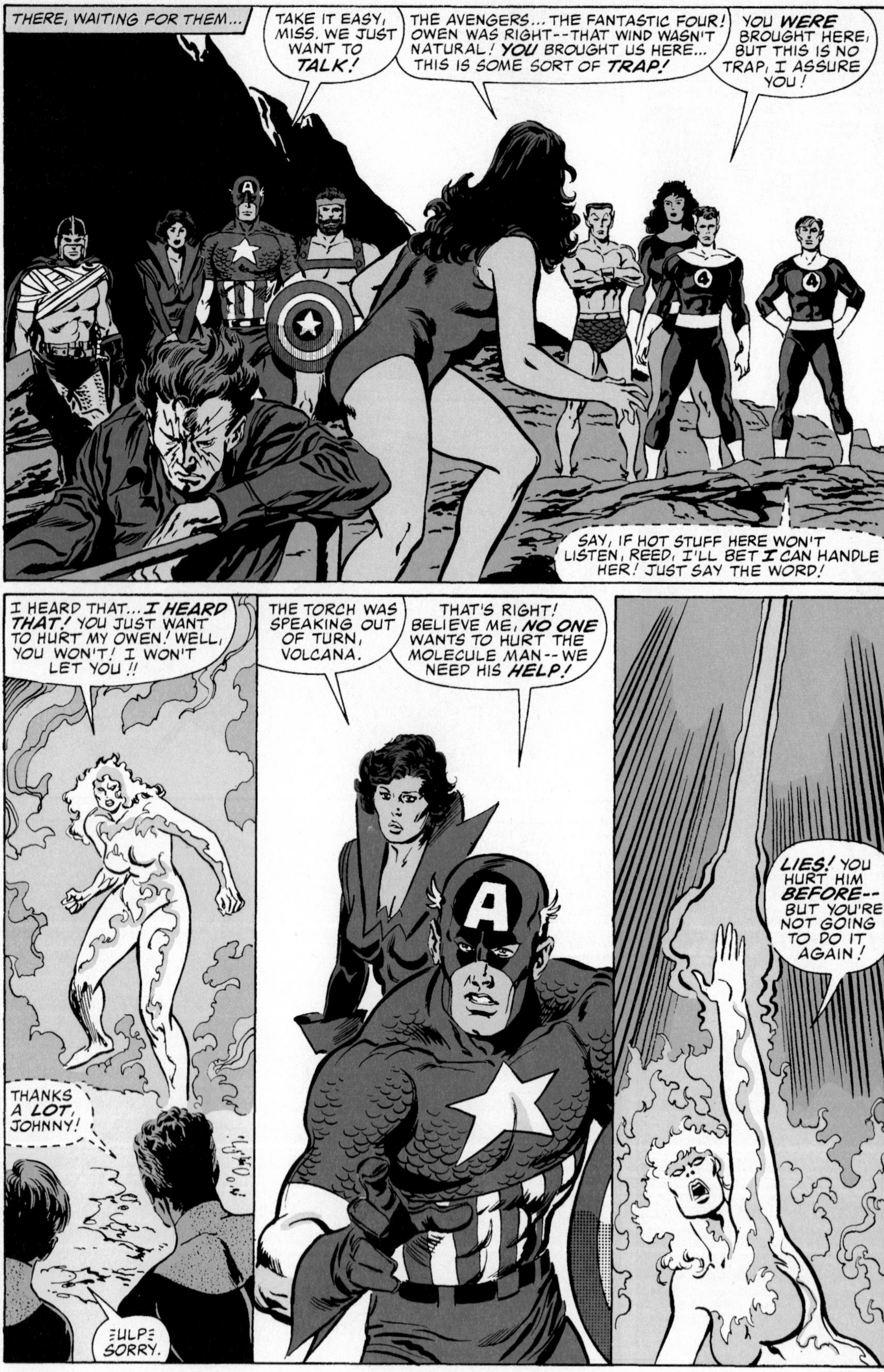
THERE, WAITING FOR THEM...
TAKE IT EASY, MISS. WE JUST WANT TO TALK!
THE AVENGERS... THE FANTASTIC FOUR! OWEN WAS RIGHT--THAT WIND WASN'T NATURAL! YOU BROUGHT US HERE... THIS IS SOME SORT OF TRAP!
YOU WERE BROUGHT HERE, BUT THIS IS NO TRAP, I ASSURE YOU!
SAY, IF HOT STUFF HERE WON'T LISTEN, REED, I'LL BET I CAN HANDLE HER! JUST SAY THE WORD!
I HEARD THAT... I HEARD THAT! YOU JUST WANT TO HURT MY OWEN! WELL, YOU WON'T! I WON'T LET YOU!!
THANKS A LOT, JOHNNY!
GULP SORRY.
THE TORCH WAS SPEAKING OUT OF TURN, VOLCANA.
THAT'S RIGHT! BELIEVE ME, NO ONE WANTS TO HURT THE MOLECULE MAN--WE NEED HIS HELP!
LIES! YOU HURT HIM BEFORE--BUT YOU'RE NOT GOING TO DO IT AGAIN!

FWHOOSH

VOLCANA CAN POUR OUT THE HEAT OF A SMALL STAR, BUT IT DOESN'T EVEN FEEL *STUFFY* IN HERE!

EVERYONE HOLD YOUR POSITIONS!

NICE SAVE, SUE.

THANKS, JENNIFER! I THOUGHT THAT WE MIGHT NEED AN *INVISIBLE* ACE-IN-THE-HOLE!

HOW'S YOUR FORCE-FIELD TAKING THE HEAT, SUE?

SO FAR SO GOOD, DEAR--

"-- BUT I DON'T THINK WE HAVE TO WORRY ABOUT *THAT* ANY LONGER!"

OWIE... I'LL NEVER BE ABLE TO BEAT *ALL* OF THEM! OH, OWIE, I FAILED YOU AGAIN!

VOLCANA, CAN'T YOU SEE THAT WE DON'T WANT TO HURT ANYBODY! WE NEED YOUR MAN'S HELP! JUST HEAR US OUT-- AND THEN IF YOU STILL WANT TO LEAVE NOBODY WILL STOP YOU! I GUARANTEE IT!

SHE SPEAKS TRULY, THOUGH THERE WILL SOON BE NO PLACE TO WHICH YOU CAN FLEE!

THE IMPENDING CATASTROPHE THREATENS THE ENTIRE PLANET!

YOU THINK I DON'T KNOW THAT, SURFER?

THE "CATASTROPHE" WOULD HAVE *HAPPENED* BY NOW IF NOT FOR *ME!*

EVEN AS WE SPEAK, I'M LITERALLY *HOLD-ING THIS PLANET TOGETHER...*

...AND LET ME TELL YOU, IT'S NOT EASY GIVEN MY CONDITION.

THEN... CAN YOU UNDO THE DAMAGE WROUGHT HERE, OWEN REECE?

*NO!* I'M TELLING YOU GUYS, I'M *WOUNDED! INJURED! HURT!* IT'S ALL I CAN DO TO *SLOW DOWN* THE EARTH'S DESTRUCTION!

IF I TRIED TO USE ANY MORE ENERGY THAN I'M USING NOW, I'D JUST TEAR UP MY INSIDES EVEN WORSE! I MIGHT BURN OUT MY POWER COMPLETELY! IT MIGHT EVEN *KILL* ME!

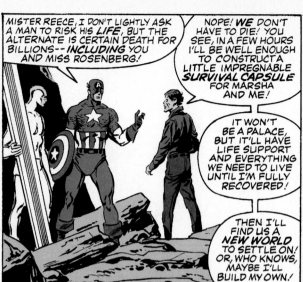

MISTER REECE, I DON'T LIGHTLY ASK A MAN TO RISK HIS *LIFE*, BUT THE ALTERNATE IS CERTAIN DEATH FOR BILLIONS-- *INCLUDING* YOU AND MISS ROSENBERG!

NOPE! *WE* DON'T HAVE TO DIE! YOU SEE, IN A FEW HOURS I'LL BE WELL ENOUGH TO CONSTRUCT A LITTLE IMPREGNABLE *SURVIVAL CAPSULE* FOR MARSHA AND ME!

IT WON'T BE A PALACE, BUT IT'LL HAVE LIFE SUPPORT AND EVERYTHING WE NEED TO LIVE UNTIL I'M FULLY RECOVERED!

THEN I'LL FIND US A *NEW WORLD* TO SETTLE ON! OR, WHO KNOWS, MAYBE I'LL BUILD MY OWN!

LET'S SEE... FROM THAT LOOK IN YOUR EYES I'D GUESS THAT YOUR QUIETLY CONSIDERING *JUMPING* ME AND TRYING TO *FORCE* ME TO COOPERATE! OR MAYBE YOU'RE EVEN THINKING OF THREATENING MARSHA--!

WE'RE THE *AVENGERS*, MR. REECE! WE DON'T WORK THAT WAY...

USUALLY.

YEAH? WELL, I WARN YOU, I'M WEAK, BUT I'M *NOT* HELPLESS.

YOU AREN'T *REALLY* GOING TO JUST SAVE YOURSELF AND LET EVERYTHING ELSE GO TO PIECES ARE YOU?

THE WORLD DIDN'T DO A WHOLE HECK OF A LOT FOR ME MOST OF MY LIFE!

BUT, *THINK* ABOUT IT--! NO MORE SAK'S, NO MORE CHILDREN PLAYING HIDE AND SEEK, NO MORE SUNRISES OFF CAPE COD...

HMM... NO MORE OF MY FAVORITE T.V. SHOWS, EITHER! MARSHA AND I SURE WOULD MISS THE *F TROOP* RERUNS!

IF I TRY TO SAVE THE EARTH AND *FAIL*... I DEFINITELY WON'T HAVE ENOUGH ENERGY LEFT TO SAVE MARSHA AND ME!

THAT SEEMS VERY PROBABLE...

EVEN IF I *SUCCEED*, THE EFFORT MAY KILL ME, OR CRIPPLE ME... OR, WORST OF ALL, BURN OUT MY POWER!

DO YOU REALIZE WHAT THAT WOULD MEAN? I'D BE DEFENSELESS-- EASY PREY FOR THE GOVERNMENT OR ANYBODY ELSE WHO WANTED TO WIRE ME UP AND TRY TO FIND OUT HOW MY POWERS USED TO WORK! AND YOU *KNOW* THEY WOULD--!

WE WON'T LET THAT HAPPEN, MR. REECE! YOU HAVE *RIGHTS*... NO MATTER WHAT YOU'VE DONE-- OR BEEN-- IN THE PAST!

WHAT DO YOU THINK, MARSHA?

I--I DON'T KNOW, OWIE! *YOU'RE* THE MOST IMPORTANT THING TO ME!

UH-HUH...

STILL, I KNOW THAT IT'S SO HARD FOR A TRULY *COSMIC* BEING, LIKE ME, TO START OVER ON A WHOLE NEW WORLD...

...BUT IT'S A WHOLE 'NOTHER THING FOR A RELATIVELY NORMAL HUMAN LIKE YOU!

OKAY, I'LL DO IT.

SEVERAL HOURS LATER... TIME IS GROWING SHORT, OWEN REECE. WE MUST MOVE QUICKLY.

I'M READY.

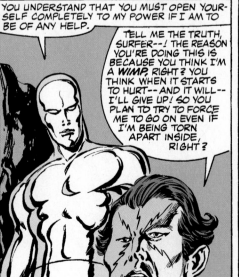

YOU UNDERSTAND THAT YOU MUST OPEN YOURSELF COMPLETELY TO MY POWER IF I AM TO BE OF ANY HELP.

TELL ME THE TRUTH, SURFER--! THE REASON YOU'RE DOING THIS IS BECAUSE YOU THINK I'M A *WIMP*, RIGHT? YOU THINK WHEN IT STARTS TO HURT-- AND IT WILL-- I'LL GIVE UP! SO YOU PLAN TO TRY TO FORCE ME TO GO ON EVEN IF I'M BEING TORN APART INSIDE, RIGHT?

LET'S FACE IT, YOU GUYS WOULD *RATHER* I WAS DEAD OR DE-POWERED! YOU DON'T LIKE THE IDEA OF A GUY AS POWERFUL AS ME WALKING AROUND!

WELL, YOU'RE GOING TO GET YOUR *CHANCE*, SURFER! 'CAUSE NOW OUR ENERGIES ARE *LINKED*! A LITTLE PUSH FROM YOU AT THE CRITICAL POINT-- AND I'M HISTORY!

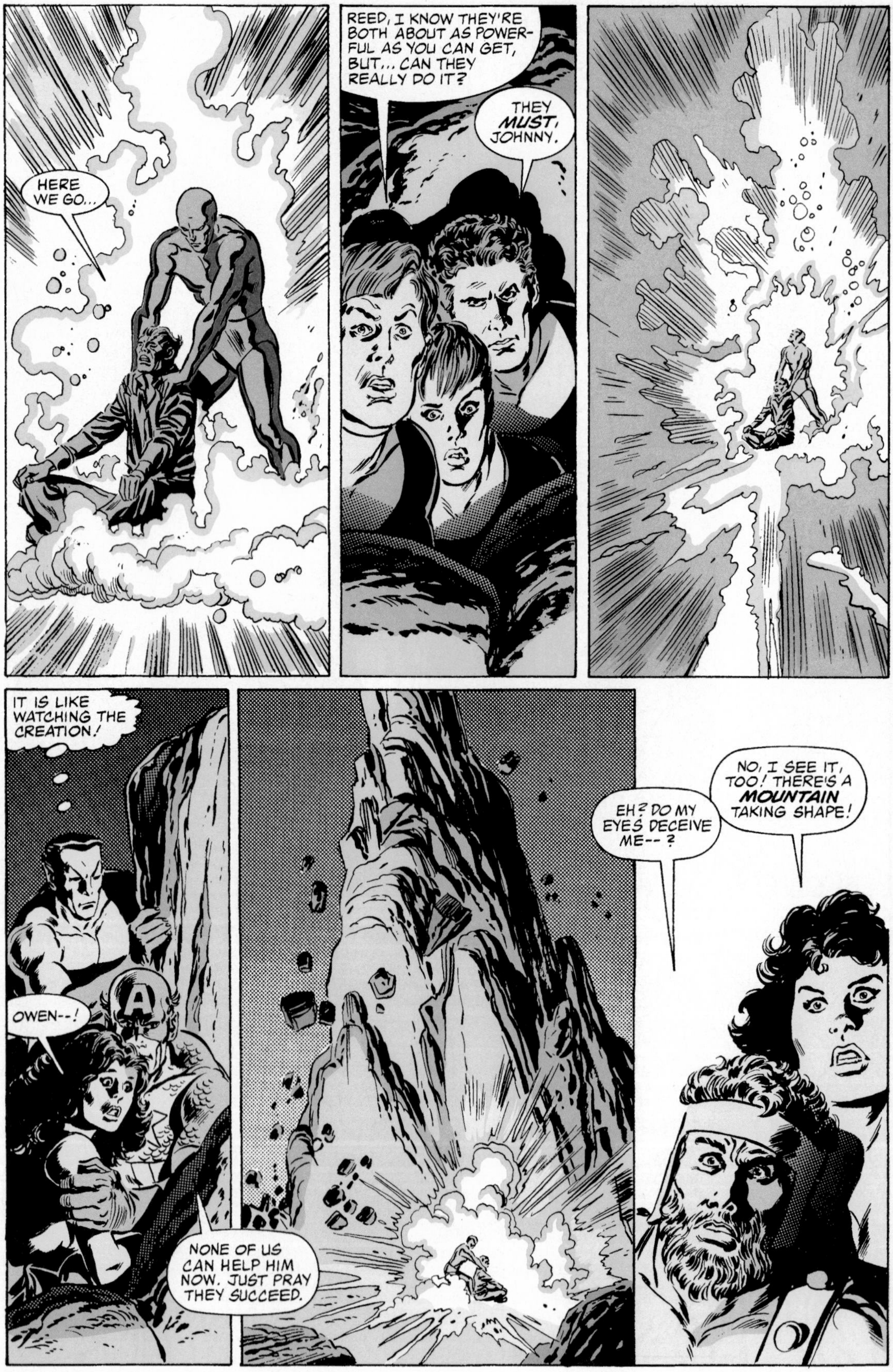

HERE WE GO...
REED, I KNOW THEY'RE BOTH ABOUT AS POWERFUL AS YOU CAN GET, BUT... CAN THEY REALLY DO IT?
THEY MUST, JOHNNY.
IT IS LIKE WATCHING THE CREATION!
OWEN--!
NONE OF US CAN HELP HIM NOW. JUST PRAY THEY SUCCEED.
EH? DO MY EYES DECEIVE ME-- ?
NO, I SEE IT, TOO! THERE'S A MOUNTAIN TAKING SHAPE!

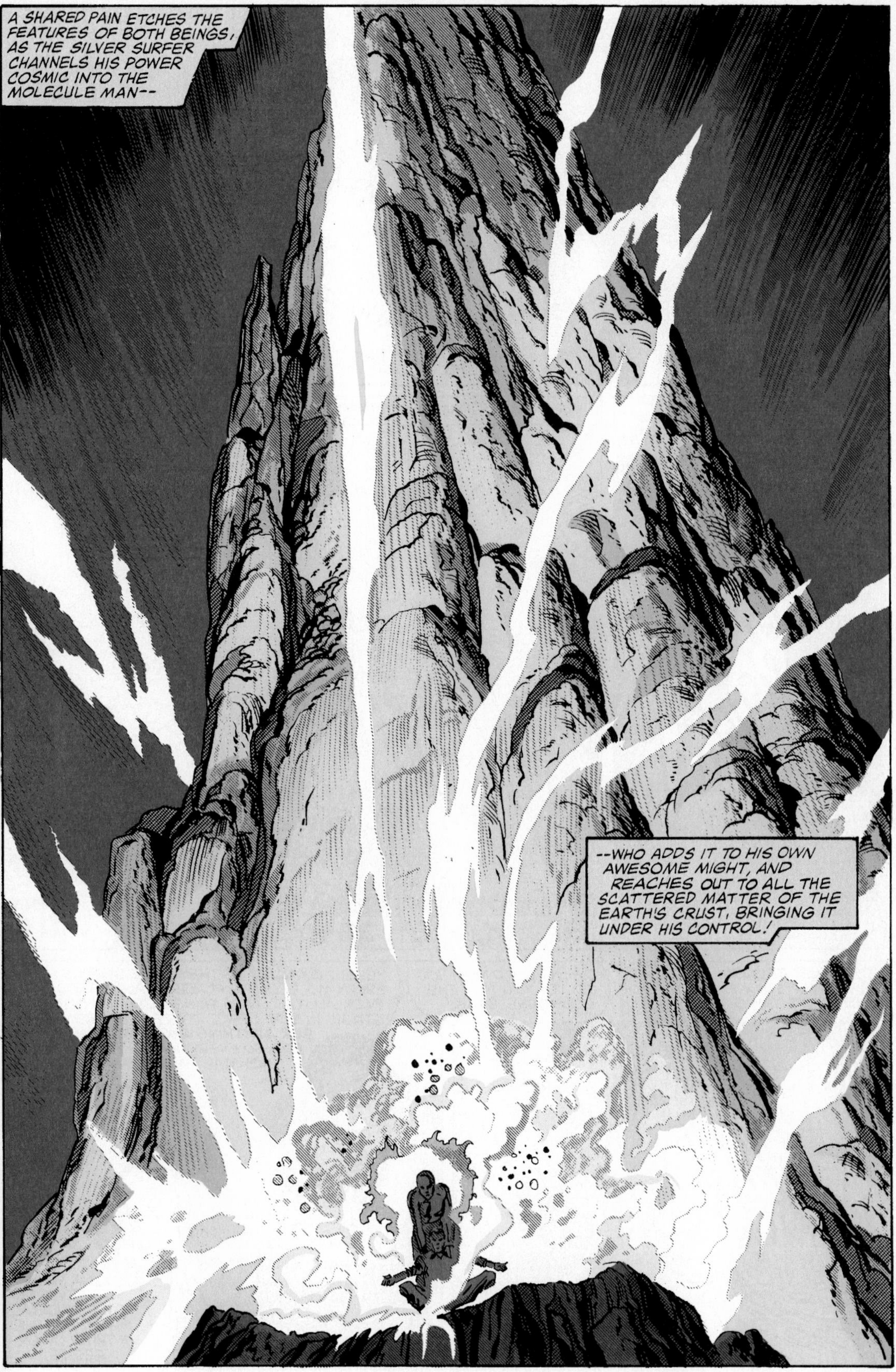
A SHARED PAIN ETCHES THE FEATURES OF BOTH BEINGS, AS THE SILVER SURFER CHANNELS HIS POWER COSMIC INTO THE MOLECULE MAN--
--WHO ADDS IT TO HIS OWN AWESOME MIGHT, AND REACHES OUT TO ALL THE SCATTERED MATTER OF THE EARTH'S CRUST, BRINGING IT UNDER HIS CONTROL!

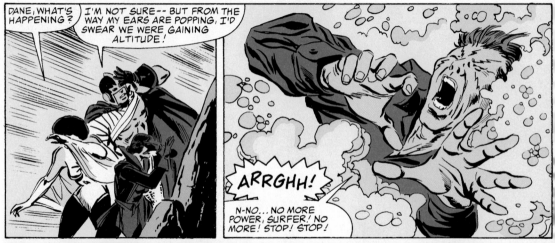

DANE, WHAT'S HAPPENING?

I'M NOT SURE-- BUT FROM THE WAY MY EARS ARE POPPING, I'D SWEAR WE WERE GAINING ALTITUDE!

ARRGHH!

N-NO... NO MORE POWER, SURFER! NO MORE! STOP! STOP!

THE AIR IS SPLIT BY A MIGHTY CRACK OF THUNDER AS THE SURFER BREAKS CONTACT WITH THE MOLECULE MAN--

--DRAWING THE AMBIENT COSMIC ENERGY BACK WITHIN HIM!

KRABOOM

IT IS OVER AT LAST! I PRAY THAT I HAVE DONE THE RIGHT THING!

OWEN! OH, OWEN, YOU DID IT! YOU PUT THE MOUNTAINS BACK!

YEAH... EXACTLY AS THEY WERE BEFORE... EVERY MOLECULE IN PLACE! I ALSO BROUGHT BACK ALL THE LIVING THINGS I'D PUT INTO STASIS IN SUB-SPACE. THEY WON'T REMEMBER ANYTHING ABOUT WHAT HAPPENED... SO EVERYTHING'S BACK TO NORMAL, INCLUDING ME!

WHAT?

YOUR FRIEND HAS REVERTED TO HIS ORIGINAL FORM. NOW HE IS TRULY OWEN REECE.

SOON... MR. REECE, I REALIZE THAT MERE THANKS CAN'T REPAY YOU FOR THE SACRIFICE YOU'VE MADE, BUT--!

THAT'S OKAY, CAP! I GUESS I SHOULDN'T HAVE EXPECTED TO LIVE AN ORDINARY LIFE WITH THE POWERS I HAD. MAYBE THIS IS ALL FOR THE BEST!

THERE'S A SENTIMENT I CAN SUPPORT! IT'S GOOD THAT REECE'S SACRIFICE WAS SO THOROUGH. THE WORLD WILL BE A MUCH SANER PLACE, WITHOUT A MAN WHO CAN CONTROL MOLECULES!

WELL, REECE, THE AUTHORITIES ARE UNAWARE OF YOUR PART IN THIS. IF YOU LIKE, WE'LL KEEP IT THAT WAY.

THANK YOU, DR. RICHARDS. LIKE I SAID BEFORE, MARSHA AND I JUST WANT TO GO BACK TO DENVER AND BE LEFT ALONE.

THAT IS EASILY ARRANGED!

AND SO...

TO THINK THAT SUCH A MORTAL COULD POSSESS A POWER TO DWARF THAT OF THE GODS, AND LOSE IT IN SUCH SERVICE! VALOR SURELY WEARS STRANGE GUISES!

C'MON, MUSCLES, IT'S TIME FOR US TO TAKE OFF, TOO! THE WASP FOUND ONE OF OUR QUINJETS ON THE FAR SIDE OF THE MOUNTAIN.

VERY WELL, I...EH? HOW TALL ARE YOU, WOMAN?

SIX-FOOT-SEVEN... AND A SMIDGE. DON'T TELL ME YOU FEEL THREATENED!

THREATENED? NOT I! DID I EVER TELL YOU ABOUT THE TIME I WAS SURROUNDED BY A HUNDRED AMAZON WARRIORS?

NOOO. WHY DON'T YOU TELL ME ABOUT IT OVER DINNER?

125

SHORTLY, AT A MODEST APARTMENT IN A SUBURB OF DENVER...

OWIE! OUR APARTMENT IS ALL FIXED UP--! BUT IT WAS A *WRECK* LAST TIME WE WERE HERE!*

YEAH, I KNOW! WHEN I WAS PUTTING THE ROCKIES BACK, I FIGURED, WHILE I WAS AT IT, WHY NOT PUT OUR PLACE BACK TOGETHER!

I ALSO UNDID SOME OF THE MISCELLANEOUS DAMAGE DONE BY THE BEYONDER IN THE LAST FEW DAYS!

*SECRET WARS II #9.

I REBUILT THE *X-MEN'S* MANSION HEADQUARTERS, FIXED SOME OF THE DAMAGE DONE BY AN EARTHQUAKE HE CAUSED IN SAN FRANCISCO... AND SOME OTHER THINGS...

BUT IF YOUR POWER WAS BURNING OUT, OWIE, WHY DID YOU DO ALL THAT *EXTRA* STUFF? UNLESS YOU SOMEHOW *FORCED* HIM TO, SURFER!

NO, MARSHA HE DIDN'T.

IN FACT, HE *COULD* HAVE PUSHED ME TOO FAR... OR POSSIBLY EVEN HAVE SUCKED MY POWER OUT OF ME WHEN HE BROKE CONTACT!

BUT HE *DIDN'T*. ALL HE DID WAS *HELP* ME. AND HE WAS SO UNSELFISH, HE GAVE ME SO MUCH POWER, THAT I DIDN'T HAVE TO STRAIN MYSELF AS MUCH AS I THOUGHT I WOULD--

--SO I DIDN'T LOSE *ANYTHING*, BABE!

OWEN, YOUR FACE--! YOU MEAN, YOU'RE STILL--?!

YEP, STILL THE MOLECULE MAN... THOUGH IT'LL BE WEEKS BEFORE I'M FULLY RECOVERED AND BACK TO NORMAL STRENGTH!

I CONFESS... I WAS SORELY TEMPTED TO PUT AN END TO YOUR POWERS.

BUT TO DO SO WOULD HAVE BEEN AN ACT BORN OF FEAR-- WHILE YOUR LEAVING YOURSELF OPEN TO ME WAS AN ACT OF COURAGE!

EVIL STEMS FROM FEAR, WHILE TRUE COURAGE IS A SIGN OF GOOD WITHIN!

I SIMPLY ALLOWED YOUR COURAGE TO INSPIRE MINE!

THANKS FOR BELIEVING IN ME, SURFER!

AND THANKS FOR NOT LET- TING ON TO THE OTHERS THAT I WAS FAKING HAVING LOST MY POWERS!

YEAH, I HATED TO FOOL THEM. BUT IF THEY KNEW I WAS STILL THE MOLECULE MAN, THEY'D CONSTANTLY BE WORRIED ABOUT WHAT I WAS UP TO!

THEY'RE CONTENT, AND I KEEP MY PRIVATE LIFE... AS WELL AS MY POWERS.

I ENVY YOU.

I LOST THE FREEDOM OF THE COSMOS IN DEFENDING THIS PLANET-- WHILE YOU RISKED ALL TO SAVE THE EARTH, YET KEPT YOUR LIFE AND LOVE!

YOU ARE A LUCKY MAN, OWEN REECE. MAY WE ALL ONE DAY KNOW SUCH HAPPINESS!

END

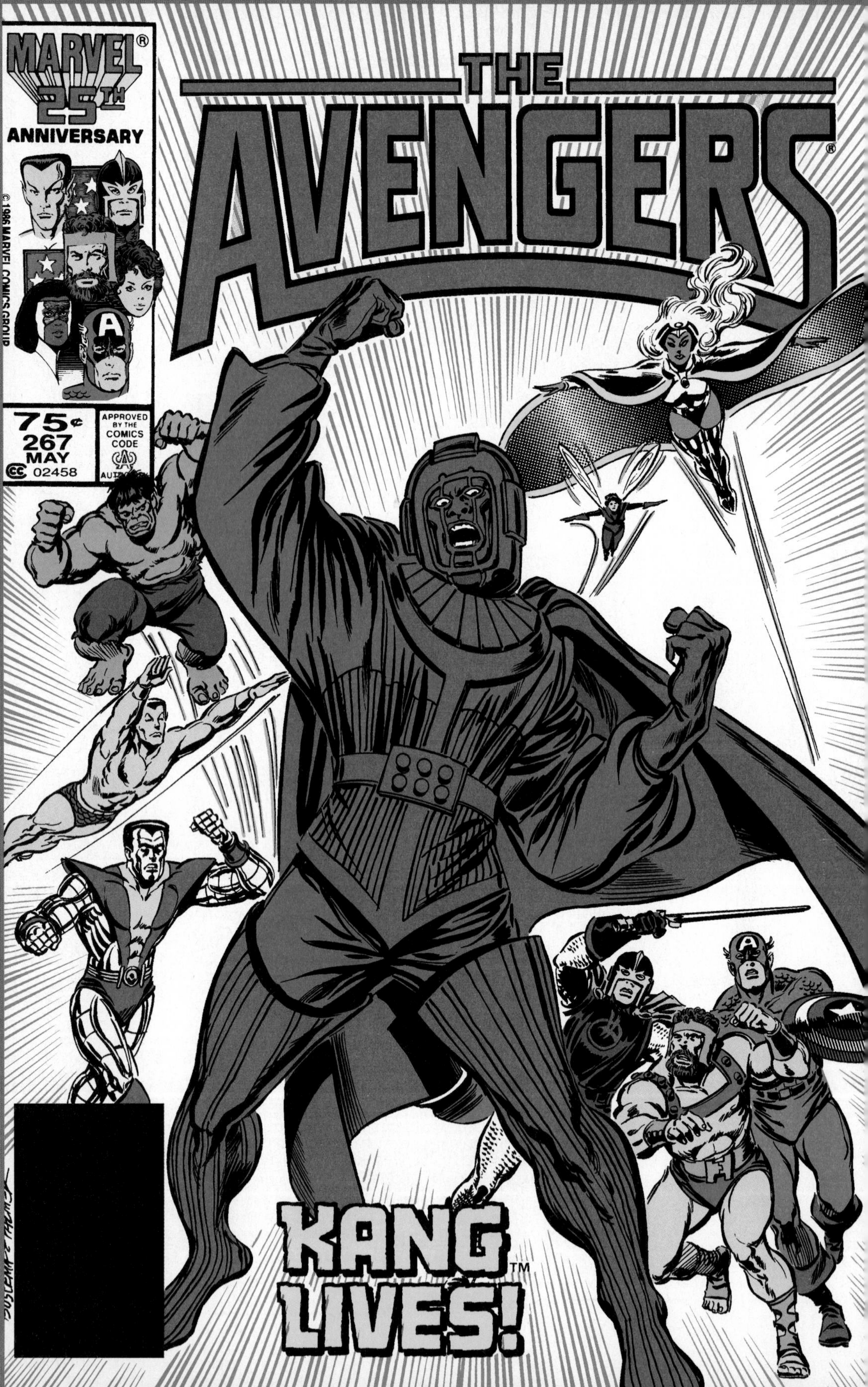
MARVEL® 25TH ANNIVERSARY
© 1986 MARVEL COMICS GROUP
THE AVENGERS®
75¢
267
MAY
02458
APPROVED BY THE COMICS CODE
KANG™ LIVES!

# TIME--AND TIME AGAIN!

THEY CALL HER *STORM*, FOR ALL WIND AND WEATHER IS AT THE COMMAND OF HER AMAZING MUTANT POWERS! IN HER YOUNG LIFE, SHE HAS BEEN BOTH SINNER AND SAINT--

--BUT NOW, AT LONG LAST, SHE HAS TAKEN HER RIGHTFUL PLACE AMONG THE GREATEST OF HEROES.

NOW, SHE IS AN AVENGER!

| ROGER STERN WRITER | JOHN BUSCEMA BREAKDOWNS | TOM PALMER FINISHER | JIM NOVAK LETTERER | CHRISTIE SCHEELE COLORIST | MARK GRUENWALD EDITOR | JIM SHOOTER EDITOR IN CHIEF |

WELCOME HOME, STORM... AND CONGRATULATIONS! YOU DID A GREAT JOB OF BLUNTING THAT GULF COAST HURRICANE!

THANK YOU, *WASP*. I DIDN'T EXPECT SUCH A LAVISH *RECEPTION!*

OH... THE REPORTERS? WELL, ACTUALLY, THEY'RE HERE BECAUSE OF OUR NEW MEMBER. HE'S INSIDE NOW, CONFERRING WITH THE *PRESIDENT!*

HEADS UP! HERE THEY COME!

I-I AM VERY NERVOUS, MR. PRESIDENT!

JUST FOLLOW MY LEAD, *COLOSSUS* ...I'M AN OLD HAND AT THIS!

MR. PRESIDENT, IS THE INDUCTION OF A *SOVIET CITIZEN* INTO THE AVENGERS A SIGN OF--?

WHOA, LET'S BACK UP THERE A MINUTE! COLOSSUS IS A *FORMER* SOVIET CITIZEN-- AND I'M SURE HE'LL MAKE A FINE AMERICAN!

BEFORE THE CHIEF EXECUTIVE CAN CONTINUE, THE AIR IS SUDDENLY SPLIT BY THE WHINE OF POWERFUL JETS AND...

*IRON MAN!* WE WERE BEGINNING TO WONDER IF YOU'D SHOW!

SORRY I'M LATE, *CAPTAIN AMERICA!* SOME PERSONAL BUSINESS CAME UP AT THE LAST MINUTE--

-- BUT I SETTLED IT FAST! I WOULDN'T HAVE MISSED THIS FOR THE WORLD!

LADIES AND GENTLEMEN, HERE IS THE MAN WHO'S CHIEFLY RESPONSIBLE FOR BRINGING COLOSSUS TO OUR SHORES!

YOU FLATTER ME, MR. PRESIDENT!

NONSENSE! IF YOU HADN'T HELPED COLOSSUS SMUGGLE HIS FAMILY OUT OF SIBERIA, HE'D STILL BE AT THE MERCY OF THE KREMLIN.

JUST DOING MY DUTY, SIR.

ARNIE, GET A CLOSE-UP OF IRON MAN WITH THE PRESIDENT! THIS IS BIG!

BY THE WAY, MY EMPLOYER, TONY STARK, ASKED ME TO GIVE YOU THIS!

SO SOON? WELL, THAT IS GOOD NEWS! WE CAN ALL TAKE PRIDE IN THE WORK OF MEN LIKE ANTHONY STARK! IT JUST GOES TO SHOW HOW MUCH CAN BE ACCOMPLISHED WITH A LITTLE OLD-FASHIONED HARD WORK--

--AND YANKEE ƎUUNGHƎ OOFFƎ ...CAN'T GET THE BLASTED THING OPEN!

MAY I ASSIST YOU, COMRADE... I MEAN, MISTER PRESIDENT?

I THINK THE CHIEF CAN HANDLE IT, COLOSSUS!

JUST TUG A LITTLE HARDER, SIR!

SUDDENLY...

DON'T! STOP!!

WHAT THE--? HOW'D THIS BUM GET PAST THE FRONT GATE?

STOP HIM! DON'T LET HIM GET CLOSE TO THE PRESIDENT!

YOU'VE MADE A BIG MISTAKE, BUDDY!

NO, YOU DON'T UNDERSTAND! THE PRESIDENT'S IN DEADLY DANGER! THAT'S NOT IRON MAN!!

OH, AND I SUPPOSE YOU ARE?

YES, I'M ANTHONY STARK, AND--!

BUT AS THE SECRET SERVICE AGENTS WRESTLE TONY STARK TO THE GROUND--

--THE PRESIDENT FINALLY YANKS THE METAL BOX OPEN.

132

WHEN THE GREAT MUSHROOM CLOUD FINALLY SETTLES, THERE IS LITTLE LEFT STANDING ON THE ISLAND OF MANHATTAN.

I DID IT! I KILLED THEM ALL!

AND YET, ONE MAN STILL LIVES, PROTECTED FROM THE AWFUL HEAT AND RADIATION BY A GLISTENING *FORCE FIELD*...

AND THE FOOLS NEVER SUSPECTED FOR A MOMENT THAT THEIR TEAMMATE'S ARMOR DISGUISED *KANG THE CONQUEROR!*

NOW THERE ARE NONE LEFT ALIVE TO STOP MY PLANS OF=

=CONQUEST. *EH?* WHERE AM I?

WHO DARES INTERRUPT MY GREATEST TRIUMPH?!?

BE *STILL*, FOOL!

FOOL?!? YOU ADDRESS KANG THE CONQUEROR, MASTER OF TIME!

KANG THE *IDIOT!* THERE'S *NOTHING LEFT* ON THAT 20TH CENTURY EARTH FOR YOU TO CONQUER! AMERICAN ARMED FORCES IMMEDIATELY RETALIATED FOR WHAT WAS THOUGHT A SOVIET ATTACK!

YOU SPARKED A GLOBAL THERMONUCLEAR WAR OF WHICH YOU WERE THE *SOLE SURVIVOR!* ONLY YOUR COUNTERPART WAS LESS SUCCESSFUL!

133

WHAT DO YOU MEAN-- "COUNTERPART"?

FOR A "MASTER OF TIME", YOU DON'T KNOW MUCH ABOUT ITS *NATURE!* HAVEN'T YOU REALIZED THAT ONE OR MORE *ALTERNATE REALITIES* MAY DIVERGE AT CRITICAL POINTS IN TIME?

HERE, SEE FOR YOURSELF...WE PLUCKED YOU FROM THE REALITY IN WHICH YOU SURVIVED--BUT THERE WAS ANOTHER REALITY IN WHICH THINGS TURNED OUT QUITE DIFFERENTLY!

ANOTHER KANG? *DEAD?!*

JUST ONE OF *MANY* KANGS--AND SETS OF AVENGERS!

YOU TIME-TRAVELERS ARE A MAJOR PROBLEM...THE *MORE* YOU JUMP ACROSS TIME, THE MORE DIVERGENT REALITIES YOU *CREATE!* THIS COUNCIL HAS CONVENED TO *END* THAT CHAOS!

I DON'T *BELIEVE* IT! EVEN IF IT WERE TRUE, WHAT *RIGHT* HAVE YOU--?

BRING UP THE LIGHTS, BROTHER, AND *SHOW* HIM!

THERE, *NOW* DO YOU SEE? WE HAVE EVERY RIGHT!

ENOUGH! LET'S BE DONE WITH HIM!

NO! *NO!!* N-!!!

OH, SHUT UP!

PATHETIC WRETCH!

HOW MANY MORE OF THESE INFERIOR DOUBLES MUST WE BE FORCED TO EXTERMINATE? I SWEAR--

--EACH NEW DIVERGENT DOUBLE WE ISOLATE IS MORE *IGNORANT* THAN THE ONE BEFORE! IT'S ENOUGH TO MAKE ME WISH I'D NEVER *BUILT* A TIME MACHINE.

TAKE HEART, BROTHER! MOST OF THEM ARE SO *INCOMPETENT* THAT THEY *DIE* IN THEIR OWN FAILED SCHEMES!

AND IN THIS NULL-TIME ZONE WE CAN *TERMINATE* THE OTHERS WITHOUT CREATING MORE BAD COPIES!

YES. HOWEVER, THIS DUTY DOES TAKE US AWAY FROM OUR PRIME INTEREST -- *CONQUEST!* I MOVE THAT WE *ADJOURN* UNTIL OUR NEXT SCHEDULED MEETING!

AGREED!

SIMULTANEOUSLY, THE THREE KANGS VANISH FROM THEIR SEATS.

BUT THEN, ACROSS THE CHAMBER...

*HAH!* TOOK ME A YEAR OF CALCULATIONS, BUT I FINALLY FOUND THE CHRONO-COORDINATES NECESSARY TO GET ME INTO THE COUNCIL CHAMBERS *BEFORE* THE NEXT MEETING.

THIS PLACE INTRIGUES ME.

I'M CERTAIN THAT OUR CAPED BROTHER IS HIDING SOMETHING HERE THAT--AH-*HA!*

PING-PING

A POSITIVE SENSOR PULSE! MUST BE A SECRET *PANEL* RIGHT ABOUT HERE!

VERY GOOD, BROTHER! I *THOUGHT* YOU'D BE THE ONE TO COME EXPLORING!

135

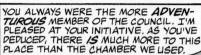

YOU ALWAYS WERE THE MORE *ADVENTUROUS* MEMBER OF THE COUNCIL. I'M PLEASED AT YOUR INITIATIVE. AS YOU'VE DEDUCED, THERE *IS* MUCH MORE TO THIS PLACE THAN THE CHAMBER WE USED.

SHALL I SHOW YOU AROUND?

AH... *YES*, BROTHER. PLEASE!

WHAT'S HIS GAME?

UNLIKE YOURSELF AND OUR OTHER COUNCIL-BROTHER, I AM NOT PRESENTLY RULING A SINGLE REALITY. I HAVE ESTABLISHED MY BASE OF OPERATIONS IN *THIS* REGION THAT IS BEYOND TIME AND SPACE!

HERE IS MY CENTRAL ROBOTICS PLANT.

IMPRESSIVE. THIS DWARFS ANYTHING *I* POSSESS. HE IS A MORE *DANGEROUS* VERSION OF MYSELF THAN I *SUSPECTED!*

AND THROUGH THERE IS ONE OF MY ARMAMENT FABRICATORS.

I'M PUZZLED, BROTHER-- WHY HAVE YOU KEPT THIS HIDDEN FROM THE COUNCIL?

*HIDDEN?* I KEEP NOTHING HIDDEN! YOU'RE *HERE*, AREN'T YOU?

THIS IS THE *NERVE CENTER* OF MY BASE! FROM HERE I SCAN THE MANY REALITIES IN SEARCH OF OUR INFERIOR AND EMBARRASSING DOUBLES.

AH, *THIS* MAY INTEREST YOU! WHENEVER OUR COUNCIL BROTHER RETURNS TO HIS 41ST CENTURY EMPIRE--

--HE FIRST REASSURES HIMSELF OF HIS OWN AUTHORITY BY REVIEWING HIS TROOPS.

YOU... SPY ON *US*?

LET US SAY, I WATCH AFTER YOU. THESE REVIEWS TAKE *HOURS*... LET'S JUMP AHEAD A BIT.

"HAH! HE'S SO PREDICTABLE! HE SPENDS HALF OF EACH DAY AT THE TOMB OF HIS LOVELY *RAVONNA.* HE'S MOURNED HER FOR OVER FIFTY OF HIS YEARS..."

...POOR OLD DOTARD! ALL THAT TIME WASTED!

YOU... YOU *HEARTLESS*--! I MOURN FOR MY RAVONNA, AS WELL! HOW CAN YOU-- ?

TUT-TUT, YOUNG ONE! I CALL IT A *WASTE*--

--BECAUSE I HAVE NO NEED TO MOURN HER!

RAVONNA? *ALIVE* ?!?

OH, RAVONNA! I--! ≡GAUGHK!≡

ZAAK

MY LORD, WAS THAT REALLY NECESSARY?

IT WAS. I AM SORRY I HAD TO PUT YOU THROUGH THAT, RAVONNA... BUT SOON IT WILL BE ALL OVER.

NOW THERE IS ONLY *ONE LEFT* TO ELIMINATE!

ON OUR WORLD, IN OUR TIME-- A SLEEK LIMOUSINE WINDS ITS WAY THROUGH A GROWING CROWD IN FRONT OF AVENGERS MANSION.

NO OUTLAW AVENGERS! NAMOR MUST *GO!*

OUT NOW!

OUT, OUT!

AVENGERS YES-- NAMOR NO!?

MS. VAN DYNE, IS IT TRUE THAT THE *SUB-MARINER* HAS BEEN MADE AN AVENGER?

WHY NO OFFICIAL WORD? WHAT ARE YOU TRYING TO *HIDE!*

NO ONE'S HIDING ANYTHING, BOYS! WE'VE JUST BEEN *BUSY!* NOW, IF YOU'LL EXCUSE ME--

--I'LL ISSUE A STATEMENT LATER!

HEROES --NOT OUTLAWS!

AVENGERS YES! SUB-MARINER NO!

HOLEE--! SHE SHRUNK DOWN TO THE SIZE OF A *BIRD*... JUST LIKE THAT!

GOOD MORNING, MS. VAN DYNE!

'MORNING, *JARVIS!* HOW LONG HAS THE "FAN CLUB" BEEN OUT FRONT?

IT'S BEEN GATHERING EVER SINCE THE MORNING *TABLOIDS* HIT THE STREET! EVIDENTLY, SOMEONE IN THE CAPITAL LEAKED WORD ABOUT OUR NEWEST AVENGER!

GREAT, WELL IT'S PARTLY *MY* FAULT-- I SHOULD HAVE ANNOUNCED SUB-MARINER'S MEMBERSHIP EARLIER. HAVE YOU CALLED THE POLICE?

YES, MADAME. THEY ASSURED ME THEY'D HAVE SOME OFFICERS KEEP AN EYE ON THE CROWD.

GOOD, I'D BETTER PREPARE A *STATEMENT* OF SOME KIND. I JUST HOPE MY DELAYING HASN'T TARNISHED OUR REPUTATION TOO MUCH!

I SHOULDN'T WORRY, MADAME. THE AVENGERS HAS SURVIVED BAD PRESS BEFORE!

OH, THIS *CABLE* ARRIVED FOR YOU EARLIER.

WONDERFUL! PROBABLY MORE BAD NEWS!

"DUE BACK IN THE STATES AT THE END OF THE MONTH... KEEP YOUR WEEKENDS FREE... LOVE, *PALADIN*"!

AM I TO ASSUME THAT IT'S *NOT* BAD NEWS?

YOU ASSUME CORRECTLY, YOU OLD DEAR! MMM-*MWAH*!

JARVIS! YOU'VE *LOST* A FEW POUNDS, HAVEN'T YOU?

I...ER...THAT IS, Y-YES, MADAME.

WELL, THE RESULTS ARE VERY *BECOMING*!

SAY, WHERE IS EVERYBODY?

THE TWO CAPTAINS AND THE SUB-MARINER ARE EN ROUTE TO *HYDROBASE*--

--BUT HERCULES AND THE BLACK KNIGHT ARE AT WORK *BELOW*!

OH, OF COURSE! THIS IS THE DAY WE'D PLANNED TO START *REMODELING* THE SECOND SUB-BASEMENT!

AS THE AVENGERS' DEVOTED BUTLER LOOKS ON, *JANET VAN DYNE* WILLS HERSELF TO SHRINK BY TWELVE INCHES, AND SOARS AWAY ON THE GOSSAMER WINGS OF THE *WASP*!

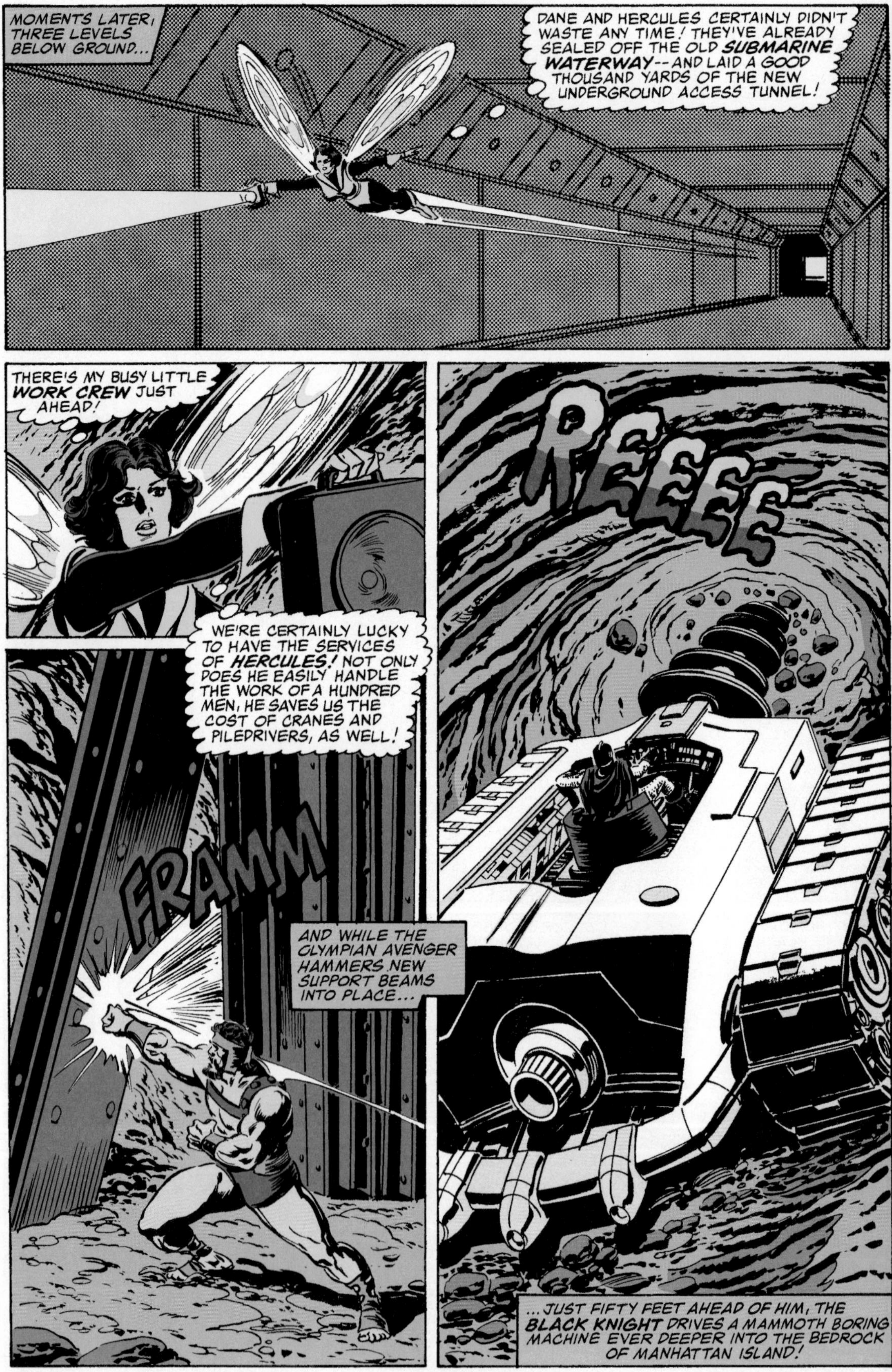
MOMENTS LATER, THREE LEVELS BELOW GROUND...
DANE AND HERCULES CERTAINLY DIDN'T WASTE ANY TIME! THEY'VE ALREADY SEALED OFF THE OLD SUBMARINE WATERWAY-- AND LAID A GOOD THOUSAND YARDS OF THE NEW UNDERGROUND ACCESS TUNNEL!
THERE'S MY BUSY LITTLE WORK CREW JUST AHEAD!
WE'RE CERTAINLY LUCKY TO HAVE THE SERVICES OF HERCULES! NOT ONLY DOES HE EASILY HANDLE THE WORK OF A HUNDRED MEN, HE SAVES US THE COST OF CRANES AND PILEDRIVERS, AS WELL!
FRAMM
AND WHILE THE OLYMPIAN AVENGER HAMMERS NEW SUPPORT BEAMS INTO PLACE...
REEEE
...JUST FIFTY FEET AHEAD OF HIM, THE BLACK KNIGHT DRIVES A MAMMOTH BORING MACHINE EVER DEEPER INTO THE BEDROCK OF MANHATTAN ISLAND!

HEY, DANE! LOOKS GREAT!

WHAT? OH...HI, JAN! LET ME TURN THIS OFF A MINUTE, SO WE CAN TALK WITHOUT SCREAMING!

REEE--

YOU'VE REALLY MADE GREAT PROGRESS!

HMM

YEAH, BUT THE HARD PART'S JUST AHEAD!

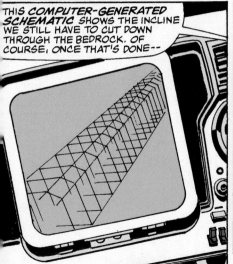

THIS COMPUTER-GENERATED SCHEMATIC SHOWS THE INCLINE WE STILL HAVE TO CUT DOWN THROUGH THE BEDROCK. OF COURSE, ONCE THAT'S DONE--

--WE LINK UP WITH AN OLD ABANDONED TUNNEL THAT A.I.M. DUG UNDER THE EAST RIVER.* THEN, SETTING UP THE REST OF OUR NEW UNDERGROUND SHUTTLE-LINK TO HYDROBASE WILL BE A SNAP!

*THE SUBVERSIVE ADVANCED IDEA MECHANICS GROUP'S TUNNEL PROJECT WAS REVEALED WAY BACK IN MARVEL FEATURE #10.

DANE WHITMAN, WHY DOES YOUR MACHINE GLOW IN THAT MANNER?

EH? IT'S NOT SUPPOSED TO-- WAIT A MINUTE! THAT'S NOT COMING FROM THE AUGER MODULE! WHAT THE DEVIL--?!

AS SUDDENLY AS IT CAME, THE EERIE GLOW DISAPPEARS, TAKING THE THREE AVENGERS WITH IT!

THE NEXT THING THEY KNOW...

WHAT WAS *THAT?*

I DON'T KNOW... MAYBE A *TRANSPORT BEAM* OF SOME SORT! ONE THING'S FOR SURE, WE'RE *NOT* WHERE WE *WERE!*

NOT EVEN IN THE STYGIAN DEPTHS OF THE NETHERWORLD HAVE I E'ER ENCOUNTERED SUCH *FOG* AS THIS!

I BELIEVE IT! AT ITS WORST, *LONDON* WAS NEVER THIS BAD!

THERE ARE FIGURES MOVING OUT THERE, BUT I CAN'T MAKE THEM OUT! I...

...OH, *NO!* IT'S *THE HULK!*

STAND YE BACK, AVENGERS! THE HULK HAS ESCAPED ME BEFORE--

--BUT HE SHALL NOT DO SO *AGAIN!*

AND NOW, MONSTER--!

HERCULES, *WAIT!* THERE'S SOMETHING STRANGE ABOUT THIS! I'VE NEVER SEEN THE HULK HIT SO HARD THAT HE DIDN'T GET RIGHT BACK UP!

YOU'RE RIGHT, WASP! I DON'T THINK HERCULES IS RESPONSIBLE FOR THE HULK'S CURRENT STATE... HE'S NOT UNCONSCIOUS, HE'S IN SOME SORT OF *TRANCE!*

HEY, AM I STARTING TO LOSE IT, OR IS THE HULK BECOMING *TRANSPARENT?*

I-IT CAN'T BE! HE COULDN'T HAVE TURNED INTO...

...GIANT-MAN?!?

GIANT-MAN? THAT'S THE NAME JAN'S *EX-HUSBAND* USED IN THE EARLY DAYS OF THE AVENGERS!

SURELY THIS IS SOME HIDEOUS JEST! THIS CAN- NOT BE *HENRY PYM!*

BUT IT IS, HERCULES! I-I'D KNOW THIS FACE ANYWHERE...

...IT'S REALLY *HANK!*

143

SEVERAL MILES SOUTHEAST OF NEW YORK HARBOR...

ANY TROUBLE WITH THE NAVIGATIONAL COMPUTER, CAP?

NOT A BIT! WITH ALL THE DATA I FED IT--

--THE SUB SHOULD SAIL RIGHT UP TO OUR NEW DOCK AT HYDROBASE.

SAY, YOU LOOK GREAT, CAPTAIN MARVEL! IS THAT A NEW HAIRDO?

THANK YOU, YES! I THOUGHT IT WAS TIME FOR A CHANGE!

WHERE'S THE SUB-MARINER?

ABOUT A QUARTER-MILE OFF THE PORT... LOOKS LIKE HE'S FOUND SOME COMPANY, TOO!

HAH-HAH! THOSE PORPOISES ARE IN FOR QUITE A RACE! I'VE SEEN NAMOR OUT-SWIM SAILFISH!

NAMOR REALLY SEEMS TO BE ENJOYING HIMSELF. I NEVER KNEW HE COULD BE SO... PLAYFUL!

THERE'S A LOT THAT PEOPLE DON'T REALIZE ABOUT OUR SUB-MARINER. NAMOR CONFIDED IN ME A FEW TIMES DURING THE WAR, AND...

...WELL, LET'S JUST SAY HE HASN'T HAD THE HAPPIEST OF LIVES.

HE HASN'T DONE MUCH TO MAKE IT BETTER! LOTS OF PEOPLE STILL THINK HE'S AS DANGEROUS AS THE HULK! AND I HAVE TO ADMIT THAT THERE ARE TIMES WHEN HE MAKES ME UNEASY!

HE HAS SUCH A TEMPER... SUCH AN EGO!

HE CAN BE DIFFICULT! THAT'S FOR CERTAIN. STILL, THERE'S A VERY DECENT MAN HIDING BETWEEN THOSE POINTED EARS!

I THINK BEING AN AVENGER WILL BRING THAT MAN OUT IN THE OPEN!

I HOPE YOU'RE RIGHT, CAPTAIN!

NO NEED TO BE SO *FORMAL*, C.M. THERE ARE NO CIVILIANS IN EARSHOT-- IT'S ALL RIGHT TO CALL ME *STEVE*.

I'LL CALL YOU STEVE, IF YOU'LL CALL ME *MONICA*.

MONICA-- ?

MONICA RAMBEAU... THAT'S *MY* NAME.

MONICA, YOU DIDN'T *HAVE TO* TELL ME THAT.

I'VE BEEN WANTING TO CONFIDE IN AN AVENGER I CAN TRUST. WHO BETTER THAN *YOU?*

HO, AVENGERS--

--WE'LL DINE WELL TONIGHT!

NOT MORE LOBSTER!

PAY NO ATTENTION TO MR. MEAT-AND-POTATOES, NAMOR! AS FAR AS *I'M* CONCERNED, YOU CAN STOCK THE AVENGERS LARDER FROM NOW TILL *DOOMSDAY!*

BUT YOU STILL DON'T COMPLETELY *TRUST* HIM-- DO YOU, MS. RAMBEAU? HOW LONG WILL IT BE UNTIL YOU TELL *HIM* TO CALL YOU MONICA?

145

ELSEWHERE...

WE'LL GET TO THE BOTTOM OF THIS, JAN. THERE MUST BE *SOME* EXPLANATION.

TH--THAT'S ALL RIGHT, DANE... I'M GETTING A SNEAKING SUSPICION I *KNOW* WHAT'S WHAT HERE.

HERCULES, PULL HIS *MASK* BACK INTO PLACE ...PLEASE.

AS YOU WISH. I STILL DO NOT UNDERSTAND HOW THE HULK COULD TURN INTO HENRY PYM... OR WHY HE WOULD WEAR SUCH *GAUDY* GARB!

THIS WAS HANK'S *FIRST* GIANT-MAN UNIFORM... HE DIDN'T KEEP THIS STYLE FOR LONG. AND I SUSPECT THAT HANK *REPLACED* THE HULK HERE--

--BUT IF I'M RIGHT, HE WON'T STAY HERE FOR LONG.

OH! THERE HE GOES.

G-GOOD-BYE, HANK.

I'LL BE--! HE'S BEING REPLACED BY *IRON MAN!*

EH? THIS BE NOT ANY IRON MAN *I* HAVE E'ER SEEN!

THIS IS THE ARMOR HE WORE WHEN THE AVENGERS WAS FOUNDED. NOW I *KNOW* WHAT'S HAPPENING!

YEARS AGO, ON THE AVENGERS' FIRST OFFICIAL MISSION, WE FOUGHT A BIZARRE CREATURE--

"-- WHO CALLED HIMSELF THE *SPACE PHANTOM.** HE COULD DUPLICATE THE APPEARANCE AND POWERS OF ANY MORTAL BEING, AND WHOEVER HE DUPLICATED WAS DIS-PLACED INTO A SHADOWY *LIMBO* WORLD..."

*IN THE NOW-CLASSIC *AVENGERS #2.*

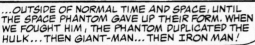
...OUTSIDE OF NORMAL TIME AND SPACE, UNTIL THE SPACE PHANTOM GAVE UP THEIR FORM. WHEN WE FOUGHT HIM, THE PHANTOM DUPLICATED THE HULK...THEN GIANT-MAN...THEN IRON MAN!

YOU THINK WE'RE IN THIS *LIMBO*?

THAT YOU ARE, AVENGERS--

--AND I AM MOST HEARTENED THAT YOU WERE ABLE TO *DEDUCE* THAT ON YOUR OWN! WELCOME ALL...

...WELCOME TO *MY DOMAIN*!

*KANG!*

WE SHOULD HAVE KNOWN THAT YOU'D BE BEHIND ANYTHING INVOLVING TRICKS WITH *TIME*!

WHO IS THIS FIEND? THE MIGHTY THOR TOLD ME THAT LIMBO WAS RULED BY A BEING CALLED *IMMORTUS*!

IMMORTUS IS NO *MORE*! *KANG* IS NOW *SUPREME* RULER OF LIMBO! AND THE EXTENT OF MY POWER IS BEYOND YOUR *IMAGININGS*!

YOU DIDN'T BRING US HERE JUST TO TELL US *THAT*!

OF COURSE NOT! I BROUGHT YOU HERE FOR MY *AMUSEMENT*!

BUT I'M WILLING TO BE SPORTING ABOUT THIS! TO RETURN HOME, ALL YOU MUST DO IS *DEFEAT* ME!

OTHERWISE, YOU'LL STAY IN LIMBO FOR THE REST OF *ETERNITY*!

IN THAT CASE, I PICK THE *FIRST* CHOICE!

REALLY, WASP! YOUR *BIO-ELECTRIC STING* MAY MAKE SHORT WORK OF LESSER FOES, BUT SURELY YOU DIDN'T EXPECT IT TO PENETRATE MY PROTECTIVE FIELD?

NO, BUT IT MAKES A GREAT DIVERSION! MY *SWORD*, ON THE OTHER HAND, SHATTERS JUST ABOUT ANYTHING --INCLUDING *FORCE-FIELDS!*

*YOUR* TURN, HERC!

KROOM

AYE!

FOOLS! HAVE YOU SO SOON FORGOTTEN THAT KANG IS ALSO A MASTER OF *ROBOTICS?!?*

EH?!

148

IF YOU CAN'T DO ANY BETTER THAN THIS, YOU'LL *NEVER* GO HOME! HAH-HAH-HAH-HAH-HA!

KRAM

*MARVELOUS!* IT'S GOING EVEN BETTER THAN I'D HOPED, RAVONNA! I HAVE THESE AVENGERS RIGHT WHERE I WANT THEM!

BEFORE THEY BREATHE THEIR LAST, I'LL HAVE THEM *DOING* EXACTLY AS I WISH!

BUT WHAT *IS* IT YOU WISH, MY LORD?

I KNOW YOU WANT TO **DESTROY** YOUR GREATEST FOES, BUT I DON'T FULLY UNDERSTAND **HOW--**?

THAT, MY DEAR, IS BECAUSE YOU HAVE NOT HAD MY EXPERIENCE IN THE ARTS OF SUBTERFUGE AND DECEPTION.

I HAVE MANAGED TO ELIMINATE **ALL** OF MY DIVERGENT DUPLICATES, SAVE **ONE.** I AM NOW GOING TO LURE THAT LAST SURVIVING **DOUBLE** INTO A BATTLE WITH THESE AVENGERS...HERE IN THE HEART OF LIMBO!

THAT WILL BE THE **END** OF MY RIVAL-SELF. I'LL THEN REPLACE HIM IN HIS FUTURE-TIME WITH A **ROBOTIC COPY--** AS I HAVE ALREADY WITH SO MANY OTHERS-- AND RULE HIS EMPIRE BY **PROXY.**

BUT WILL THREE AVENGERS BE ENOUGH TO SLAY YOUR... YOUR **TWIN?**

OF COURSE NOT! HE IS THE LONGEST LIVED OF **ALL** KANGS, AND VERY NEARLY MY **EQUAL!** I EXPECT **HIM** TO EXTERMINATE **THEM!**

BUT THE BATTLE SHOULD WEAKEN HIM SUFFICIENTLY TO ENABLE ME TO SAFELY DELIVER THE **KILLING BLOW!**

THEN, WITH THE AVENGERS' RANKS HALVED, AND MYSELF ESTABLISHED AS THE ULTIMATE KANG-- **I SHALL** CONQUER ALL TIMES!

NEXT: **THE KANG DYNASTY!**

MARVEL
25TH
ANNIVERSARY
THE AVENGERS
75¢
268
JUNE
CC 02458
APPROVED BY THE COMICS CODE AUTHORITY

# THE KANG DYNASTY!

HOURS AGO, THE WASP ENTERED THIS CONSTRUCTION AREA DEEP BENEATH NEW YORK'S AVENGERS MANSION, TO JOIN HERCULES AND THE BLACK KNIGHT. BUT NOW...

YOU'RE SURE THAT NONE OF THEM CAME BACK UP INTO THE MANSION, *JARVIS?*

STAN LEE PRESENTS:
ROGER STERN – WRITER
JOHN BUSCEMA – BREAKDOWNS
TOM PALMER – FINISHED ART
JIM NOVAK – LETTERER
CHRISTIE SCHEELE – COLORIST
MARK GRUENWALD – EDITOR
JIM SHOOTER – EDITOR-IN-CHIEF

I'M POSITIVE, *CAPTAIN AMERICA.* I KNOW IT SOUNDS ABSURD, BUT THREE AVENGERS HAVE SIMPLY *VANISHED!*

STRANGER THINGS HAVE HAPPENED.

THERE'S NO SIGN OF A *BREAK-IN* FROM BELOW... OR OF ANY STRUGGLE! I CAN'T IMAGINE AVENGERS NOT PUTTING UP A FIGHT, IF THEY WERE ATTACKED, BUT--!

HERE'S SOMETHING ODD, CAP! THE ENERGY-SENSOR CORE IN THE BLACK KNIGHT'S EXCAVATION MACHINERY HAS SUF-FERED A FORM OF POWER OVERLOAD!

THAT'S NOT MUCH TO GO ON, *NAMOR*, BUT WE'D BETTER CHECK IT OUT! CAN YOU HAUL THAT CORE UP TO OUR ELECTRONICS LAB?

CERTAINLY! *CAPTAIN MARVEL*, IF YOU'LL LIGHT THE WAY--?

O-OF COURSE.

I CAN'T GET OVER HOW THE *SUB-MARINER* CAN HEFT A MODULE THAT WEIGHS A TON--AND STILL *FLY!* HOW DOES HE DO IT WITH JUST THOSE TINY WINGS ON HIS ANKLES?!

SOON...

THAT'S THE FINAL CONNECTION, CAP... THE CORE IS ALL HOOKED UP TO THE *SYSTEMS ANALYZER.*

GOOD, LET'S HOPE THERE'S ENOUGH FUNCTIONAL MEMORY IN THE CORE'S DATA CHIPS--

--TO GIVE US AN IDEA OF... WHAT'S THIS?!?

THESE READINGS INDICATE THAT THE SENSOR-CORE'S MEMORY WAS SCRAMBLED BY SOME SORT OF *CHRONAL DISPLACE-MENT WAVE!*

"CHRONAL DISPLACEMENT WAVE"? THAT'S THE JARGON IRON MAN CAME UP WITH TO EXPLAIN IT, C.M. THE PULP WRITERS OF MY BOYHOOD WOULD PROBABLY HAVE CALLED IT A "TIME-TELEPORT-RAY"!

IT CAN ONLY MEAN THAT OUR TEAMMATES HAVE BEEN SPIRITED AWAY BY KANG!

KRANG?! IMPOSSIBLE! THAT OLD ATLANTEAN TRAITOR HASN'T THE TECHNOLOGY TO DO THIS!

NOT KRANG...KANG! KANG THE CONQUEROR-- I KNOW ABOUT HIM FROM SCANNING THE AVENGERS DATA-FILES. HE'S A TIME-TRAVELING WARLORD FROM HUNDREDS OF YEARS IN THE FUTURE.

I CAN TELL YOU FROM FIRST-HAND EXPERIENCE THAT HE'S ONE OF OUR MOST DANGEROUS ENEMIES!

BUT WHAT COULD KANG BE UP TO? WHY WOULD HE KIDNAP HALF OF THE AVENGERS?

YES, AND WHERE HAS HE TAKEN THEM?

THAT'S THE BIG QUESTION, NAMOR! THEY COULD BE ANYWHERE IN TIME!

INDEED, BEYOND ALL SPACE AND TIME, IN THE SHADOWY REALM OF LIMBO--

-- THE THREE MISSING AVENGERS ARE LOST ON A FOGBOUND PLANE WITH THE COMATOSE FORM OF IRON MAN...AN IRON MAN FROM LONG AGO.

HERCULES, DID YOU HAVE TO COMPLETELY PULVERIZE THE ROBOT KANG SICCED ON US?*

IF YOU'D LEFT A FEW CIRCUITS INTACT, I MIGHT'VE BEEN ABLE TO COBBLE TOGETHER SOMETHING TO HELP GET US OUT OF THIS PEA-SOUP!

MY APOLOGIES, DANE WHITMAN. THE ROBOT'S TAUNTS LEFT ME SORELY VEXED--

*LAST ISSUE.

--AS HAVE THESE APPARITIONS. FIRST, IT WAS THE HULK...THEN, GIANT-MAN! NOW I FACE AN IRON MAN OUTFITTED IN UNFAMILIAR ARMOR.

THE WASP CLAIMS THAT ALL THREE WERE DISPATCHED TO LIMBO IN THE FIRST YEAR OF THE AVENGERS' FOUNDING. HOW CAN THIS BE? HOW IS IT THAT WE HAVE SEEN THEM HERE NOW?

IT'S NOT EASY TO EXPLAIN, HERC. LIMBO APPARENTLY TOUCHES ALL TIMES, BUT IS PART OF NONE. NOTHING ABOUT LIMBO FITS THE CONCEPTS OF TIME AS WE KNOW THEM...THERE IS NO "NOW" IN THIS PLACE.

HERE, TIME IS SPACE...AND VICE VERSA. YOU SEE--!

MERCY, SIR KNIGHT! I BEG YOU, EXPLAIN NO MORE...

...ELSE I SHALL UNDERSTAND EVEN LESS THAN I DO A'READY! EH, WHAT IS THIS--?

THE ENTRANCED IRON MAN AT LAST BEGINS TO FADE FROM VIEW. DOES THIS MEAN WE ARE TO BE SPARED FURTHER VISITATIONS FROM THE PAST?

NO, HERCULES, THERE'S ONE MORE ON HIS WAY--THE ONE I'VE BEEN WAITING FOR--

...THE ONE RESPONSIBLE FOR THE APPEARANCES OF THE ORIGINAL AVENGERS! HE CALLS HIMSELF THE *SPACE PHANTOM!*

≥?!≤

WHO ARE YOU? WHAT ARE YOU DOING HERE?

DON'T YOU RECOGNIZE ME, PHANTOM? YOU JUST FINISHED BATTLING MY TEAMMATES!

Y-YOU RESEMBLE THE *WASP!* BUT YOU CAN'T BE--!

OH, YES, I CAN! AND I'M A MUCH TOUGHER WASP THAN THE ONE YOU ONCE ATTACKED!* SO, BELIEVE ME, IT'S IN YOUR BEST INTERESTS TO *COOPERATE!*

W-W-WHAT DO YOU WANT?

*AVENGERS #2.*

WE'LL START WITH A LITTLE INFORMATION!

≥GEEEK!≤

I THINK NOT!

KANG! YOU--!

I PROMISED TO RETURN YOU HOME, IF YOU COULD FIND AND DEFEAT ME, AVENGERS! I DIDN'T PROMISE YOU A GUIDE THROUGH LIMBO!

ENOUGH OF YOUR INFERNAL *ROBOTS,* KANG! FACE US LIKE A MAN!

I'M NO ROBOT THIS TIME, HERCULES... JUST A PROJECTION OF LIGHT AND SOUND! IF YOU WANT THE REAL ME, JUST FOLLOW YOUR *NOSES!*

HAH-HAH-HA-HAH-HA!

AND, AN INCALCULABLE DISTANCE AWAY...

**HAH-HAH-HA-HAH-HA!**

SURELY, THERE CAN BE NO SWEETER *REVENGE* THAN THIS...

...TO SEE ONE'S ENEMIES FLOUNDER ABOUT HELPLESSLY, UNSURE OF WHAT TO DO OR WHERE TO TURN!

THE MIGHTY AVENGERS ARE MERE PLAYTHINGS IN MY HANDS, *RAVONNA!*

SO IT WOULD APPEAR, MY LORD!

I CAN HARDLY WAIT TO USE THEM IN ELIMINATING MY LAST REMAINING *DOUBLE...*

--MY DEAR, DIVERGENT BROTHER-IN-TIME! YOU SEE, RAVONNA? THERE HE IS--

-- CONFERRING WITH THE LIEUTENANTS OF HIS 41ST CENTURY EMPIRE, UNAWARE THAT MY MACHINES MONITOR HIS EVERY *MOVE.*

HE'S ACTUALLY MY PHYSICAL ELDER, YOU KNOW...NOT THAT HIS YEARS OF EXPERIENCE HAVE KEPT ME FROM MANIPULATING HIM.

I ALLOWED HIM TO THINK HIMSELF MY *EQUAL* IN CUNNING, ENLISTING HIM TO HELP EXTERMINATE THE MANY ALTERNATE-REALITY KANGS WHO HAD BEEN BROUGHT INTO EXISTENCE THROUGH MY...

...OR RATHER, THROUGH *OUR* TRAVELS THROUGH TIME! HE HAS NO IDEA HOW *SUCCESSFUL* WE'VE BEEN. ALL THE DIVERGENT LIVES OF KANG HAVE BEEN ELIMINATED, SAVE FOR *MINE* AND *HIS!* AND HE, TOO, SHALL SOON FALL!

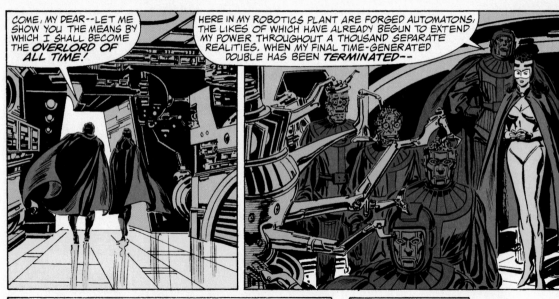

COME, MY DEAR--LET ME SHOW YOU THE MEANS BY WHICH I SHALL BECOME THE *OVERLORD OF ALL TIME!*

HERE IN MY ROBOTICS PLANT ARE FORGED AUTOMATONS, THE LIKES OF WHICH HAVE ALREADY BEGUN TO EXTEND MY POWER THROUGHOUT A THOUSAND SEPARATE REALITIES. WHEN MY FINAL TIME-GENERATED DOUBLE HAS BEEN *TERMINATED*--

--HE WILL ALSO BE *REPLACED* BY A ROBOTIC COPY UNDER MY CONTROL. THEN, I WILL RULE A GREAT DYNASTY, REACHING FROM THE HEART OF LIMBO TO ACROSS ALL SPACE AND TIME!

*OH!* MY LORD...

...THE BODY OF THE PREVIOUS DOUBLE YOU SLEW*...I THOUGHT YOU'D...DISPOSED OF IT.

*LAST ISSUE.

NO, THAT DOUBLE IS YET OF VALUE TO ME! I INTEND TO USE IT AGAINST MY *LAST* RIVAL!

I DON'T UNDERSTAND! I THOUGHT YOU WERE USING THE AVENGERS AGAINST YOUR TWIN.

THE AVENGERS ARE BUT *PART* OF THE TRAP.

AND BEFORE THEY ARE TRULY READY FOR ME TO USE, I WANT TO PLAY WITH THEM A BIT MORE...FRUSTRATE THEM... GET THEM REALLY FIGHTING MAD!

ELSEWHERE...

"FOLLOW YOUR NOSES," HE SAID! WE'RE LUCKY TO *SEE* OUR NOSES IN THIS PEA SOUP!

IF I EVER LAY MY HANDS 'PON THE *REAL* KANG, HE WILL NE'ER FIND HIS NOSE AGAIN!

HOLD ONTO THAT THOUGHT, HERCULES! I'M GOING TO SEE IF VISIBILITY GETS ANY BETTER WITH ALTITUDE!

WASP! YOU HAVE ALL BUT VANISHED FROM SIGHT!

THIS HASN'T GAINED ME MUCH EITHER! I CAN'T SEE... WAIT A MINUTE! THERE'S SOME SORT OF MOVEMENT JUST AHEAD. IT LOOKS LIKE...

"...OH, *NO!* DIRE WRAITHS!"

FORWARD, SISTERS! FORWARD TO THE KILL!

"I'D FORGOTTEN THAT THE SPACEKNIGHT ROM HAD BANISHED THESE MONSTERS TO LIMBO!*"

TO THE KILL!

LOOK OUT, THEY'RE COMING FROM ALL SIDES!

*MOST PUBLICLY IN *ROM* #66.

HOLEE--!

THERE BE NOTHING HOLY ABOUT THESE INFERNAL CREATURES! THEIR FOUL ATTACK MUST BE ANSWERED IN KIND!

KILL!

159

IF I LET THEM GET TOO CLOSE, THEY'LL--*ULP!*--SUCK MY BRAIN OUT!

HERCULES...DANE... HOW ARE YOU HOLDING UP?

NEVER FEAR, WASP! YOU SPEAK TO HIM WHO HAS FACED THE HORDES OF THE *UNDER-WORLD!*

LET ALL OF WRAITHDOM DESCEND UPON ME! THEY SHALL NOT FIND THE PRINCE OF POWER WANTING!

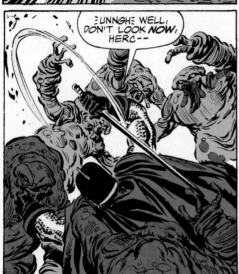

∃UNNGH∃ WELL, DON'T LOOK *NOW*, HERC--

-- BUT I THINK YOU'VE JUST *GOTTEN* YOUR WISH!

BAH! IT MATTERS NOT WHETHER MY FOES NUMBER A HUNDRED OR A HUNDRED TIMES A HUNDRED--

--THE SON OF ZEUS SHALL NOT FAIL!

I HOPE HERCULES' STRENGTH IS AS GREAT AS HIS CONFIDENCE! THESE WRAITHS KEEP ATTACKING IN WAVES, AND THERE DOESN'T SEEM TO BE ANY END TO THEM!

HERCULES *MAY* BE THE STRONGEST AVENGER WE'VE EVER HAD, BUT THERE'S A LIMIT EVEN TO *HIS* POWER!

WHILE, ON EARTH...

YOU **DEFEND** THAT FISH-MAN?

THAT "FISH-MAN" SAVED MY UNCLE'S LIFE!

A HERO THEN--A HERO NOW

NAMOR OUR ALL!

SUBBY OUT

INSIDE AVENGERS MANSION...

NEWS OF THIS MORNING'S PROTEST AGAINST THE SUB-MARINER* SPREAD FASTER THAN I THOUGHT. THE CROWDS ARE BACK...

...AND NOW, THERE ARE COUNTER DEMONSTRATORS, AS WELL.

*LAST ISSUE.

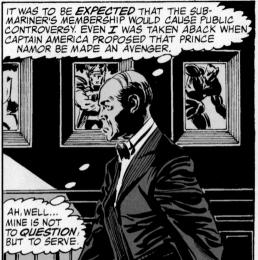

IT WAS TO BE **EXPECTED** THAT THE SUB-MARINER'S MEMBERSHIP WOULD CAUSE PUBLIC CONTROVERSY. EVEN **I** WAS TAKEN ABACK WHEN CAPTAIN AMERICA PROPOSED THAT PRINCE NAMOR BE MADE AN AVENGER.

AH, WELL... MINE IS NOT TO **QUESTION**, BUT TO SERVE.

SOON...

PARDON MY INTERRUPTION, SIR-- BUT THE AFTERNOON IS NEARLY GONE, AND YOU'VE YET TO **EAT!**

I KNOW, BUT WE DON'T... IS THAT FRESH COFFEE?

UMMPH= JARVIS, YOU'RE A **LIFE-SAVER.** I HADN'T REALIZED HOW **HUNGRY** I WAS.

WHAT WOULD THE AVENGERS DO WITHOUT YOU?

PROBABLY MISS MORE MEALS, SIR. MY WORD, WHAT **IS** THAT CONTRAPTION YOU'RE WORKING ON?

CAPTAIN AMERICA CLAIMS IT IS A DEVICE FOR TRANSCENDING **TIME!**

RIGHT. THE *TIME PLATFORM* WAS USED BY THE *LEADER* TO SCATTER AVENGERS THROUGH TIME.* AFTER WE WRECKED HIS PLANS, IRON MAN BROUGHT THE DEVICE BACK HERE TO STUDY.

FORTUNATELY FOR US, THE MACHINE SEEMS TO BE FULLY OPERATIONAL.

*IN *HULK* #284-285.

THEN YOU INTEND TO USE THIS DEVICE TO GO LOOKING FOR--? *GOOD HEAVENS!*

I'VE BEEN ALL THROUGH THE INTERNAL CIRCUITRY AND THE CONNECTIONS TO OUR THERMO-ELECTRIC GENERATORS, CAP! EVERYTHING CHECKS OUT *POSITIVE!*

GOOD WORK, C.M. YOU'D BETTER TAKE FIVE NOW. AS SOON AS NAMOR AND I GET THE PROPER COORDINATES DOWN, WE'LL BE TAKING OFF.

WILL DO. OH, JARVIS, I'M *SORRY!* I DIDN'T MEAN TO STARTLE YOU!

Q-QUITE ALL RIGHT, MADAME.

I JUST MISTOOK YOUR ENERGY FOR AN ELECTRICAL DISCHARGE. NO HARM DONE.

SAND-WICH?

*BLAST!* EVERY TIME I COME CLOSE TO GETTING A COORDINATE FIX ON THE CHRONAL WAVE, THE READINGS SUDDENLY SHIFT!

TAKE IT EASY, NAMOR!

WITHOUT AN EXACT FIX, WE HAVEN'T A CHANCE OF LOCATING THE OTHERS.

I KNOW IT'S *FRUSTRATING,* BUT WE WON'T HELP THEM BY LOSING OUR HEADS.

YES...YES, YOU ARE RIGHT, CAP.

CAP CALMED HIM DOWN WITH JUST A FEW WORDS. I DIDN'T THINK NAMOR RESPECTED *ANYONE* THAT MUCH.

WHAT WOULD THE PROTESTORS SAY, IF THEY COULD SEE THE SUB-MARINER'S CONCERN?

LIMBO...

WRAM

EXCUSE ME IF I DON'T AGREE, HERC!

KILL! KILL!

AH, TO AGAIN FACE AN INTRACTABLE FORCE ON THE FIELD OF BATTLE! SURELY THERE IS NOTHING MORE *GLORIOUS* THAN THIS!

FROM WHERE I STAND, THIS IS JUST ANOTHER ROTTEN WAR... AND I DON'T SEE ANYTHING GLORIOUS ABOUT WAR!

THE SHE-AVENGER GROWS IN STATURE, SISTER... HER WINGS VANISH!

SHE SEEKS TO *CONFUSE* US-- BUT SHE'LL NOT KEEP US FROM THE KILL!

NEVER SEEN ANYTHING ATTACK LIKE THIS BEFORE. THEY MAY HAVE KILLED THOUSANDS BACK ON EARTH... BUT HERE THEY'RE PRACTICALLY TRYING TO LEAP ONTO MY SWORD.

I HATE TO USE SO MUCH FORCE--

--BUT THE WAY THEY KEEP COMING, THEY GIVE US NO CHOICE!

163

EVENTUALLY...

IS THAT ALL?

THAT'S *MORE* THAN ENOUGH FOR ME! THERE MAY BE NO SUCH THING AS NORMAL TIME IN THIS PLACE, BUT IT SEEMS LIKE WE'VE BEEN FIGHTING FOR *DAYS!*

I FEEL SICK.

NO, WAIT--

--YOU CAN'T STOP NOW! *KILL* US! *ALL* OF US!

EH? YOU *WANT* TO DIE?

KANG SENT US TO SLAY YOU! THE PRICE FOR FAILURE IS *DEATH!* BETTER FOR YOU TO SLAY US QUICKLY MERCIFULLY-- THAN FOR KANG TO SLOWLY *TORTURE* US TO DEATH!

THOSE WRAITHS MAY HAVE BEEN INHUMAN *MONSTERS* BUT WHAT KANG DID TO THEM IS EVEN MORE *INHUMAN!*

HE'LL *PAY* FOR THAT!

KANG SENT YOU? WHERE IS HE?

I-IF I TELL YOU, WILL YOU KILL ME?

IF YOU DO *NOT,* I SHALL SEE TO IT THAT YOU SURVIVE IN LIMBO FOR ALL ETERNITY!

MINUTES--OR WEEKS--LATER...

'TWOULD APPEAR THAT WRAITH'S DIRECTIONS WERE *TRUE* ...THIS CAN ONLY BE THE LAIR OF KANG!

NOW THAT FIEND SHALL LEARN WHAT IT MEANS TO TOY WITH A *GOD!*

WE *ALL* HAVE A SCORE TO SETTLE! JUST THINKING OF WHAT KANG TRICKED US INTO DOING TO THOSE WRAITHS--

--MAKES ME *ILL!*

DON'T DWELL ON IT, JAN. WE NEED YOU AS GROUP LEADER. WE CAN'T LET HERC JUST GO CHARGING IN!

YOU'RE RIGHT, THANKS, DANE.

OKAY, LISTEN...THERE'S NO TELLING WHAT KANG HAS IN THERE, SO WE'LL HAVE TO DO THIS VERY *CAREFULLY!*

WHAT'S THE PLAN, BOSS?

AFTER A QUICK CONSULTATION WITH HER TEAMMATES, JANET VAN DYNE AGAIN SHRINKS TO THE SIZE OF A TINY INSECT, AND...

AT MY SMALLEST, I SHOULDN'T TRIGGER ANY PROXIMITY ALARMS THAT KANG MAY HAVE SET UP. HMMM...THIS SMALL SIDE-DOOR DOESN'T LOOK LIKE IT GETS MUCH USE--IT SHOULD BE AN IDEAL PORT-OF-ENTRY!

THAT SHOULD DEACTIVATE ANY ALARMS BUILT INTO THE DOORWAY, BUT THE LOCKING MECHANISM IS A LOT MORE STUBBORN!

FORTUNATELY, THAT'S NOT A BIG PROBLEM!

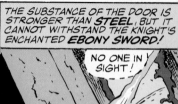

THE SUBSTANCE OF THE DOOR IS STRONGER THAN *STEEL*, BUT IT CANNOT WITHSTAND THE KNIGHT'S ENCHANTED *EBONY SWORD!*

NO ONE IN SIGHT!

THAT WON'T LAST LONG. STAY CLOSE TOGETHER--

--KANG'S SURE TO DISCOVER THAT WE'RE HERE SOON. BUT WITH A LITTLE LUCK MAYBE WE CAN FIND HIM *FIRST!*

SHORTLY...

WHAT?! WE COULDN'T HAVE BEEN SO LUCKY AS TO CATCH KANG *NAPPING!*

MUST BE ANOTHER *ROBOT.*

BUT...

THIS IS NO ROBOT! IT'S A MAN...AND HE'S DEAD!

KANG...*DEAD*?! WHO HAS DARED ROB HERCULES OF HIS VENGEANCE?

IT CAN'T BE KANG! THIS HAS TO BE A TRICK!

YEAH, AND I THINK IT'S ON US!

SO! YOU MAY HAVE SLAIN ONE OF MY TIME-BROTHERS, AVENGERS--

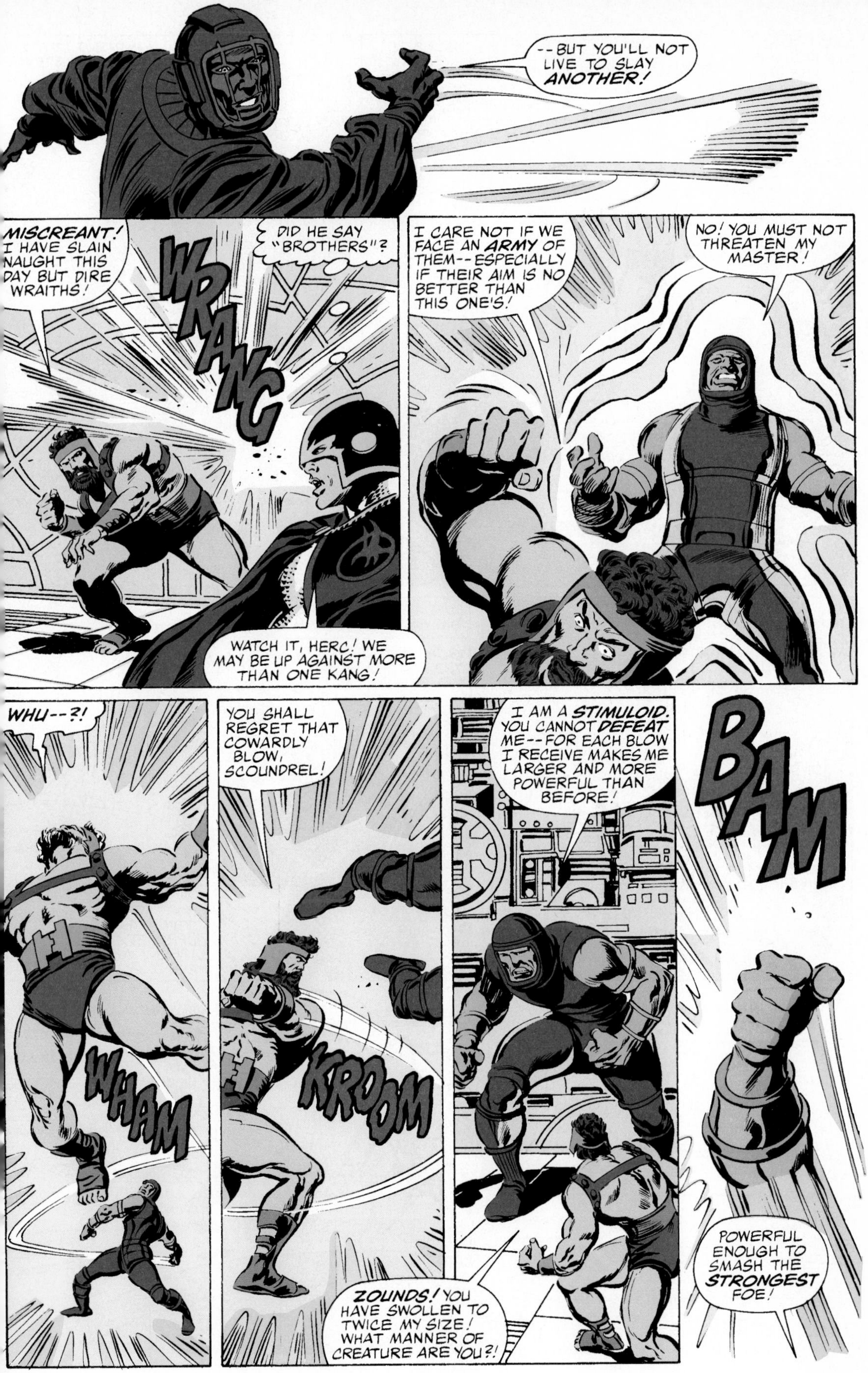
--BUT YOU'LL NOT LIVE TO SLAY ANOTHER!
MISCREANT! I HAVE SLAIN NAUGHT THIS DAY BUT DIRE WRAITHS!
WRANG
DID HE SAY "BROTHERS"?
WATCH IT, HERC! WE MAY BE UP AGAINST MORE THAN ONE KANG!
I CARE NOT IF WE FACE AN ARMY OF THEM--ESPECIALLY IF THEIR AIM IS NO BETTER THAN THIS ONE'S!
NO! YOU MUST NOT THREATEN MY MASTER!
WHU--?!
WHAM
YOU SHALL REGRET THAT COWARDLY BLOW, SCOUNDREL!
KROOM
I AM A STIMULOID. YOU CANNOT DEFEAT ME--FOR EACH BLOW I RECEIVE MAKES ME LARGER AND MORE POWERFUL THAN BEFORE!
BAM
ZOUNDS! YOU HAVE SWOLLEN TO TWICE MY SIZE! WHAT MANNER OF CREATURE ARE YOU?!
POWERFUL ENOUGH TO SMASH THE STRONGEST FOE!

BACK AT AVENGERS MANSION...

WE'VE FINALLY GOTTEN SOME SOLID **COORDINATES** TO SHOOT FOR, JARVIS! YOU KNOW WHAT TO DO--!

Y-YES, SIR. ONCE YOU'RE ALL IN PLACE, I'M TO THROW THE **MAIN POWER** SWITCH.

I MUST ADMIT TO SOME TREPIDATION, THOUGH. ARE YOU CERTAIN THIS IS SAFE?

NO, BUT IT'S A CHANCE WE HAVE TO TAKE!

≡SIGH≡ YES, SIR.

THE PLATFORM IS SET FOR PERIODIC RECALL. IF ALL GOES WELL, WE SHOULD REAPPEAR IN A MATTER OF MINUTES!

ALL SET, JARVIS. LET 'ER RIP!

BUT, AS THE AVENGERS' BUTLER THROWS THE FATEFUL SWITCH...

**GOOD HEAVENS!** THE PLATFORM IS VANISHING, TOO!

THIS WASN'T SUPPOSED TO HAPPEN! WHAT HAVE I **DONE?!**

WHAT IN BLAZES--?

THIS FOG FEELS MOST **UNNATURAL.**

THE FOG'S THE LEAST OF OUR WORRIES--

—THE TIME PLATFORM MATERIALIZED HERE **WITH US!**

WHAT?!

**JUMP!**

**BRA-BA-BOOM**

IS EVERYONE ALL RIGHT?

SHAKEN, BUT OTHERWISE UNHARMED. CAPTAIN MARVEL——?

SAME HERE, BUT IT LOOKS LIKE WE'VE LOST OUR TICKET **HOME.**

MAYBE I'D BETTER SCOUT AROUND——

——SEE IF I CAN FIND OUT WHERE WE ARE!

WITH A THOUGHT, THE SILVER-CLAD AVENGER TRANSFORMS HER BODY INTO A STREAK OF LIGHT AND VANISHES INTO THE HAZE.

LATER...

BACK SO SOON?

SOON? IT TOOK ME HOURS TO FIND MY WAY BACK HERE?

SHE WAS GONE ONLY A MINUTE!

MAYBE NOT, NAMOR. THIS PLACE FITS THE DESCRIPTION THOR FILED ON THE **LIMBO** DIMENSION. TIME DOESN'T FOLLOW ANY RULES THERE.

BUT, IN SUCH A PLACE, WE MIGHT **NEVER** FIND THE OTHERS!

IN KANG'S LAIR...

FRAM

YOU DO NOT FALL! WHY DON'T YOU FALL?

THE LION OF OLYMPUS *FALL*?

BTOW

NEVER!

BROK

BLAST IT, HERC'S TUSSLE WITH THIS BIG LUG IS KEEPING US FROM GETTING TO KANG!

YOU CANNOT DEFEAT ME, LITTLE MAN! ONCE I FREE MYSELF FROM THIS WALL, I WILL CRUSH YOU LIKE A FLEA!

OH, YOU WISH TO BE FREE OF THAT WALL?

SPROOM

WELL, THEN--

--FREE YOU SHALL BE!

SOME DISTANCE AWAY...

LISTEN! DID YOU HEAR THAT?

IT SOUNDED LIKE A MUFFLED **EXPLOSION**.

WHY IS IT GETTING DARKER?

LOOK OUT! INCOMING MISSILE!

**SKA-RAMM**

THAT'S NO MISSILE!

BLAZES! THIS IS ONE OF KANG'S **GROWING MAN** ANDROIDS! THE MORE YOU HIT THEM THE BIGGER THEY GET!

SOMETHING MUST HAVE WALLOPED ITS **GROWING** CIRCUITRY!

HERCULES!

HE MUST BE THIS WAY!

MEANWHILE...

ELIMINATING MY STIMULOID WILL NOT SAVE YOU, AVENGERS! I HAVE ENOUGH WEAPONRY ON MY PERSON TO DESTROY AN **ARMY**!

ZZRAK

YOU MEAN, YOU *HAD* ENOUGH WEAPONRY--!

ARRRHH!

Y-YOU ERUPTED FROM MY POWER HARNESS! BUT HOW--? MY FORCE-FIELD--!

IT COULDN'T SCREEN OUT AN *ENERGY TRANSFORMER* LIKE ME!

I HAD NO TROUBLE FRYING THE CIRCUITS IN YOUR BATTLE-SUIT!

LOOKS LIKE WE'VE MISSED OUT ON THE ACTION!

CAP... NAMOR! HEY, THE GANG'S ALL *HERE*!

ALL RIGHT, MR. MASTER-OF-TIME, I WANT SOME *ANSWERS* OUT OF YOU... LIKE WHERE'D THAT *OTHER* KANG COME FROM? AND WHAT'S THE *REAL* REASON YOU BROUGHT US TO LIMBO?

WHAT ARE YOU TALKING ABOUT? I NEVER--! I RECEIVED A MESSAGE THAT *YOU* WERE ATTACKING--!

NO... *NO!* WE'VE *ALL* BEEN PLAYED FOR FOOLS!

QUITE RIGHT, DEAR BROTHER! BUT NOW THE GAME DRAWS TO A *CLOSE*!

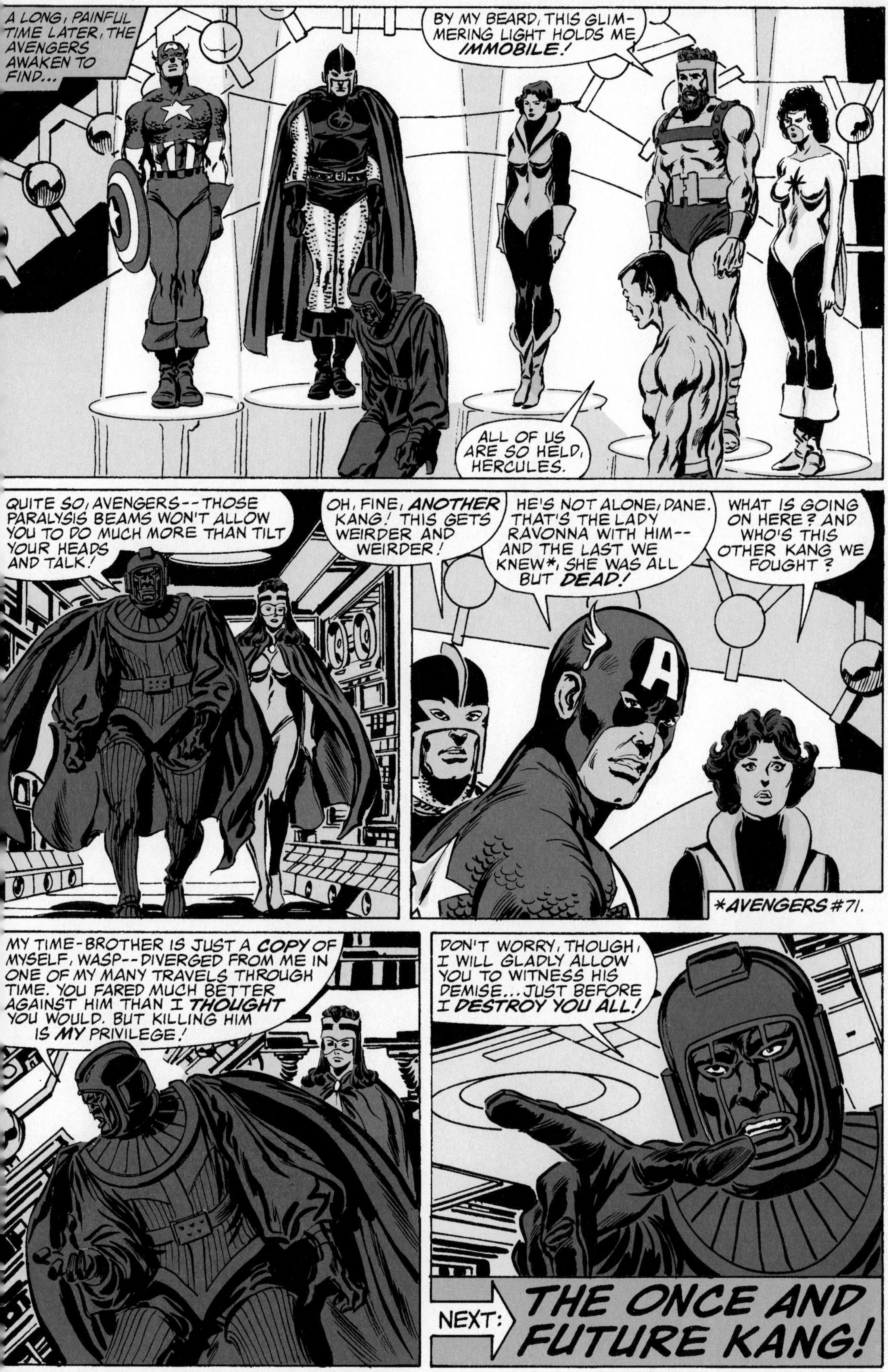
A LONG, PAINFUL TIME LATER, THE AVENGERS AWAKEN TO FIND...
BY MY BEARD, THIS GLIMMERING LIGHT HOLDS ME IMMOBILE!
ALL OF US ARE SO HELD, HERCULES.
QUITE SO, AVENGERS--THOSE PARALYSIS BEAMS WON'T ALLOW YOU TO DO MUCH MORE THAN TILT YOUR HEADS AND TALK!
OH, FINE, ANOTHER KANG! THIS GETS WEIRDER AND WEIRDER!
HE'S NOT ALONE, DANE. THAT'S THE LADY RAVONNA WITH HIM--AND THE LAST WE KNEW*, SHE WAS ALL BUT DEAD!
WHAT IS GOING ON HERE? AND WHO'S THIS OTHER KANG WE FOUGHT?
*AVENGERS #71.
MY TIME-BROTHER IS JUST A COPY OF MYSELF, WASP--DIVERGED FROM ME IN ONE OF MY MANY TRAVELS THROUGH TIME. YOU FARED MUCH BETTER AGAINST HIM THAN I THOUGHT YOU WOULD. BUT KILLING HIM IS MY PRIVILEGE!
DON'T WORRY, THOUGH, I WILL GLADLY ALLOW YOU TO WITNESS HIS DEMISE... JUST BEFORE I DESTROY YOU ALL!
NEXT: THE ONCE AND FUTURE KANG!

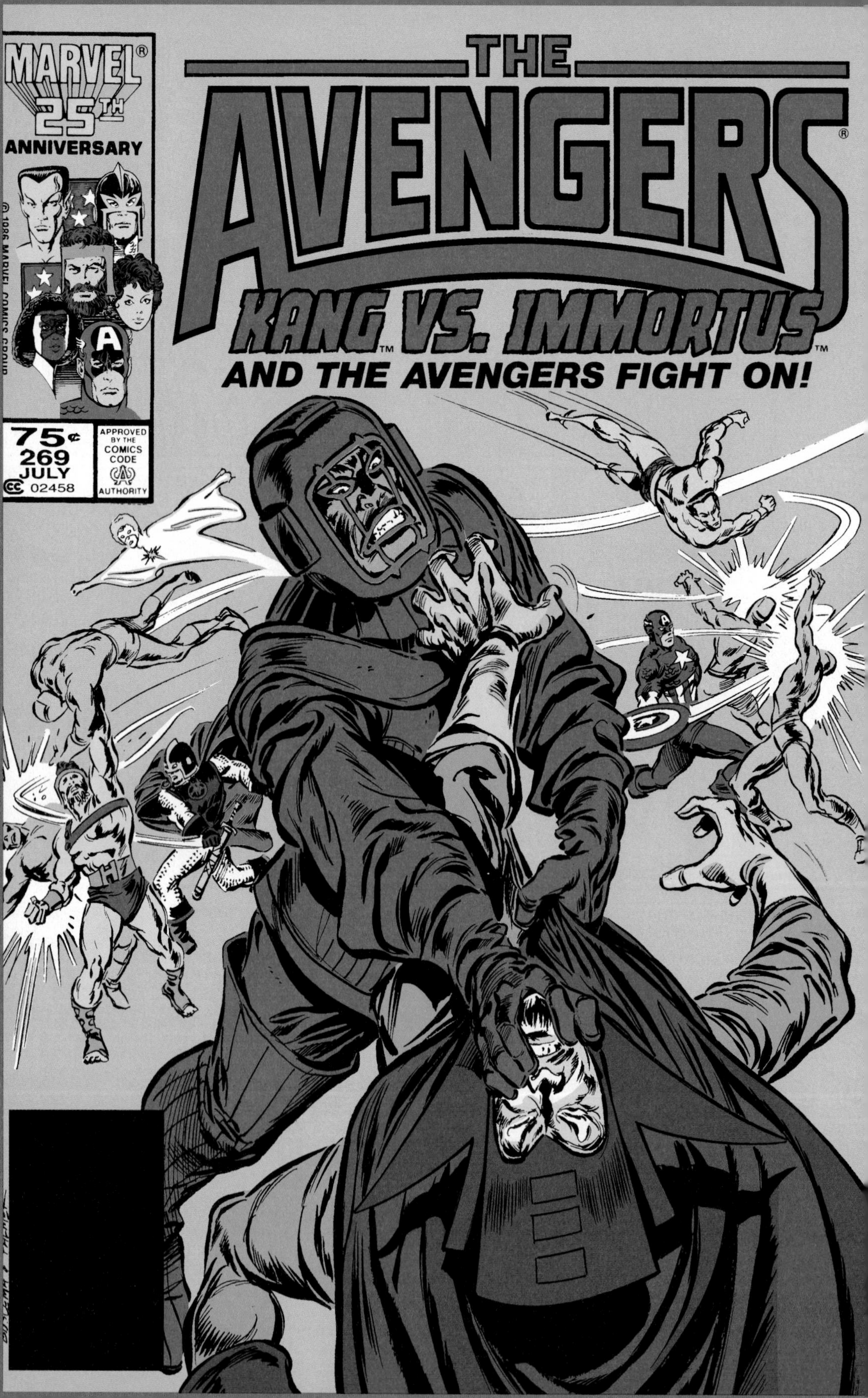
MARVEL®
25TH
ANNIVERSARY
© 1986 MARVEL COMICS GROUP
75¢
269
JULY
02458
APPROVED BY THE COMICS CODE AUTHORITY
THE AVENGERS®
KANG™ VS. IMMORTUS™
AND THE AVENGERS FIGHT ON!

STAN LEE PRESENTS: THE INCREDIBLE STORY OF
**THE ONCE AND FUTURE KANG!**

SURELY, MY LORD KANG, THIS IS YOUR GREATEST TRIUMPH!

YES, RAVONNA...THE MIGHTY AVENGERS ARE MY HELPLESS PRISONERS--AS IS MY SOLE-SURVIVING DOUBLE!

NOW THERE IS NOTHING WHICH CAN STOP MY CONQUEST OF ALL TIME--ALL REALITY!

ROGER STERN-WRITER / JOHN BUSCEMA-BREAKDOWNS
TOM PALMER-FINISHED ART / JIM NOVAK-LETTERER
CHRISTIE SCHEELE-COLORIST/MARK GRUENWALD-EDITOR
JIM SHOOTER-EDITOR-IN-CHIEF

JUST WHO'S CONQUERING **WHOM**? KANG SUPPOSEDLY PULLED US INTO THIS **LIMBO**-DIMENSION... BUT THE FIRST REAL KANG WE ENCOUNTERED WAS **DEAD!** BUT THEN, WE WERE ATTACKED BY A **SECOND** KANG--

--AND THE WHOLE LOT OF US WERE KNOCKED OUT BY A **THIRD** KANG! HOW MANY KANGS **ARE** THERE?!?

THERE **WERE** THOUSANDS, **WASP**--BUT IT SEEMS ONLY **TWO OF US** REMAIN ALIVE! MY CAPED TIME-BROTHER LURED ME HERE WITH A MESSAGE THAT YOU AVENGERS WERE ATTACKING OUR COUNCIL CHAMBERS...

...BUT I SEE NOW THAT **HE** WAS THE ONE WHO KILLED THE KANG YOU FOUND. IT WAS HE WHO BROUGHT YOU HERE--HE HAS DECEIVED US **ALL**.

HAH-HAH-HA! BUT OF COURSE, DEAR BROTHER! I KNEW YOU'D FIGURE IT OUT EVENTUALLY ...YOU ALWAYS WERE MY MOST WORTHY **DIVERGENT DOUBLE!**

IT WAS QUITE A CHALLENGE, DEVELOPING A STRATEGY TO ENTRAP YOU. I WILL ALMOST REGRET YOUR TERMINATION.

ANYBODY UNDERSTAND THIS "DIVERGENT DOUBLE" TALK?

I THINK **I** DO, **CAPTAIN AMERICA**. IN THEORY, ALTERNATE REALITIES CAN BE FORMED AT CRITICAL MOMENTS IN TIME. SAY THERE'S A BATTLE WHICH COULD HAVE TWO OR MORE CRUCIAL OUTCOMES--

--THEN TWO OR MORE REALITIES COULD **DIVERGE**, THE BATTLE IN EACH REALITY HAVING A DIFFERENT OUTCOME.

AND SINCE KANG HAS TRAVELED IN TIME--!

EXACTLY, **BLACK KNIGHT**-- MY TRAVELS HAVE RESULTED IN THE CREATION OF DIVERGENT REALITIES... AND **COPIES** OF MYSELF!

MY VERY **ANCESTRY** IS DERIVED FROM DIVERGENT REALITIES!

"THE EARTH OF MY BIRTHING HAD DIVERGED FROM YOURS CENTURIES AGO. WE ESTABLISHED LUNAR COLONIES, WHILE YOU STILL WALLOWED IN YOUR DARK AGES.

"BUT OUR SCIENTIFIC ADVANCES ALSO BROUGHT US DEVASTATING **WARS!**

"THEN, ONE DAY, A *STRANGER* CAME TO OUR WORLD. HE WAS, HE SAID, A *SCIENTIST.* HE TOOK A WIFE, BEGAT A SON, AND PULLED A RUINED EARTH BACK FROM THE BRINK OF OBLIVION."

"HE WAS MY *ANCESTOR,* AND--AS I WAS TO ONE DAY LEARN-- A TIME-TRAVELER FROM *YOUR* REALITY!"

"BY THE TIME WHICH CORRE-SPONDS TO YOUR YEAR 3000 A.D., HIS LABORS AND THOSE OF HIS LINE HAD BROUGHT FORTH AN AGE OF PEACE AND ENLIGHTEN-MENT. HOW I *HATED* IT!

"I WAS THEN A YOUNG MAN... I CRAVED THE GLORY OF *BATTLE!* BUT THERE WAS NONE OF THAT TO BE HAD IN MY TIME...THERE WAS ONLY MADDENING, UNENDING *PEACE!*

"FINALLY, DESPERATE FOR ADVENTURE, I VISITED A *CITADEL* ERECTED BY MY ANCESTOR..."

PERHAPS HERE I WOULD FIND SOME RELEASE!

"WHAT I FOUND IN A LONG-SEALED CHAMBER WAS PART OF A *TIME MACHINE,* AND THE PLANS FOR ITS OPERA-TION! THERE WAS MY ESCAPE FROM A LIFE OF BOREDOM!

"IT TOOK YEARS TO RE-BUILD AND REDESIGN THE MACHINE TO MY NEEDS-- BUT THEN, AT LAST, I WAS PLUNGED INTO THE DIS-TANT *PAST...*

"...BACK TO ANCIENT EGYPT, WHERE I ESTABLISHED MYSELF AS THE *PHARAOH RAMA-TUT!*

177

"BUT, THEN, FOUR MORE TIME-TRAVELERS WERE BROUGHT BEFORE ME... THE ACCURSED *FANTASTIC FOUR!*

"I THOUGHT THEM *ENSLAVED* BY MY SUPERIOR TECHNOLOGY--

"--BUT I WAS *WRONG!* THEY BROKE FREE OF MY CONTROL AND TURNED ON ME IN MY OWN THRONE ROOM!"

"UNABLE TO STOP THEM, I WAS FORCED TO *QUIT* MY KINGDOM AND FLEE ACROSS TIME! BUT IN FLEEING, I FOUND AN EVEN *GREATER DESTINY!*

"I HAD JUST FINISHED REMOVING MY CEREMONIAL BEARD, WHEN MY SHIP RAN INTO UNEXPECTED *CHRONAL TURBULENCE*--

"--WHICH FORCED ME TO EXIT THE TIME-STREAM INTO YOUR 20TH CENTURY! AND THERE, NEAR THE ORBIT OF JUPITER, I ENCOUNTERED YOUR ERA'S GREATEST DESPOT-- THE INFAMOUS *DOCTOR VICTOR VON DOOM!*

"I KNEW OF HIS EPIC BATTLES WITH THE FANTASTIC FOUR FROM REMNANTS OF HISTORY TAPES MADE OF YOUR REALITY BY MY ANCESTOR...

"...BUT I *PRETENDED* NOT TO RECOGNIZE HIM. HE WAS DISORIENTED FROM HIS ORDEAL IN SPACE, AND I TOOK ADVANTAGE OF THAT TO FEED HIM MISINFORMATION THAT WOULD LEAD HIM TO ACCEPT ME AS AN *ALLY.*

"FOR YOU SEE, I *ADMIRED* DOCTOR DOOM... BUT I ALSO *FEARED* HIM!"

"I KNEW THAT DOOM WAS THE MOST CUNNING MAN OF YOUR TIME--A GENIUS INTELLECT WHO, GIVEN THE CHANCE, MIGHT EASILY TURN MY OWN TECHNOLOGY *AGAINST* ME.

"STILL, I COULD NOT BRING MYSELF TO *STRIKE DOWN* A MAN WHO HAD SO DOGGEDLY BATTLED THE FANTASTIC FOUR, SO..."

I SHALL TAKE YOU BACK TO EARTH...WHILE *I* RETURN TO THE FUTURE.

"EAGER TO WORK HIS REVENGE UPON OUR MUTUAL FOES, DOOM ACCEPTED MY OFFER. I SOON SENT HIM ON HIS WAY IN A PRE-PROGRAMMED LANDING MODULE..."

*YOU* SET THAT FIEND LOOSE ?!

WHEN I AM *FREE* OF THIS PARALYZING RAY, KANG, I WILL *REPAY* YOU FOR THAT ACT OF MADNESS!

BOLD TALK, *SUB-MARINER!*

BUT I CAN UNDERSTAND YOUR *RAGE.* DOOM HAS PLAYED YOU FOR THE *FOOL* MANY TIMES--BOTH BEFORE AND AFTER I AIDED HIM--*HASN'T HE?*

REMEMBER THIS MOMENT, KANG...*I WILL!*

I HAVE HEARD ENOUGH! *HERCULES* WILL NOT BE HELD BY THE MACHINATIONS OF A MERE MORTAL!

I SHALL *NOT* YIELD TO THIS PARALYZING BEAM ...IF IT TAKES *EVERY BIT* OF MY MIGHT, I SHALL BE *FREE!*

AND, ACROSS THE CHAMBER...

WHAT'S THAT STRANGE FLUCTU-ATION IN THE PARALYSIS BEAM'S *POWER SUPPLY?*

OH, I'LL REMEM-BER, SUB-MARINER. MY MEMORY IS QUITE *EXCELLENT.*

I REMEMBER HOW I FOUGHT MY WAY BACK INTO THE TIME-STREAM, BUT THE TURBU-LENCE PROVED *TOO MUCH* FOR MY CRAFT. BY THE TIME I'D REGAINED CONTROL, I FOUND MYSELF ON A WAR-TORN EARTH OF 4000 A.D.

"THE WARRIORS OF THAT TIME FOUGHT ON WITH WEAPONS FROM STOCKPILES CREATED CENTURIES EARLIER--

"--FOR THEY HAD FALLEN INTO SUCH A STATE OF *BARBARISM,* THEY HAD NO UNDERSTANDING OF HOW THEIR EQUIPMENT WORKED OR HOW TO MAKE MORE."

WITH MY OWN GREAT SCIEN-TIFIC TALENT AND THE WEAPONS AND INVENTIONS OF THIS FAR-FUTURE AGE, I CAN RULE THIS *WORLD!*

"I LOCKED MYSELF INSIDE ONE RESEARCH COMPLEX--

"--AND WITHIN HOURS I HAD MASTERED A SCORE OF MIRACULOUS DEVICES. INSPIRED BY MY MEETING WITH DOCTOR DOOM, I CREATED A *BATTLE SUIT* CONTAINING A SMALL ARMORY OF WEAPONS.

"THAT DAY, *KANG THE CONQUEROR* WAS TRULY BORN!

"WITH MY SKILL AND WEAPONRY, IT WAS SIMPLE TO RALLY THE BARBARIAN *RABBLE* TO MY SIDE.

"IN A FEW SHORT WEEKS I CARVED OUT A *NEW EMPIRE!* BUT THAT DID NOT SATISFY ME!

"THE WORLD I RULED WAS DYING. I CRAVED *DOMINION* OVER AN EARTH STILL GREEN AND VITAL.

"MY THOUGHTS IMMEDIATELY WENT TO THE GLORIOUS *LIVING* WORLD OF MY ANCESTOR...20TH CENTURY EARTH.' AND WHY NOT? THOUGH IT WAS THE TIME OF DOCTOR DOOM, I NOW FELT *MORE* THAN A MATCH FOR HIM!

"I ACTUALLY WELCOMED THE CHALLENGE OF PITTING MY WEAPONRY AGAINST DOOM'S IN A CONTEST FOR WORLD DOMINATION. BUT IT WAS NOT *DOOM* WHO CHALLENGED ME UPON MY RETURN TO THE 20TH CENTURY...

"...IT WAS A FLEDGLING GROUP OF SUPER-BEINGS CALLED THE *AVENGERS!*"

I REMEMBER THAT DAY MYSELF, KANG!

AS I RECALL, WE SENT YOU RUNNING BACK TO THE FUTURE WITH YOUR TAIL BETWEEN YOUR LEGS!

LUCK!

WHAT--?

YOU HEARD ME! IT WAS SHEER *LUCK* YOU THWARTED ME THAT DAY!

THWARTED *US*, BROTHER!

AFTER ALL, YOUR LIFE DID NOT DIVERGE FROM MINE UNTIL *AFTER* THAT FIRST ENCOUNTER WITH THE AVENGERS. WOULD YOU LIKE TO KNOW *WHEN* IT DID?

YOU MEAN, WHEN *YOUR* LIFE DIVERGED FROM *MINE*, UPSTART! NO, I WILL YET HAVE THE UPPER HAND IN THIS, AND THEN I SHALL *FIND OUT* FOR MYSELF!

MEANWHILE...

HERCULES IS BEGINNING TO OVERLOAD THE SYSTEM. I SHOULD *WARN* KANG--BUT IF I DO, HE MIGHT *KILL* THE AVENGERS OUTRIGHT.

YET, IF I *DON'T--*!

I... *WILL*... BE... *FREE*!

SO, MY COUNTERPART THINKS ME AN *UPSTART*! AND WHAT DO *YOU* THINK, CAPTAIN?

I COULDN'T REPEAT THAT IN MIXED COMPANY!

DEFIANT TO THE END, EH? YOU WERE JUST AS OBSTINATE THE *LAST* TIME I HELD YOU CAPTIVE!

I WOULD HAVE DESTROYED YOU THEN... HAD IT NOT BEEN FOR MY LOVELY RAVONNA!

OH! WHAT--?

SURELY, YOU MUST RECALL, MY DEAR--

"-- HOW, AFTER MY ARMY HAD SEIZED YOUR FATHER'S KINGDOM, MY LIEUTENANT, *BALTAG,* DEMANDED YOUR DEATH... AND TURNED AGAINST ME WHEN I REFUSED.

"I WAS DRIVEN TO *JOIN FORCES* WITH CAPTAIN AMERICA AND HIS NEOPHYTE AVENGERS AGAINST MY OWN ARMIES.

"IN RETURN FOR YOUR *AID*, CAPTAIN, I RETURNED YOU AVENGERS TO YOUR PROPER PLACE IN TIME...CONFIDENT THAT I COULD HAVE MY *REVENGE* UPON YOU ANOTHER TIME.

"BUT AS I WAS SENDING YOU ON YOUR WAY, THE TRAITOROUS *BALTAG* BROKE FREE FROM HIS GUARDS AND SEIZED A *WEAPON*..."

DEATH TO KANG, WHO HAS BETRAYED US ALL!

"EVEN AS I TURNED, THE LOVE OF MY LIFE HURLED HERSELF INTO THE LINE OF FIRE!"

RAVONNA!

"BALTAG WAS BROUGHT DOWN IN AN INSTANT--BUT HE HAD LEFT MY SOUL WITH A *WOUND* MORE SERIOUS THAN ANY HE COULD EVER HAD INFLICTED ON MY BODY!"

RAVONNA... HAVE I *GAINED* YOUR LOVE, ONLY TO HAVE *LOST* IT?

"NOTHING IN ALL MY SCIENCE COULD RESTORE HER LIFE. AT BEST, I COULD BUT PRESERVE HER BODY IN STASIS."

THE YEARS THAT FOL- LOWED ARE A BLUR TO ME NOW. I SET OUT THROUGH TIME AND SPACE, IN SEARCH OF ADVENTURE-- ANY ADVENTURE-- WHICH WOULD HELP ME FORGET.

BUT NOTHING DID.

"EVENTUALLY, MY VENTURES BROUGHT ME BACK TO YOUR 20TH CENTURY, AND A CHANCE ENCOUNTER WITH THE MIGHTY THOR!

"I'D THOUGHT I HAD HIM AT MY MERCY...

"...BUT HE'D ONLY FEIGNED HELPLESSNESS, TO LEARN MY INTENTIONS. AS I PREPARED TO DEPART IN MY CAMOUFLAGED TIME-SPHERE--

"-- HE USED THAT ACCURSED HAMMER OF HIS TO ENVELOPE MY CRAFT IN AN INFINITY VORTEX. MY TIME-SPHERE WAS OBLITERATED...

"...AND I WAS FLUNG INTO THIS MISTY REALM OF LIMBO. HOW LONG I WANDERED HERE IS IMPOSSIBLE TO SAY, FOR--AS YOU'VE LEARNED--LIMBO EXISTS BEYOND ALL CONCEPTS OF TIME AND SPACE.

"BUT FINALLY I CHANCE UPON A SPRAWLING FORTRESS... AND THE REMAINS OF THE ONE WHO HAD BEEN THIS DIMENSION'S MASTER--THE ONE CALLED IMMORTUS!

"I DO NOT KNOW WHAT HAD KILLED IMMORTUS, NOR DO I CARE--

"-- FOR IN DEATH, HE COULD NOT CHALLENGE MY CLAIM TO HIS DIMENSION, OR HIS WONDROUS DEVICES!

"THERE WERE ENDLESS SCORES OF *VIEWSCREENS,* ALL FOCUSED ON DIFFERENT POINTS IN REAL TIME AND SPACE. MASTERY OF THE CONTROLS CAME TO ME QUITE NATURALLY..."

"...AND I SOON FOUND MYSELF FACING THAT MOMENT IN TIME I HAD MOST TRIED TO FORGET."

"AS I GROPED FOR THE CONTROLS, MY HAND FELL UPON AN UNTRIED SWITCH. AND SUDDENLY--"

"--I WAS NO LONGER *ALONE* IN LIMBO!"

R-RAVONNA?

WHAT? MY LORD KANG... WHERE *ARE* WE?

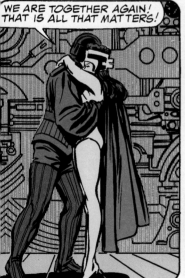

WE ARE TOGETHER AGAIN! THAT IS ALL THAT MATTERS!

"BUT I WAS *WRONG.* FOR AS WE EMBRACED, I SAW SOMETHING THAT MADE MY BLOOD RUN COLD!"

"THE SCREEN WHICH HAD SHOWN RAVONNA ABOUT TO SACRIFICE HERSELF, NOW DISPLAYED THE BODY OF KANG!

"IN SAVING MY LOVE, I HAD DIVERGED A NEW REALITY IN WHICH I *DIED!*"

"I SOON DISCOVERED THAT MY ADVENTURES HAD TRIGGERED AN *ABUNDANCE* OF DIVERGENT REALITIES, MANY OF WHICH HELD *COPIES* OF MYSELF..."

WHY DO THEY WORRY YOU SO?

BECAUSE THEY'RE SUCH *IDIOTS*--

--AND THEY'RE DIVERGING *MORE* IDIOTS! I MUST PUT AN *END* TO THIS BEFORE THE NAME OF *KANG* BECOMES SYNONYMOUS WITH "*FOOL!*"

"LIMBO ITSELF PROVIDED A SOLUTION. THE LESSER KANGS COULD BE EXTERMINATED WITHIN THIS TIMELESS REALM *WITHOUT* PRODUCING MORE DIVERGENT DOUBLES!

"OBSERVATION REVEALED THAT TWO 'BROTHERS' WERE TOO *CLEVER* TO BE EASILY ELIMINATED. SO I ENLISTED THEM INTO A *COUNCIL OF TIME*, LETTING THEM THINK THEY WERE PART OF MY PLAN..."

...WHEN THEY WERE ACTUALLY LITTLE MORE THAN *STOOGES!*

YOU WILL SUFFER A THOUSAND TORTURES FOR THIS!

WHILE, ALL BUT UNNOTICED...

I WOULD HARDLY HAVE BELIEVED IT POSSIBLE! HERCULES IS NOT ONLY OVERCOMING THE PARALYSIS BEAM--

"-- HE'S CAUSING A *POWER DRAIN* ON THE ENTIRE SYSTEM!"

CAP, DO YOU FEEL--?

THE PARALYSIS FADING? YES!

IF I COULD MOVE JUST A *LITTLE MORE*--!

MERE MOTION IS NOT THE ONLY THING ON *CAPTAIN MARVEL'S* MIND..

I'VE BEEN FIGHTING TO UNLEASH MY ENERGY POWERS, BUT THIS BEAM'S HELD ME BACK. IF IT'S STARTING TO *WEAKEN*--!

YOU'RE IN NO POSITION TO THREATEN TORTURE, BROTHER! YOU... *WHAT?!*

YOU'RE *MOVING!* BUT YOU *CAN'T!* IT'S NOT POSSIBLE!

IS THAT *FEAR* IN YOUR VOICE, BROTHER? IS YOUR PRECIOUS SCHEME UNRAVELING!

AND THEN, THE EXPLOSIVE FORCE AT CAPTAIN MARVEL'S COMMAND ERUPTS FROM HER BODY IN ONE DEVASTATING BURST OF ENERGY!

CHO KOOM

THAT DID IT! I CAN MOVE AGAIN, BUT... I FEEL *STIFF!*

LIMBER UP FAST, AVENGERS!

YOU'VE CUT OFF THE PARALYSIS BEAMS! BUT *HOW?* THERE ARE SAFEGUARDS...

...WARNING SYSTEMS--! THERE WOULD HAVE BEEN *SIGNS* OF AN OVERLOAD!

THERE *WERE* SIGNS, MY LORD!

RAVONNA, YOU *KNEW--?* YOU *BETRAYED* ME?!?

MAYHAP SHE BUT CAME TO HER *SENSES!*

THICK-WITTED FOOL! MY PROTECTIVE ARMOR HAS RESISTED THE HAMMER OF THOR--IT CAN EASILY STAVE OFF YOUR CLUMSY ATTACK!

BUT HOW WELL IS YOUR FORCE-FIELD *ROOTED?*

KT

OOM

HA! NOT WELL AT ALL, 'TWOULD SEEM!

LET'S GO! WE CAN'T LET HIM GET AWAY FROM US NOW!

RAVONNA, ARE YOU--?

I WILL BE FINE, WASP. I HAVE *THIS ONE* WELL IN HAND.

GO ON AFTER THE *OTHER* KANG. JUST... TRY TO TAKE HIM ALIVE.

WE WILL IF HE LETS US!

THIS IS BIZARRE! I THOUGHT RAVONNA AND KANG WERE LOVERS, BUT IT LOOKS LIKE *SHE* LET US GET FREE!

THE WASP IS GONE NOW. PUT DOWN YOUR *WEAPON.*

NO.

RAVONNA... *PLEASE!*

188

SEVERAL CHAMBERS BEYOND... THESE ROBOT HORDES WILL NOT KEEP ME FROM KANG!

NO, BUT THEY MIGHT *SLOW US DOWN*, HERCULES--AND GAIN KANG *TIME!* STEP UP THE PACE!

CAP-- *LOOK OUT!*

I SAW HIM COMING, JAN, BUT THANKS!

WHERE'S CAPTAIN MARVEL?

SHE FLEW ON AHEAD--

"--TO MAKE SURE KANG WOULDN'T GET TOO FAR AWAY!"

YOU SQUANDER YOUR ENERGIES, WOMAN--

--NOTHING CAN BREECH MY FORCE-FIELD!

WANT TO BET? I'VE SHATTERED FIELDS GENERATED BY WHOLE *STARSHIPS!*

SHE'S RIGHT-- SHE'LL *OVER-LOAD* MY SHIELDS IN MOMENTS!

BUT I HAVE A MEANS OF DEALING WITH HER LIVING ENERGY!

KLIK

THERE ARE WAYS TO COUNTER *EVERY* ATTACK, MARVEL! AS YOU HAVE BECOME A CREATURE OF LIGHT AND LIGHTNING, A SMALL DOSE OF *DARKFORCE* WILL PUT YOU IN YOUR PLACE--

--AND SLOWLY DRAIN YOUR *LIFE* AWAY!

NOT IF *WE* CAN HELP IT, MISTER!

KTANG

WHAT?

N-NEVER FELT SO C-C-COLD!

YOU'VE OVERCOME MY ROBOTS *ALREADY*? IMPRESSIVE...BUT I'VE STILL ENOUGH POWER AT MY COMMAND TO HUMBLE YOU *ALL*!

THINK HE'S BLUFFING, CAP?

ONLY ONE WAY TO *FIND OUT*, JAN!

AVENGERS ATTACK!

WHILE...

PLEASE, RAVONNA --GIVE ME THE WEAPON.

NO. NO, YOU WANT TO KILL MY... THE OTHER KANG.

RAVONNA, I LOVE YOU MORE THAN HE! I HAVE MOURNED FOR YOU FOR HALF-A-CENTURY OF TIME!

IF YOU TRULY LOVE ME, THEN PROMISE YOU WILL NOT HARM YOUR TIME-BROTHER.

I COULD NEVER PROMISE THAT! I MUST HAVE MY REVENGE FOR THE WAY HE USED ME!

I SEE.

GO THEN... GET IT OVER WITH!

YOU'RE LETTING ME GO ...JUST LIKE THAT?

IF YOU'RE SO DETERMINED TO GET YOURSELF KILLED, IT IS POINTLESS TO TRY AND STOP YOU. BUT I WON'T GIVE YOU MY WEAPON-- YOU'LL HAVE TO KILL ME FIRST.

KEEP YOUR TOY! CAPTAIN MARVEL WRECKED MOST OF MY BATTLE-SUIT'S WEAPONRY, * BUT I STILL HAVE THE MEANS TO ELIMINATE MY COMPETITION! I'M NOT THE ONE WHO WILL DIE, MY LOVE!

*LAST ISSUE.

HE'S SO WRONG! THEY WERE ALL SO WRONG...WHY COULDN'T THEY SEE?

THEY WEREN'T CAPABLE OF SEEING THEIR ERRORS, RAVONNA.

I HAD TO GIVE HIM A CHANCE. I HAD TO TRY!

I KNOW.

I'LL USE MY DOUBLE'S OWN STRATEGY AGAINST HIM. LET THE *AVENGERS* SOFTEN HIM UP, THEN *I* WILL STRIKE!

BAM

TOOM

WE NEED MORE *COVER*, HERCULES! RIP OUT THAT MACHINERY AND--!

SAY NO MORE, WASP.

KRAK

DOES THE WOMAN TAKE ME FOR AN *IDIOT*?

I NEED NO DIRECTION FOR SO *SIMPLE* A TASK!

A MOST FORMIDABLE *MISSILE*, OLYMPIAN ...FOR A LESSER FOE!

SKRAKOW

GOT TO MOVE NOW!

AH-*HA*! I THOUGHT HERCULES' ATTACK MIGHT BE A DIVERSION!

UNFF EVEN WITH MY *SHIELD* SHUNTING OFF MOST OF THE BLAST, IT STILL HAS THE KICK OF A MISSOURI MULE!

I'M SURPRISED YOU'D TRY SO *OBVIOUS* A TACT, CAPTAIN! I...WHA--?

NOT AS OBVIOUS AS YOU THOUGHT, KANG! YOU SHOULD'VE KEPT YOUR EYE ON THE MAN WITH THE *MAGIC SWORD*!

ZZAK

YOUR CAPTAIN MARVEL HAS YET TO FULLY RECOVER--MY *BACK-UP SYSTEMS* WILL SHIELD ME BEFORE *ANY* OF YOU CAN STRIKE AGAIN!

WRONG, BRO--

--THERRR=

ZRAM

DISRUPTING MY FIELD GAINS YOU LITTLE, AVENGER!

WELL, NOW--

--COULD *THIS* BE THE KANG WHO VOWED TO GET THE UPPER HAND? HAH-HAH-HA! THE FOOL NEVER EVEN *CONSI-DERED* THAT I MIGHT HAVE TAMPERED WITH HIS WEAPONRY BE-FORE HE WENT UNDER THE *PARALYSIS BEAM!*

YOU *SEE,* AVENGERS? I PLANNED FOR *EVERYTHING!* DESPITE YOUR INTERFERENCE, YOU COULDN'T THWART MY GREATEST SCHEME!

NOW AT LAST, I AM *THE ONE AND ONLY* KANG!

OH, YEAH? HOW DO YOU *KNOW* THERE AREN'T A FEW *MORE* KANGS WANDERING AROUND LOOSE?

BECAUSE I HAVE COMPUTED *ALL POSSIBLE DIVERGENCES,* AND ELIMINATED THEM ALL! I AM THE *SOLE* MASTER OF TIME!

*NOT SO,* BROTHER...

...YOU WILL NEVER BE MASTER, AS LONG AS *I* YET LIVE!

IMMORTUS!

NO! YOU...YOU CAN'T BE IMMORTUS! THIS IS SOME TRICK!

NOT AT ALL! WHAT HAS GONE BEFORE HAS BEEN THE TRICK!

I ALLOWED YOU TO ELIMINATE ALL THE DIVERGENT KANGS, BECAUSE IT SERVED MY PURPOSES! BUT THERE WAS ONE DIVERGENCE WHOSE EXISTENCE I KEPT HIDDEN FROM YOU... MINE!

YOU'RE SAYING THAT YOU DIVERGED FROM ME? BUT THERE WERE NO SIGNS--!

SOUNDS LIKE IMMORTUS DID A GOOD JOB OF KEEPING YOU IN THE DARK, MISTER! THE AVENGERS LEARNED LONG AGO THAT IMMORTUS WAS ANOTHER MANIFESTATION OF KANG*-- BUT WE'D ALSO BEEN TOLD HE WAS DEAD.

THE RUMORS OF MY DEMISE WERE A NECESSARY DECEPTION, CAPTAIN.

DIVERGENCE OR NOT, YOU'LL NOT STOP ME FROM--!

*GIANT-SIZE AVENGERS #3.

OH, DO BE STILL! I WAS STOPPING YOU LONG BEFORE YOU EVER ENTERED LIMBO! WHO DO YOU THINK ENGINEERED THAT TURBULENCE IN THE TIME STREAM THAT FIRST BROUGHT YOU TO THE 20TH AND 40TH CENTURIES?

NOR WAS IT MERE CHANCE THAT LED YOU TO MY ERSATZ REMAINS.

I MENTALLY MANIPULATED YOUR RESCUE OF MY LOVELY RAVONNA. AND SHE, IN TURN, HELPED ME KEEP YOUR COUNTER-DIVERGENCY PROJECT UNDER OBSERVATION.

IT'S ALL TRUE. I'M SORRY, MY LORD, BUT IMMORTUS IS ALL THAT WAS EVER GOOD IN KANG. AND YOU... YOU ARE STILL SO FULL OF HATE!

NO... NO, I AM MASTER OF TIME!

YOU ARE NOT EVEN THE *LAST* OF THE KANGS... *THIS IS!* THE *PSYCHE-GLOBE* HAS AB-SORBED THE *MEMORIES* OF ALL THE KANGS YOU HAVE *SLAIN.*

BY ITS POWER AM *I* THE *SUPREME MASTER OF LIMBO!*

THEN YOU WILL BE SUPREME NO MORE!!

NOW IT IS *KANG* WHO RIGHTFULLY RULES!

HAH! *LOOK* AT YOU ALL...FROZEN WITH *FEAR!* AND WELL *SHOULD* YOU BE!

NO LONGER WILL KANG BE MADE A *FOOL* OF!

THE POWER OF THIS GLOBE IS *MINE!*

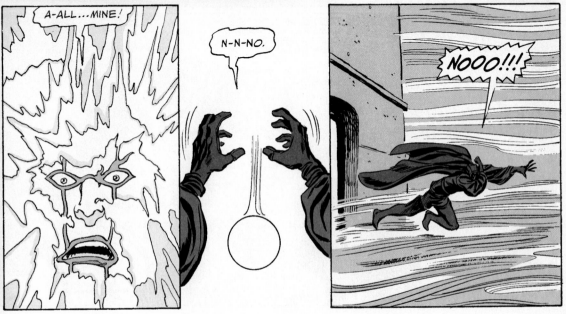

A-ALL...MINE!

N-N-NO.

NOOO!!!

195

WHY ARE WE JUST STANDING HERE? HE'S GETTING AWAY!

THERE'S NO NEED TO CHASE AFTER HIM, CAPTAIN-- KANG IS NO LONGER A *PROBLEM*.

AND IN HIS *CURRENT* STATE OF MIND, HE WILL *NEVER* FIND HIS WAY OUT OF LIMBO.

YOU...YOU SOMEHOW KEPT US FROM *STOPPING* KANG! YOU *WANTED* HIM TO GRAB THAT SPHERE!

NO, I GAVE KANG THE OPPORTUNITY TO EITHER *CONDEMN* OR *REDEEM* HIMSELF. WHEN HE SEIZED THE SPHERE, HE CHOSE THE *FORMER* COURSE ...MORESO THE PITY.

WHAT WAS *REALLY* IN THAT GLOBE?

EXACTLY WHAT I SAID-- THE *LIFE MEMORIES* OF ALL THE SLAIN KANGS. THEY WERE *NOT* THE SOURCE OF MY POWER, THOUGH I HAD LEARNED MUCH ABOUT ALTERNATE REALITIES BY EXAMINING THEM, ONE BY ONE.

BUT KANG WAS *FORCE-FED* ALL THOSE MEMORIES *AT ONCE!*

YES.

THOUSANDS OF MEMORIES IN AN INSTANT! THAT WOULD BE MORE THAN ANY *MORTAL MIND* COULD STAND!

*THOSE* MEMORIES ESPECIALLY, NAMOR... FOR EACH AND EVERY ONE HAS ENDED IN KANG'S DEFEAT AT HIS OWN HANDS!

BUT WHY DEAL WITH KANG IN SUCH A *ROUND-ABOUT* WAY?

UNDERSTAND, CAPTAIN MARVEL, THAT AS *RULER OF LIMBO* IT IS MY *DUTY* TO UNTANGLE THE REALITIES BROUGHT ABOUT BY MY DIVERGENT COUNTERPARTS. IT IS AN ONEROUS AND OFTEN *DISTASTEFUL* DUTY.

I FOUND IT PREFER-ABLE TO LET ONE KANG ELIMINATE THE OTHERS, THAN TO INTERVENE *DIRECTLY* MYSELF.

YOU CALL LETTING ONE KANG WIPE OUT THOUSANDS, AND THEN DRIVING HIM MAD *"PREFERABLE"*?!

I CALL IT *VILLAINY!*

CALL IT WHAT YOU WILL! I HAVE THE RESPONSIBILITY TO OVERSEE MANY MILLENNIA OF TIME... AND TO MAIN-TAIN THE STABILITY OF MORE REALITIES THAN YOUR POOR MINDS CAN *IMAGINE!* EVERYTHING I DO IS *NECESSARY!*

WHY SHOULD WE BELIEVE YOU ANY MORE THAN WE WOULD *KANG?*

WHETHER OR NOT YOU BELIEVE ME IS *MOOT!* MY PURPOSES HAVE BEEN SERVED. YOU HAVE PLAYED YOUR PARTS WELL, BUT THERE IS NO LONGER A NEED FOR YOU IN LIMBO--

--BEGONE, BACK TO YOUR 20TH CENTURY EARTH!

MY LORD, WHY DID YOU DIS-MISS THEM SO *IMPERIOUSLY?*

NOW, THE AVENGERS WILL *NEVER* TRUST YOU.

I COULD NEVER *HOPE* TO WIN THEIR TRUST, RAVONNA-- NOR WOULD I *WANT* IT. HEROES MUST *ALWAYS* BE WARY OF BEINGS AS POWERFUL AS I.

FAR BETTER I BE THOUGHT A *VILLAIN,* THAN A WORLD LOSE THE EFFECTIVENESS OF THE MIGHTY *AVENGERS!*

END

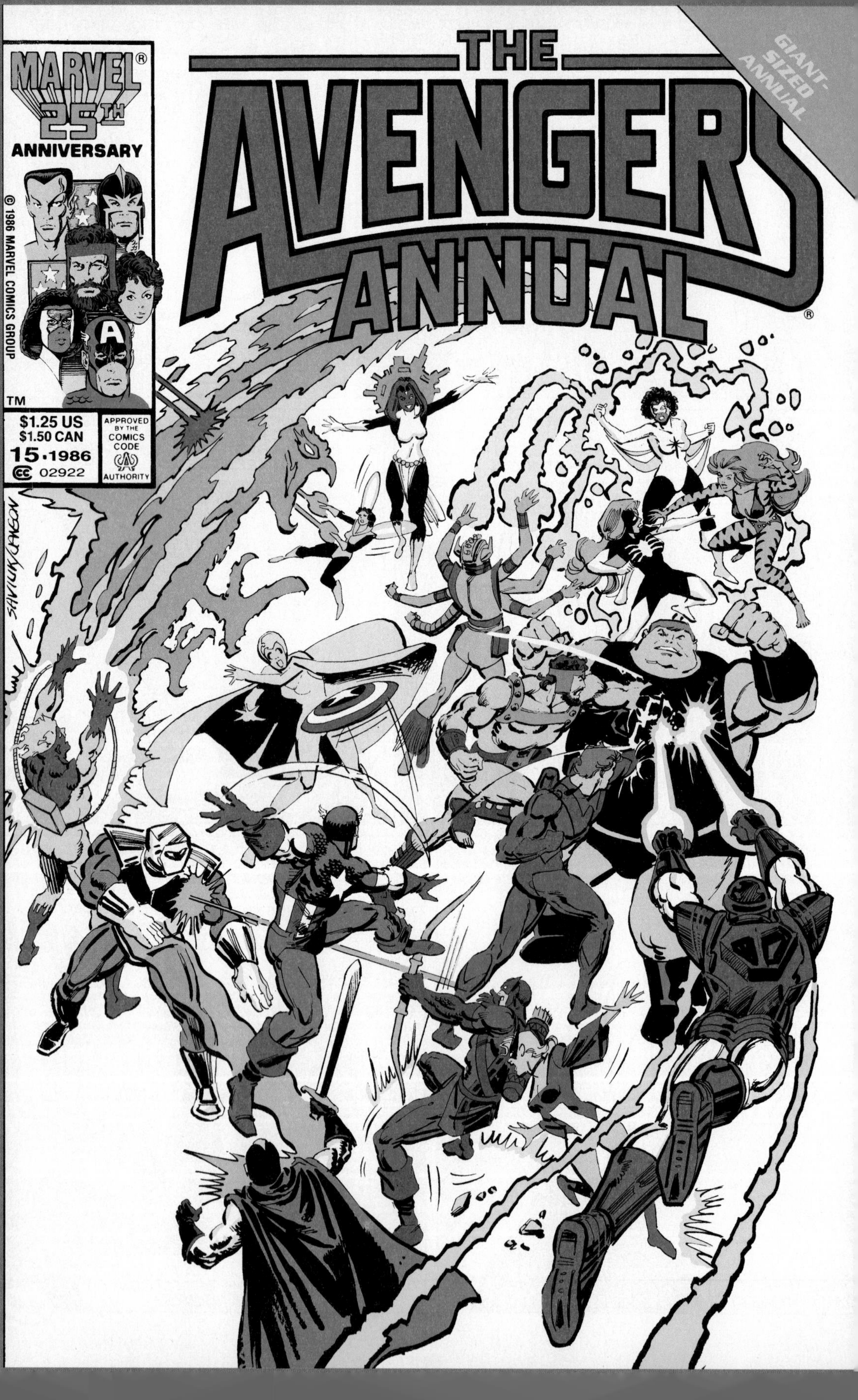

THE AVENGERS ANNUAL
GIANT-SIZED ANNUAL
MARVEL 25TH ANNIVERSARY
© 1986 MARVEL COMICS GROUP
TM
$1.25 US
$1.50 CAN
15 • 1986
02922
APPROVED BY THE COMICS CODE AUTHORITY

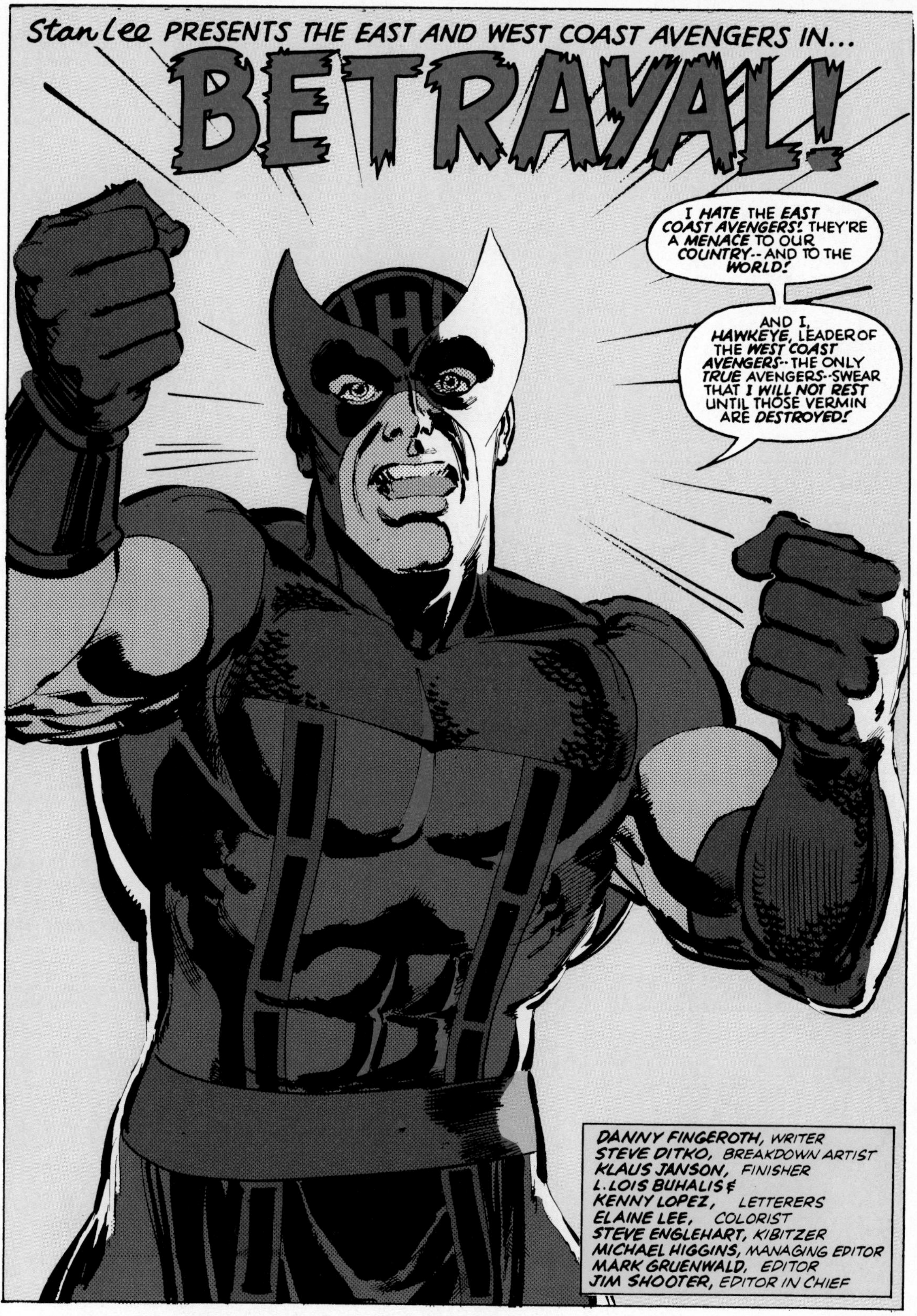

Stan Lee PRESENTS THE EAST AND WEST COAST AVENGERS IN...
BETRAYAL!
I HATE THE EAST COAST AVENGERS! THEY'RE A MENACE TO OUR COUNTRY-- AND TO THE WORLD!
AND I, HAWKEYE, LEADER OF THE WEST COAST AVENGERS-- THE ONLY TRUE AVENGERS--SWEAR THAT I WILL NOT REST UNTIL THOSE VERMIN ARE DESTROYED!
DANNY FINGEROTH, WRITER
STEVE DITKO, BREAKDOWN ARTIST
KLAUS JANSON, FINISHER
L. LOIS BUHALIS &
KENNY LOPEZ, LETTERERS
ELAINE LEE, COLORIST
STEVE ENGLEHART, KIBITZER
MICHAEL HIGGINS, MANAGING EDITOR
MARK GRUENWALD, EDITOR
JIM SHOOTER, EDITOR IN CHIEF

AW, C'MON, HONEY. DON'T BE SO UPSET JUST BECAUSE YOU *STRUCK OUT.* THIS IS JUST A FUN GAME!

BESIDES, CAP'S GOT A *MEAN* CURVE BALL.

HE SURE *DOES,* MOCKING-BIRD.

*BAP!*

HAWK, PLEASE TRY TO TAKE IT EASY AND ENJOY YOUR-SELF.

AFTER ALL, THIS FIRST ANNUAL EAST vs. WEST BASE-BALL GAME WAS *YOUR* IDEA.

I KNOW, I KNOW. I'LL TRY.

BATTER UP!

THE PLACE IS *ROYALS STADIUM, KANSAS CITY, MISSOURI.*

THE TWO AVENGERS TEAMS HAVE COME HERE, THE MID-POINT BETWEEN THEIR TWO COASTS, TO EXCHANGE IDEAS AND INFORMATION...

...BUT MOSTLY TO HAVE A *GOOD TIME.*

AT LEAST THERE WASN'T MUCH OF A CROWD HERE TO SEE ME STRIKE OUT-- JUST SOME GROUNDS-CREW MEMBERS.

I'M GLAD WE KEPT THIS THING PRIVATE, HAWK. A STADIUM FULL OF AVENGERS FANS WOULD'VE BEEN EXCITING-- BUT HARDLY *RELAXING!*

COME ON, *IRON MAN, WONDER MAN*--LET'S GET A CHEER GOING!

WEST IS BEST! EAST COAST STINKS!

THAT'S A CHEER?

FORMER AVENGER HENRY PYM IS THE GAME'S UMPIRE.

HIS EX-WIFE, THE WONDROUS WASP, IS CATCHER FOR THE EAST COASTERS.

HERE YOU GO, CAP. WE'VE GOT THESE TURKEYS *BEAT!*

DON'T BE TOO OVER-CONFIDENT, JAN. WE'VE ONLY GOT A TWO-RUN LEAD.

"ONLY" TWO RUNS? HEY, WITH *CAPTAIN AMERICA* PITCHING AND ME AND *HERCULES* MAKING UP THE INFIELD--THAT'S AS GOOD AS HAVING WON!

ZOUNDS! I DON'T THINK I SHALL *EVER* COMPREHEND THE WORKINGS OF THIS STRANGE APPAREL...!

YOU WERE SAYING, KNIGHT...?

DON'T FEEL BAD, HONEY. I'LL REDEEM YOUR HONOR WHEN IT'S MY TURN AT BAT.

MAYBE I WON'T HAVE TO WAIT THAT LONG. LOOK WHO'S UP FOR OUR SIDE--

WONDER MAN!

STEEEE-RIKE ONE!

HUH? THAT WAS WAY OUTSIDE!

BAP

OKAY, PEOPLE. I'M SENDING THE NEXT ONE TO DOWNTOWN CALCUTTA!

YEAH!

WHOK!

THAT LITTLE SUCKER'S GONNA KEEP GOING FOR MILES!

BUT SIMON WILLIAMS HAS NOT CONSIDERED THE EAST COAST AVENGERS' OUTFIELD.

HER NAME IS CAPTAIN MARVEL.

GOT TO SWITCH TO MY LIGHT-FORM--

--OVERTAKE THE BALL--

--TURN SOLID SO I CAN CATCH--

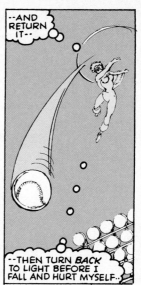

--AND RETURN IT--

--THEN TURN *BACK* TO LIGHT BEFORE I FALL AND HURT MYSELF...

--AND, OH, WHY NOT--TURN SOLID AGAIN TO *CATCH* IT!

BY OLYMPUS! WHAT A *FANTASTIC* DISPLAY OF SKILL!

BEAUTIFUL, CAPTAIN! THAT'S THE PLAY OF THE GAME!

WHAT A *SHOWBOAT!* I *LOVE* IT!

USUALLY I DON'T SHOW OFF WITH MY POWERS LIKE THAT.

I'M A LITTLE EMBARRASSED-- BUT IT *WAS* FUN.

BUT...

I WAS *ROBBED*, HANK! THAT BALL WAS OUT OF THE STADIUM BY THE TIME SHE CAUGHT IT!

THAT SHOULD COUNT AS A *HOME RUN!*

LET ME THINK...

DON'T *THINK!* THROW HER OUT OF THE *GAME!* MAKE THEM *FORFEIT!* MAKE THEM--

I'M DECLARING THAT LAST PLAY--

..A GROUND-RULE DOUBLE!

*AWRIGHT!* WHO SAID COMPLAINING NEVER GOT YOU ANYWHERE?

THANKS A LOT, HANK.

NEXT UP TO BAT--TIGRA!

BALL ONE!

BAP

BALL? THAT WAS A ST--!

NEVER MIND. BUT IF YOU WEREN'T MY EX, WHO I WAS TRYING TO STAY FRIENDS WITH-- GRRRR!

ON THE NEXT PITCH--

BUNT

HAH! WHAT A PUNY ATTEMPT!

SURELY YOU HAVE MORE STRENGTH THAN THAT, TIGRA!

ALL I NEED DO IS WAIT FOR THE FEEBLE, LITTLE THING TO GET TO ME!

NO, HERCULES--

--YOU'VE GOT TO CHARGE IT AND GRAB IT, OR ELSE--

OR ELSE "PUNY, FEEBLE" TIGRA'S GONNA LEAP OVER YOU AND BE SAFE AT FIRST!

LIKE SO!

AND THANKS TO THAT INGENIOUS BIT OF STRATEGY--

--WONDER MAN SCORES! AWRIGHT!

HERC, DON'T JUST HOLD ONTO THE BALL! TIGRA'S ALREADY PAST SECOND!

THROW IT TO THE BLACK KNIGHT AT THIRD! HE MIGHT STILL HAVE A CHANCE TO TAG HER OUT!

WHAT-- WHERE-- WHO--?

OH--THE KNIGHT!

HERE, SIR KNIGHT!

BUT, FLUSTERED, HERCULES AIMS HIS THROW TOO HIGH.

PROPELLED BY HERCULES' SUPERHUMAN MUSCLES, THE BALL STREAKS OVER DANE WHITMAN'S VALIANT, LEAPING STAB--

--AND HEADS, WITH LETHAL VELOCITY-- TOWARD SOME STARTLED, WATCHING GROUNDS-CREW--

JOHNNY, MOVE!

HE CAN'T! HE'S TOO SCARED!

HE'S GONNA GET HIT!

WHUMP

A-AN ARROW! IT SAVED ME!

I DID IT-- I KNOCKED THE BALL OFF COURSE! AT LEAST I'VE BEEN OF SOME USE TODAY.

ALL RIGHT! TIGRA SCORES! THE GAME'S TIED UP!

NOW IT'S MY TURN!

SURE YOU WANT TO USE YOUR BATTLE-STAVES INSTEAD OF A BAT, MOCKING-BIRD?

NO BOUT ADOUBT IT, HANK!

COME ON, CAP! SHOW 'ER WHO'S THE BOSS!

WELL I HEAR BRUCE SPRINGSTEEN IS --BUT I WAS BORN IN THE U.S.A., TOO!

SO HERE COMES MY "YANKEE DOODLE SPECIAL"!

WHAK

AND THERE IT GOES!

BUT, ANOTHER DARING LEAP BY THE BLACK KNIGHT STOPS THE SEARING GROUNDER!

SHAP

OWW!

HERE YA GO, HERC! CATCH IT AND STEP ON FIRST!

WHOA-- GOTTA JUMP!

Hmmm. PERHAPS I WAS TOO FORCEFUL.

WHOOMP!

SHEESH! HOW WAS I SUPPOSED TO GET TO THE BASE--WHEN I WAS BUSY LEAPING OVER THAT *FISSURE?!*

I'M GONNA *BRAIN* THAT HERCULES...!

EASY, HONEY. REMEMBER WHAT YOU TOLD ME BEFORE.

YEAH, RIGHT-- A *FUN* GAME!

*IRON MAN STEPS UP TO THE PLATE.*

*THE WIND-UP.*

*THE PITCH.*

THE *BLOB?*

YEAH. THE BLOB.

HEY, WATCH IT. YOU COULD *HURT* SOMEBODY WITH ONE 'A THESE THINGS!

CRUNCH

*AND, AFTER THE BLOB, SIX OTHER FIGURES MATERIALIZE ON THE FIELD.*

THE NEW-COMERS ARE:

--MYSTIQUE--

--PYRO--

--AVALANCHE--

--SPIRAL--

--DESTINY--

--SPIDER-WOMAN.

WELL DONE, *SPIRAL.* WE HAVE ARRIVED HERE AS PLANNED.

IT'S THE *BROTHERHOOD OF EVIL MUTANTS!* WHAT DO *THEY* WANT HERE?

THEY'RE NOT THE BROTHERHOOD ANYMORE, MOCKINGBIRD, AND SPIDER-WOMAN AND SPIRAL NEVER WERE IN THAT GROUP. THE REST HAVE REPUTEDLY GONE STRAIGHT--AND ALL OF THEM WORK FOR THE FEDERAL GOVERNMENT NOW.

YOU'RE RIGHT, HANK. THEY'RE CALLED *FREEDOM FORCE* NOW. BUT I *STILL* WOULDN'T TRUST THEM.

WE *ARE* FREEDOM FORCE. I AM *MYSTIQUE,* THE GROUP'S LEADER, AND WE ARE HERE TO *ARREST* YOU, AVENGERS.

ARREST US! FOR *WHAT?!*

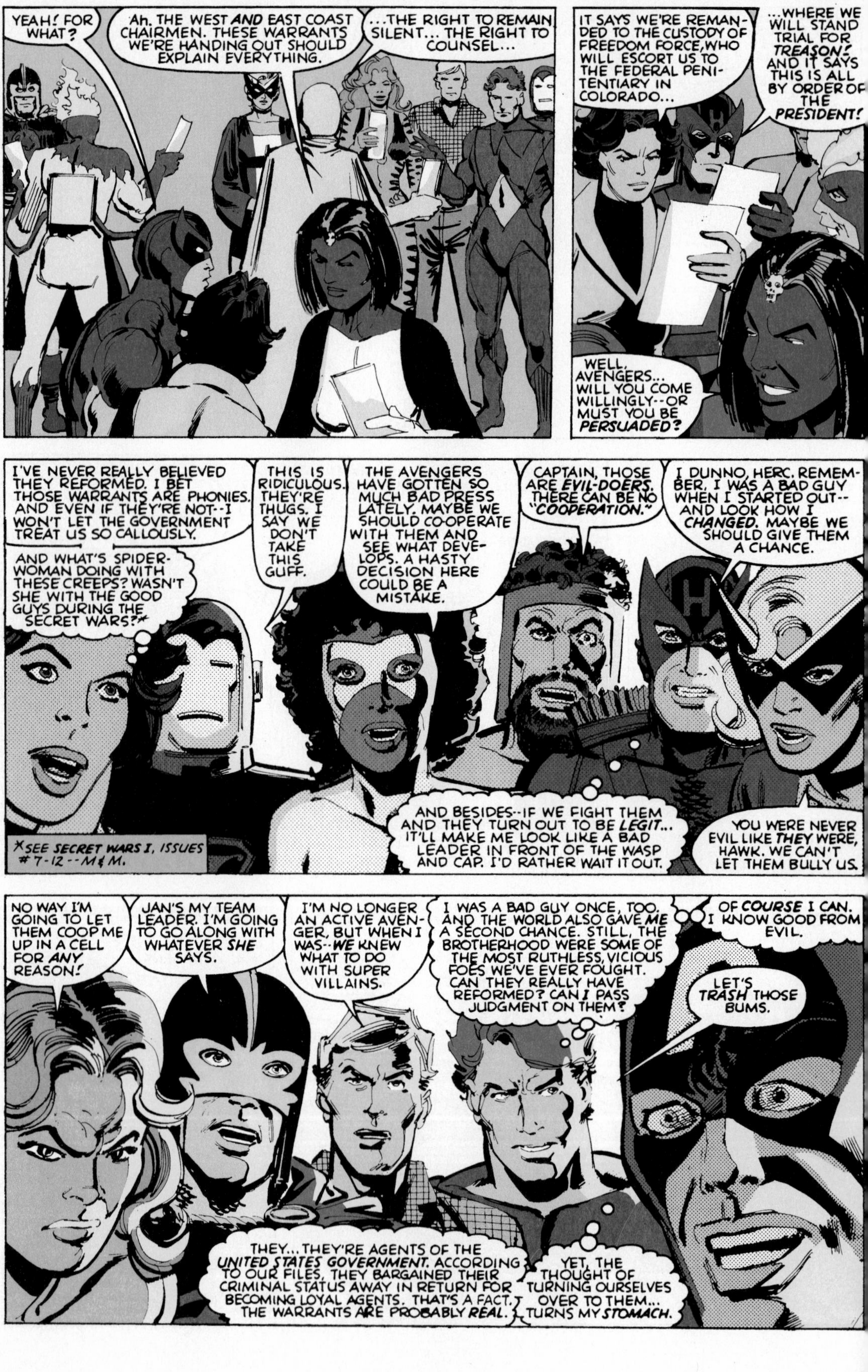
YEAH! FOR WHAT?
Ah. THE WEST AND EAST COAST CHAIRMEN. THESE WARRANTS WE'RE HANDING OUT SHOULD EXPLAIN EVERYTHING.
...THE RIGHT TO REMAIN SILENT... THE RIGHT TO COUNSEL...
IT SAYS WE'RE REMANDED TO THE CUSTODY OF FREEDOM FORCE, WHO WILL ESCORT US TO THE FEDERAL PENITENTIARY IN COLORADO...
...WHERE WE WILL STAND TRIAL FOR TREASON! AND IT SAYS THIS IS ALL BY ORDER OF THE PRESIDENT!
WELL, AVENGERS... WILL YOU COME WILLINGLY--OR MUST YOU BE PERSUADED?
I'VE NEVER REALLY BELIEVED THEY REFORMED. I BET THOSE WARRANTS ARE PHONIES. AND EVEN IF THEY'RE NOT--I WON'T LET THE GOVERNMENT TREAT US SO CALLOUSLY.
AND WHAT'S SPIDER-WOMAN DOING WITH THESE CREEPS? WASN'T SHE WITH THE GOOD GUYS DURING THE SECRET WARS?*
THIS IS RIDICULOUS. THEY'RE THUGS. I SAY WE DON'T TAKE THIS GUFF.
THE AVENGERS HAVE GOTTEN SO MUCH BAD PRESS LATELY. MAYBE WE SHOULD CO-OPERATE WITH THEM AND SEE WHAT DEVELOPS. A HASTY DECISION HERE COULD BE A MISTAKE.
CAPTAIN, THOSE ARE EVIL-DOERS. THERE CAN BE NO "COOPERATION."
I DUNNO, HERC. REMEMBER. I WAS A BAD GUY WHEN I STARTED OUT--AND LOOK HOW I CHANGED. MAYBE WE SHOULD GIVE THEM A CHANCE.
*SEE SECRET WARS I, ISSUES #7-12--M&M.
AND BESIDES--IF WE FIGHT THEM AND THEY TURN OUT TO BE LEGIT... IT'LL MAKE ME LOOK LIKE A BAD LEADER IN FRONT OF THE WASP AND CAP. I'D RATHER WAIT IT OUT.
YOU WERE NEVER EVIL LIKE THEY WERE, HAWK. WE CAN'T LET THEM BULLY US.
NO WAY I'M GOING TO LET THEM COOP ME UP IN A CELL FOR ANY REASON!
JAN'S MY TEAM LEADER. I'M GOING TO GO ALONG WITH WHATEVER SHE SAYS.
I'M NO LONGER AN ACTIVE AVENGER, BUT WHEN I WAS--WE KNEW WHAT TO DO WITH SUPER VILLAINS.
I WAS A BAD GUY ONCE, TOO. AND THE WORLD ALSO GAVE ME A SECOND CHANCE. STILL, THE BROTHERHOOD WERE SOME OF THE MOST RUTHLESS, VICIOUS FOES WE'VE EVER FOUGHT. CAN THEY REALLY HAVE REFORMED? CAN I PASS JUDGMENT ON THEM?
OF COURSE I CAN. I KNOW GOOD FROM EVIL.
LET'S TRASH THOSE BUMS.
THEY... THEY'RE AGENTS OF THE UNITED STATES GOVERNMENT. ACCORDING TO OUR FILES, THEY BARGAINED THEIR CRIMINAL STATUS AWAY IN RETURN FOR BECOMING LOYAL AGENTS. THAT'S A FACT. THE WARRANTS ARE PROBABLY REAL.
YET, THE THOUGHT OF TURNING OURSELVES OVER TO THEM... TURNS MY STOMACH.

BUT--WHAT CHOICE DO WE HAVE? THEY *ARE* REPRE-SENTATIVES OF THE GOVERN-MENT. HAVE WE THE RIGHT TO OPPOSE THEM WHEN THEY'VE, AS YET, DONE NOTHING WRONG?

WELL, WELL...IT SEEMS THE "MIGHTY" AVENGERS HAVE TURNED INTO A *DEBATING SOCIETY!*

HAVE WE MADE UP OUR MINDS YET, CHILDREN?

YES, WE HAVE.

WE REJECT YOUR AUTHORITY...

...WE *REFUSE* TO COME ALONG!

WELL, IT'S UNDER PRO-TEST, BUT...

...WE *AGREE* TO COME ALONG!

WELL, *HAWKEYE*, THAT DOESN'T SAY MUCH FOR A *UNIFIED* FRONT!

BUT I--ALL I MEANT--I THOUGHT THAT--

THIS IS MOST AMUSING, PEOPLE. BUT I REALLY *MUST* HAVE AN ANSWER.

ENOUGH OF THIS PRATTLE! THIS IS ANSWER ENOUGH!

--I HOPE IT IS *CLEAR* ENOUGH!

THAT *PITCHER'S CART!* AVA-LANCHE--!

DON'T SWEAT IT, PYRO! ALREADY TAKEN CARE OF!

WITH A WAVE OF HIS ARM, AVALANCHE LETS LOOSE HIS MUTANT POWER OF MOLECULAR LIQUIFICATION AND *DESTROYS* THE VEHICLE!

HEAR ME, *FREEDOM FORCE!* THAT WAS JUST THE *FIRST* THING I SHALL HURL AT YOU.

AND IF MY FEL-LOWS WILL NOT JOIN ME, I WILL FIGHT YOU *ALONE!*

I'M WITH HERCULES. WE'VE *GOT* TO STAND UP TO THEM!

THIS *IS* A STROKE OF LUCK, eh, CHUMS?

YEAH. HOW 'BOUT IT, MYSTIQUE. DO WE GET TO KICK SOME AVENGER *BUTT* NOW?

YES, BLOB. THE AVENGERS HAVE JUST ASSAULTED DULY AUTHOR-IZED GOVERNMENT AGENTS--

*SUBDUE THEM USING WHATEVER FORCE IS NECESSARY!*

ALL RIGHT!

BUT ONE MEMBER OF FREEDOM FORCE IS NOT SO ENTHUSIASTIC.

THE AVENGERS ARE GOOD PEOPLE. I REMEMBER THAT FROM THE BEYONDER'S PLANET. I WANTED TO BE IN A TEAM LIKE THEIR'S-- THAT'S ONE REASON I *JOINED* FREEDOM FORCE.

BUT FREEDOM FORCE *ISN'T* LIKE THEM. THEY *ARE* STILL *EVIL.*

I'LL DO MY JOB *TODAY.*

BUT TOMORROW...

THE NOVICE HEROINE'S THOUGHTS ARE DISTRACTED, AS AVALANCHE MERELY GESTURES TOWARD THE GROUND AND THE BATTLE BEGINS!

NEARBY, PYRO CREATES A RAGING FIREBIRD WHICH, UNDER HIS MENTAL CONTROL, ATTACKS ONE GROUP OF AVENGERS...

--AND, ELSEWHERE ON THE FIELD, *SPIRAL* AND *CAPTAIN MARVEL* FACE OFF...

I'LL TAKE THIS ONE OUT *FAST* WITH SOME ENERGY BLASTS.

THEY SAY YOU ARE PERHAPS THE MOST *POWERFUL* AVENGER, CAPTAIN.

SO, I SHALL HAVE TO WEAVE ONE OF *MY* MOST POWERFUL SPELLS AND SEND IT AGAINST YOU.

NO! SOMEHOW SHE HAS *NEGATED* ALL MY POWERS! MY *BLASTS* AREN'T FUNCTIONING--AND I CAN'T TURN INTO *ENERGY!*

I'M *HELPLESS!*

CAPTAIN MARVEL--IN BIG TROUBLE!

IF I REMEMBER THE AVENGERS FILES CORRECTLY, SPIRAL IS IMMENSELY *DANGEROUS*. STILL, IF I CAN SNEAK UP AND SURPRISE HER, I MIGHT HAVE A CHANCE...

*NEARBY...*

YER TRICKY, ALL RIGHT, WASP. BUT I'LL GET YA *SOONER* OR LATER, AND WHEN I DO--

YOU WANT ME, BLOBSIE?

OKAY--YOU *GOT* ME!

ZZZZT ZZZTT

*AARRRGH!* SETTIN' OFF HER STINGS IN MY EAR!

I HAD TO! YOU WOULDN'T *BELIEVE* THE WAX BUILD-UP IN THERE! YUCK!

EVERYTHING'S SPINNIN' AROUND! CAN HARDLY STAND! I'M GONNA BE *SICK!*

YOU'RE TOO LATE TO HELP YOUR FELLOW CAPTAIN.

NOW YOU SHALL EXPERIENCE ONE OF SPIRAL'S SPELLS *FIRST HAND!*

NEARBY, PYRO'S FLAME-BIRD FORCES HAWKEYE AND HANK PYM DOWN INTO A FISSURE CREATED BY AVALANCHE.

MY SHIRT'S CAUGHT *FIRE!* GOT TO GET IT OFF!

BUT THAT WON'T SAVE US FROM BEING *CRUSHED* BY FALLING EARTH AND ROCKS!

NO, BUT *I* WILL!

WONDER MAN!

*ABOVE...* YOU CAN CRUMBLE ALL THE EARTH YOU LIKE, AVALANCHE. *HERCULES* WILL NOT BE DETERRED.

ESPECIALLY IF I FIND THAT WHICH I AM SEEKING.

YOU JERK... NOBODY CAN GET TO ME WHEN I DON'T *WANT* 'EM TO! NOBODY!

MEANWHILE, CAPTAIN AMERICA FINDS HIMSELF VICTIM TO THE TIME AND SPACE MANIPULATING POWERS OF SPIRAL'S WOVEN SPELLS.

I TAKE ONE STEP AFTER ANOTHER-- BUT SOMEHOW I GET *NO CLOSER!*

ONE CHANCE--

--MY *SHIELD!*

A NOBLE TRY, NOBLE CAPTAIN.

BUT ALL I HAD TO DO WAS TRANSPORT MYSELF TO ANOTHER DIMENSION FOR THE SPLIT-SECOND YOUR SHIELD WOULD HAVE HIT ME.

NOW, PERHAPS, I SHALL ADD AN ELEMENT OF *PAIN* TO THE SPELL I HAVE YOU IN...

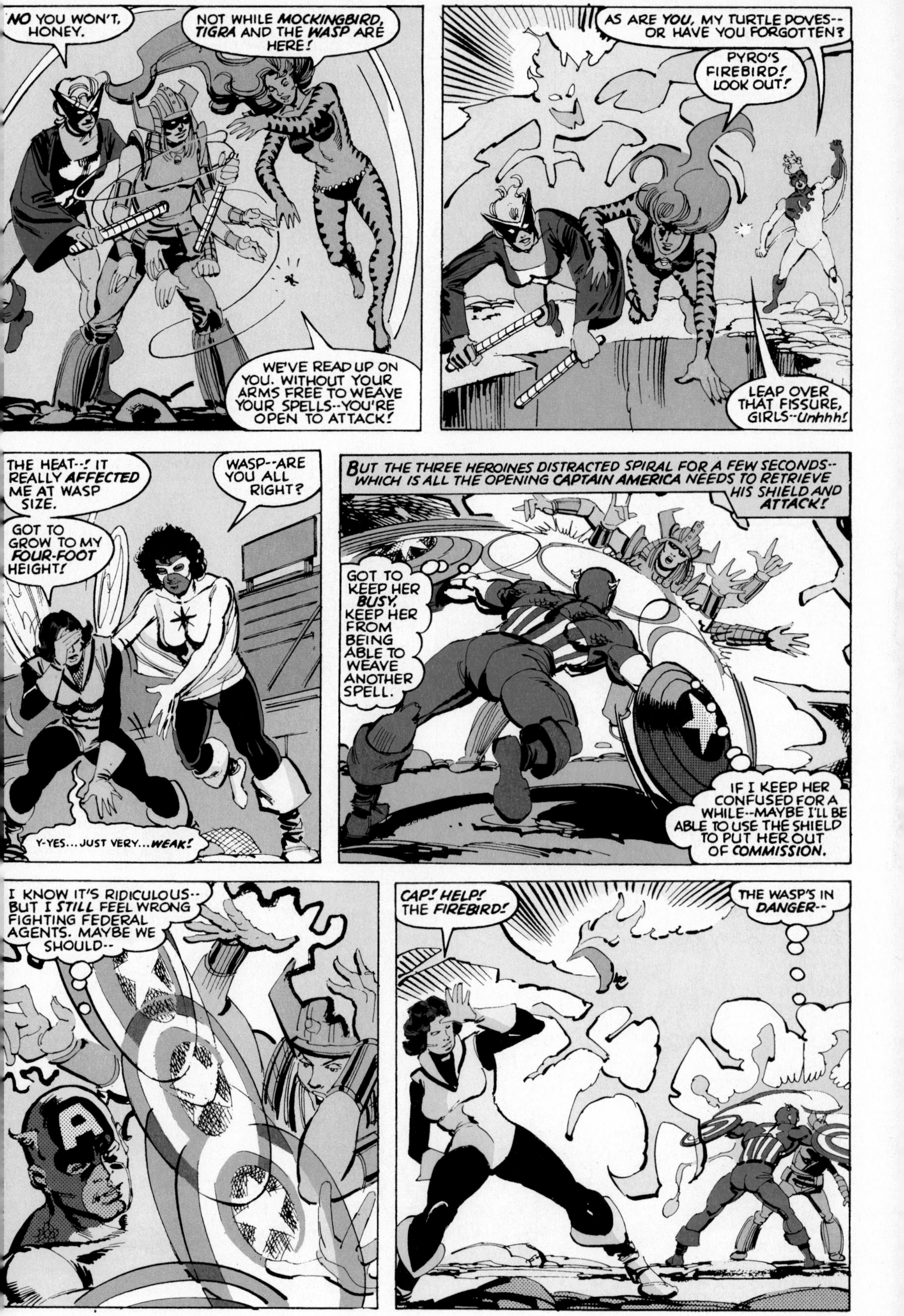
NO YOU WON'T, HONEY.
NOT WHILE MOCKINGBIRD, TIGRA AND THE WASP ARE HERE!
WE'VE READ UP ON YOU. WITHOUT YOUR ARMS FREE TO WEAVE YOUR SPELLS--YOU'RE OPEN TO ATTACK!
AS ARE YOU, MY TURTLE DOVES-- OR HAVE YOU FORGOTTEN?
PYRO'S FIREBIRD! LOOK OUT!
LEAP OVER THAT FISSURE, GIRLS--Unhhh!
THE HEAT--! IT REALLY AFFECTED ME AT WASP SIZE.
WASP--ARE YOU ALL RIGHT?
GOT TO GROW TO MY FOUR-FOOT HEIGHT!
Y-YES... JUST VERY... WEAK!
BUT THE THREE HEROINES DISTRACTED SPIRAL FOR A FEW SECONDS-- WHICH IS ALL THE OPENING CAPTAIN AMERICA NEEDS TO RETRIEVE HIS SHIELD AND ATTACK!
GOT TO KEEP HER BUSY, KEEP HER FROM BEING ABLE TO WEAVE ANOTHER SPELL.
IF I KEEP HER CONFUSED FOR A WHILE--MAYBE I'LL BE ABLE TO USE THE SHIELD TO PUT HER OUT OF COMMISSION.
I KNOW IT'S RIDICULOUS-- BUT I STILL FEEL WRONG FIGHTING FEDERAL AGENTS. MAYBE WE SHOULD--
CAP! HELP! THE FIREBIRD!
THE WASP'S IN DANGER--

GOT TO HELP-- *UNNH!*

HAVE A *STUN-BLAST*, CAPTAIN.

YOU SHOULD *NEVER* LEAVE YOURSELF OPEN LIKE THAT, YOU KNOW.

NOT WHEN THERE'S A *SHAPE-SHIFTER* LIKE MYSTIQUE AROUND.

LADIES... I BELIEVE THE SAYING IS... I'VE GOT YOU COVERED.

I CAN PREDICT ANY MOVE YOU'LL MAKE... SO YOU'D BEST MAKE NONE.

CAPTAIN MARVEL'S POWERS STILL AREN'T WORKING... AND I'M STILL WEAK FROM THE FLAMES.

SHE'S GOT US.

WHROOOSSH!

Ah! AT *LAST* I'VE FOUND WHAT I'VE BEEN LOOKING FOR!

THIS *WATER-MAIN* SHOULD TAKE CARE OF THAT FIRE CREATURE--

SHHOOOSSH!

--AND *YOU* AS WELL, *AVALANCHE!*

*UNNGGH!*

YES-- SQUEEZING THE NOZZLE LIKE THIS MAKES FOR A PERFECT *HIGH POWER JET!*

*ELSEWHERE, THE ROCK AND EARTH-SLIDE HAVING STOPPED, WONDER MAN CARRIES HIS FRIENDS BACK TO THE SURFACE, BUT--*

Uh-oh. GOTTA PUT YOU GUYS DOWN HERE. PYRO'S STARTED A BLAZE IN THE STANDS!

FREEDOM FORCE'LL DO ANYTHING TO DISTRACT US! IT LOOKS LIKE OUR GUYS ARE PUTTING UP A BETTER FIGHT THAN THEY *EXPECTED*

*SECONDS LATER...*

I CARRIED THE CREW GUYS TO SAFETY-- BUT I'VE STILL GOT TO PUT THAT *FIRE* OUT.

THIS MAINTENANCE TRUCK SHOULD MAKE A GOOD *SHOVEL*--I CAN USE IT TO SCOOP UP DIRT TO SMOTHER THE FLAMES.

NEARBY...
FINALLY RE-COVERED FROM THAT SNEAKY WASP'S ATTACK. NOW I'M GONNA--
EAT REPULSOR RAY, BLOB!
KEEP FIRING, IRON MAN--
--I CAN TAKE THIS ALL DAY.
BUT HOW DO THESE ARROWS FAZE YOU, BIG BOY?
ZOOP!
ZOOP!
ZOOP!
NOT AT ALL, HAWKEYE.
POP
POP
POP
HAH! THOUGHT YOU COULD SNEAK UP ON ME, HUH, SHELL-HEAD?
WRONG!
DIDN'T EXPECT HIM TO MOVE SO QUICKLY--!
NOW I GOTCHA!
BUT IF YOU HAVE ME, BLOB--
--THEN YOU HAVE MY CHEST LASER, ALSO!
HE LET ME GO! THE PAIN SHOULD IMMOBILIZE HIM FOR A WHILE. HE'LL KEEP.
I'LL SEE WHO ELSE NEEDS MY HELP.
AAARRGGH!
THE BLACK KNIGHT DOESN'T SEEM TO NEED ANYONE'S HELP AT THE MOMENT...
NO! IT CANNOT BE! MY SPELLS DO NOT AFFECT YOU!
MY SWORD'S ENCHANTED. IT'S ABLE TO CUT THROUGH ALL SORTS OF MAGIC FIELDS--INCLUDING SPIRAL'S, APPARENTLY.

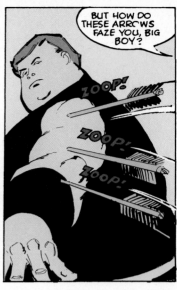

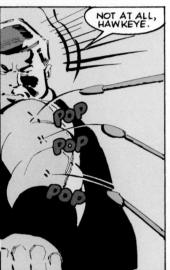

SURRENDER, SPIRAL. YOUR MAGIC IS *USELESS* AGAINST ME!

NOT REALLY, KNIGHT! WITH BUT THE SLIGHTEST GESTURE I CAN TELEPORT AWAY FROM YOU.

BUT I'LL HUNT YOU DOWN WHEREVER YOU GO.

BUT AS THE KNIGHT TURNS A CORNER TO CHASE HIS MULTI-ARMED QUARRY--

SHE LED ME INTO A *TRAP!* I'M TANGLED IN SOME SORT OF ...WEB?

WELL, I'M BETTING MY *SWORD* CAN HANDLE IT!

I DON'T KNOW IF YOUR SWORD COULD CUT THROUGH MY PSIONIC WEB OR NOT--

--BUT YOU *WON'T* GET THE CHANCE TO TRY!

SPIDER-WOMAN, DON'T-- UNH!

WHOM

NICE WORK, SPIDER-WOMAN. HE HAD ME WORRIED THERE.

THANKS.

BUT I WON'T SHAKE ANY OF YOUR HANDS. TO TELL THE TRUTH-- I'M *ASHAMED* OF WHAT WE'RE DOING.

NEARBY...

IT IS NOT MY *WISH* TO CONTINUE TO PUMMEL YOU, AVALANCHE.

MERELY *ACKNOWLEDGE* THAT I HAVE BESTED YOU.

OR DO YOU NEED TO BE FURTHER CONVINCED?

I...I SURR--

HE AIN'T GIVIN' UP, FUZZ-FACE--BUT MAYBE *YOU* OUGHTTA!

THE MISSHAPEN VILLAIN CALLED THE *BLOB!* SPIRAL MUST HAVE TELEPORTED HIM HERE!

NO MATTER. AS I DEFEATED AVALANCHE, SO SHALL I DEFEAT YOU.

BWOOP

WHAT?

STUCK!? AND NO MATTER HOW HARD I PULL, I *CANNOT* GET MY FISTS FREE!

EXACTLY, CHUMP. WHICH LEAVES YOU IN A PERFECT POSITION FOR A *HEAD-BUTT!*

BWAM BWAM BWAM

BAH! THE LION OF OLYMPUS CAN WITHSTAND BLOWS LIKE *THAT* ALL DAY LONG!

YES, BUT HOW MANY OF SPIRAL'S *SPELLS* CAN YOU WITHSTAND?

LET HIM FALL, BLOB.

UNNNHHH~!

ONE OF MY MORE *PAINFUL* SPELLS HAS ROBBED HIM OF CONSCIOUSNESS.

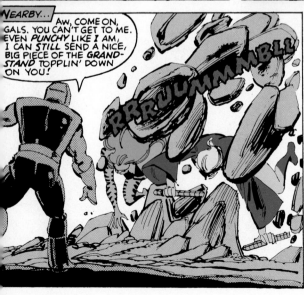

NEARBY... AW, COME ON, GALS. YOU CAN'T GET TO ME. EVEN *PUNCHY* LIKE I AM, I CAN *STILL* SEND A NICE, BIG PIECE OF THE *GRAND-STAND* TOPPLIN' DOWN ON YOU!

RRRUUMMMBLL

AND... DON'T MOVE, HAWKEYE. I'VE GOT THE DROP ON YOU.

DESTINY, I COULD LOAD AND FIRE BEFORE YOU COULD EVEN BEGIN TO SQUEEZE THAT TRIGGER.

I THINK *NOT.* I KNOW YOUR EVERY MOVE BEFORE *YOU* DO.

215

BUT YOU *DON'T* KNOW MINE.

UNH!

A TRANQUILIZER BLAST ✳

*WHILE...* GIVE IT UP, IRON MAN! I DON'T WANT TO HAVE TO *HURT* YOU!

FUNNY, I WAS JUST ABOUT TO SAY THE SAME THING TO *YOU*, PYRO.

CAN'T LET HIM KNOW IT'S TAKING MOST OF MY *POWER RESERVES* JUST TO PROTECT ME FROM HIS FLAME BARRAGE!

I CAN KEEP MAKING IT *HOTTER* AND *HOTTER* AVENGER, UNTIL--

BRRIPP

UNTIL I GET CLOSE ENOUGH TO DISCONNECT YOUR FLAME-THROWERS, PYRO?

THEY ONLY *CREATE* A FLAME FOR ME TO COMMAND. ONCE IT *EXISTS*, I CAN DO ANYTHING WITH IT--

--LIKE MAKE YOU *BEG* ME TO TURN DOWN THE HEAT.

IF I CAN GET IN A PUNCH BEFORE MY CIRCUITS OVERLOAD..

...HE'LL BE DOWN FOR THE--UNGH!

HE'S STOPPED IN HIS TRACKS, THANK HEAVEN!

THANK *SPIRAL*, PYRO.

AYE, PARTNER, THAT I DO!

SPIRAL! BEHIND YOU!

GOT 'ER! AND *SHE'S* THE MOST DANGEROUS!

KWAM

YOU'LL FIND *I'M* STILL A FORCE TO BE RECKONED WITH, WONDER MAN!

TO BLAZES WITH THAT!

UNGH!

AND JUST IN TIME. THAT WAS BEGINNING TO *SMART!*

ALL *RIGHT*, WONDER MAN! WAY TO--

*SPIDER-WOMAN!* STOP STANDING THERE LIKE A FOOL! HELP US *WIN* THIS BATTLE!

YES, MYSTIQUE.

AVENGERS! ONLY FOUR OF YOU REMAIN STANDING.

HENRY PYM AND CAPTAIN MARVEL ARE WITHOUT BENEFIT OF SUPER POWERS.

YOU, WASP, HAVE BEEN SEVERELY WEAKENED.

...AND WONDER MAN CERTAINLY CANNOT SINGLEHANDEDLY DEFEAT THE FIVE OF *US* STILL STANDING.

SURRENDER-- AVOID FURTHER NEEDLESS VIOLENCE!

WE'LL NEVER SURRENDER!

MY POWERS ARE *STILL* GONE, BUT I HAVE TO FACE THIS LIKE AN AVENGER!

I'M BEHIND YOU, JAN.

I-I'M NOT SURE WHAT *I* CAN DO, JAN.

SO FAR WE'VE BEEN LUCKY.

I DON'T *WANT* TO SURRENDER--

--BUT MAYBE WE SHOULD... BEFORE ANY-ONE GETS HURT!

217

SIMON, I APPRECIATE WHAT YOU'RE TRYING TO DO--

--BUT I'VE MADE UP MY MIND.

TAKE 'EM, AVENGERS!

COME ON, CAPTAIN! WE CAN GET SOME COVER IN THAT TRENCH!

THANKS, HANK--WE'LL DO YA PROUD!

WHAM

NOT FAST ENOUGH, PYM. I KNEW THERE WAS A STRONG PROBABILITY YOU'D DO THIS.

SHOOM

SHOOM

ENRAGED BEYOND MEASURE, WONDER MAN LEAPS TO THE FORE AND POUNDS REPEATEDLY AT THE BLOB'S HEAD.

YOU CREEPS! YOU'RE WORKING FOR THE GOVERNMENT-- AND WE'RE THE CRIMINALS?!

WHAM WHAM WHAM WHAM

IT'S A SICK JOKE!

ALREADY SOMEWHAT SHAKY FROM THE WASP'S ATTACK ON HIS EAR CANALS--

WHOOM!

ARRRGHH!

--THE BLOB SUCCUMBS!

MEANWHILE, THE WASP SUMMONS ALL HER REMAINING STRENGTH FOR A CONCENTRATED ASSAULT ON AVALANCHE!

AVALANCHE FALLS BACK, STUNNED, BUT AS HE DOES, HE INADVERTANTLY SENDS SHOCKWAVES WHICH PROPEL CHUNKS OF EARTH AT THE WASP.

UNH!

GOT YOU, MADAME CHAIRMAN!

AND THE WASP IS CAUGHT FOR THE "FINAL OUT."

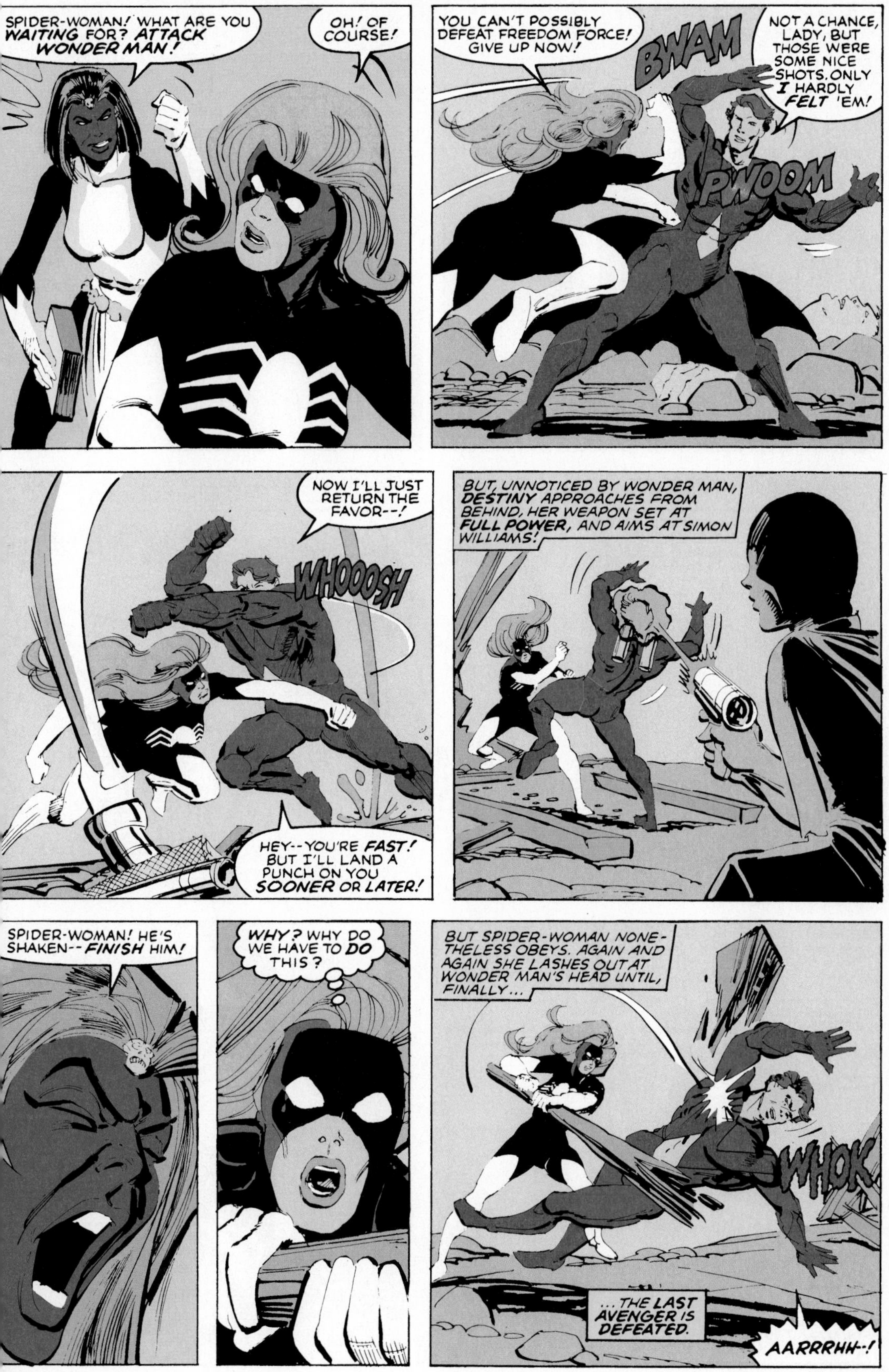
SPIDER-WOMAN! WHAT ARE YOU WAITING FOR? ATTACK WONDER MAN!
OH! OF COURSE!
YOU CAN'T POSSIBLY DEFEAT FREEDOM FORCE! GIVE UP NOW!
BWAM
NOT A CHANCE, LADY, BUT THOSE WERE SOME NICE SHOTS. ONLY I HARDLY FELT 'EM!
PWOOM
NOW I'LL JUST RETURN THE FAVOR--!
WHOOOSH
HEY--YOU'RE FAST! BUT I'LL LAND A PUNCH ON YOU SOONER OR LATER!
BUT, UNNOTICED BY WONDER MAN, DESTINY APPROACHES FROM BEHIND, HER WEAPON SET AT FULL POWER, AND AIMS AT SIMON WILLIAMS!
SPIDER-WOMAN! HE'S SHAKEN--FINISH HIM!
WHY? WHY DO WE HAVE TO DO THIS?
BUT SPIDER-WOMAN NONE-THELESS OBEYS. AGAIN AND AGAIN SHE LASHES OUT AT WONDER MAN'S HEAD UNTIL, FINALLY...
WHOK
...THE LAST AVENGER IS DEFEATED.
AARRRHH-!

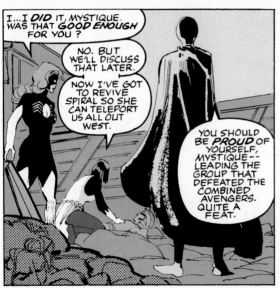

I...I **DID** IT, MYSTIQUE. WAS THAT **GOOD ENOUGH** FOR YOU?

NO. BUT WE'LL DISCUSS THAT LATER.

NOW I'VE GOT TO REVIVE SPIRAL SO SHE CAN TELEPORT US ALL OUT WEST.

YOU SHOULD BE **PROUD** OF YOURSELF, MYSTIQUE-- LEADING THE GROUP THAT DEFEATED THE COMBINED AVENGERS. QUITE A FEAT.

THANK YOU, IRENÉ. IT'S FUNNY, FOR ALL THEIR POWER, THE AVENGER I WAS **MOST** WORRIED ABOUT WAS **CAPTAIN AMERICA**. HE'S THE MOST RESOURCEFUL AND--

--AND HE'S **NOT** ON THE FIELD! HE'S **ESCAPED!**

I CAN DIVINE WHERE HE MOST LIKELY WILL BE FOUND.

HE HAS **NOT GONE** FAR.

AND, IN A FAR CORNER OF THE STADIUM...

...YES, CAP. FREEDOM FORCE **IS** UNDER THE AUTHORITY OF THE EXECUTIVE BRANCH. AND THEY **HAVE** BEEN SENT TO ARREST THE AVENGERS.

BUT **WHY,** MR. SECRETARY? WHY NOT JUST SUBPOENA US?

I'M SURE THE FOLKS AT THE TOP HAVE THEIR REASONS, CAP.

ON THE FIELD, SPIRAL DANCES AN ELABORATE SERIES OF SPELLS, **NULLIFYING** EACH AVENGER'S SPECIAL ABILITIES AND WEAPONRY...

...AND **TELEPORTING** THEM FROM THE SCENE.

SO WHAT YOU'RE TELLING ME IS THAT WE'RE SUPPOSED TO **TRUST** THESE PEOPLE WHO JUST TRIED TO KILL US--**AND** TRUST THE PEOPLE WHO SENT THEM!

PERHAPS YOU'RE OVERREACTING, CAPTAIN--

**OVERREACTING!?** LOOK, I'LL GO ALONG WITH THIS NONSENSE FOR NOW. JUST REMEMBER... EVEN **I'VE** GOT MY BREAKING POINT.

CAPTAIN-- WE HAVE COME FOR YOU. WILL YOU--?

I'VE JUST SPOKEN TO WASHINGTON. I'LL COME ALONG PEACEFULLY.

BUT **SOMEONE'S** GOING TO ANSWER FOR ALL THIS.

THE ROCKY
MOUNTAINS.

AND, DEEP INSIDE ONE PARTICULAR MOUNTAIN, THE AVENGERS, HENRY PYM AND FREEDOM FORCE MATERIALIZE--MERE MOMENTS AFTER CAP'S SURRENDER--IN A CHAMBER HEWN OUT OF THE MOUNTAIN'S IGNEOUS CENTER.

REVIVED BY SPIRAL'S SPELL EN ROUTE, THE AVENGERS STAND, DEPOWERED AND CONFUSED, UNSURE EVEN OF WHERE THEY ARE, MUCH LESS WHAT TO DO NEXT.

ONLY ONE THING SEEMS CERTAIN. THEY ARE SURROUNDED BY ENEMIES. ON ONE SIDE STANDS FREEDOM FORCE. ALL AROUND THE CHAMBER STAND ARMORED GUARDSMAN WEAPONS BRANDISHED MENACINGLY.

AND BEHIND THE BEATEN HEROES, AT THE FRONT OF THE VAST CHAMBER, STANDS A MAN WHO HATES THEM AS NO OTHER--

--HENRY PETER GYRICH, FORMER LIAISON BE-TWEEN THE AVENGERS AND THE U.S. GOVERN-MENT.

OF THE WOMAN'S IDENTITY, THEY ARE NOT CERTAIN.

THE SEATED, BESPECTACLED MAN IS RAYMOND SIKORSKY, CURRENT LI-AISON. THE AVENGERS THOUGHT OF HIM AS A FRIEND. NOW, THEY'RE NOT SO SURE.

HOW AMUSING THIS ALL IS! THE MIGHTY AVENGERS, POWERLESS TO RESIST AT ALL-- THANKS TO ME!

SPIRAL'S RIGHT. I FEEL WEAK AS A KITTEN.

THEN--WHY DIDN'T YOU DO THIS AT THE START OF OUR BATTLE?

BECAUSE NONE OF YOUR TEAMMATES WOULD STAND STILL LONG ENOUGH FOR HER TO DO IT AFTER THEY SAW YOU FALL VICTIM TO HER, MARVEL.

BUT DON'T WORRY. YOU AND YOUR PARTNERS' PRECIOUS POWERS WILL SOON RETURN. SPIRAL WASN'T ORDERED TO PERMANENTLY NULLIFY THEM. THAT WILL HAPPEN AFTER YOU ARE FOUND GUILTY.

I...I FEEL SO ASHAMED. I WANT TO RUN OVER TO THE AVENGERS AND STAND WITH THEM.

BUT... I'M AFRAID. THE CONSEQUENCES...!

TAKE YOUR SEATS IN THE PRISONERS BOX.

WELL, SINCE YOU ASKED SO *NICELY,* CUTIE--

EASY, TIGRA. WE'RE IN DEEP ENOUGH.

AND NOW, AVENGERS, WE OF FREEDOM FORCE-- HAVING PERFORMED OUR *PATRIOTIC DUTY*--

-- TAKE OUR LEAVE. *DO* HAVE A NICE DAY.

AND AS SPIRAL WEAVES A SERIES OF SPELLS TO TELEPORT HERSELF AND HER TEAMMATES AWAY...

...THE PROCEEDINGS BEGIN.

ON MY RIGHT IS *VALERIE COOPER,* NATIONAL SECURITY COUNCIL MEMBER AND GOVERNMENT LIAISON TO FREE-DOM FORCE.

AND, OF COURSE, YOU ALL KNOW *RAYMOND SIKORSKY.*

WE ARE HERE TO CONDUCT THE PRELIMINARY HEARINGS IN YOUR *TRIAL* FOR *TREASON!* WE WILL BEGIN BY--

YOU'LL BEGIN BY TELLING US THE *MEANING* OF ALL THIS, GYRICH! HOW *DARE* YOU SEND CRIMINALS TO APPREHEND US! HOW *DARE* YOU BRING US TO THIS *RACCOON LODGE* COURT!

WE'RE THE *AVENGERS!* WE'RE A FORCE FOR *GOOD* IN THE WORLD, NO MATTER WHAT YOUR PER-SONAL *BIASES* MAY BE!

NO, MISS VAN DYNE. YOU ARE *NOT* A FORCE FOR GOOD. I HAVE SUSPECTED YOUR MALEVOLENCE FOR SOME TIME --

--AND I AT LAST HAVE THE *PROOF* I NEED TO PUT YOU *ALL* BEHIND BARS!

*WHAT* PROOF?! WE DEMAND TO *KNOW!*

"YOU WANT PROOF, CAPTAIN?"

"WOULD SWORN TESTIMONY THAT THE VISION'S ATTEMPT, WHEN HE WAS YOUR TEAM'S LEADER, TO TAKE OVER ALL THE WORLD'S COMPUTER SYSTEMS..."

"...WAS NOT A PRODUCT OF SOME 'TEMPORARY INSANITY' -- BUT WAS PREMEDITATED AND PLANNED LONG IN ADVANCE BY THE VISION AND SEVERAL OF YOUR NUMBER SITTING IN THIS ROOM TODAY--"

"--WOULD THAT BE ENOUGH PROOF FOR YOU?"

"OR DO YOU REMEMBER HOW, WHEN MR. GYRICH LAST CONDUCTED HEARINGS CONCERNING AVENGERS' MISCONDUCT..."

"...THE GREY GARGOYLE 'COINCIDENTALLY' ATTACKED NEW YORK? THE AVENGERS DEFEATED THAT VILLAIN, EMERGING AS HEROES OF THE DAY."

"WELL, AVENGERS, WE NOW HAVE SWORN TESTIMONY THAT YOU WERE IN LEAGUE WITH THE GARGOYLE -- THAT HE WAS WORKING AS YOUR AGENT TO HELP YOU DISCREDIT THE HEARINGS!"

"THESE INSTANCES ARE NOT EVEN THE WORST OF THE CRIMES WE WILL PROVE YOU ALL COLLECTIVELY RESPONSIBLE FOR."

"AND SOON WE WILL BEGIN ROUNDING UP THE CULPABLE INACTIVE AVENGERS!"

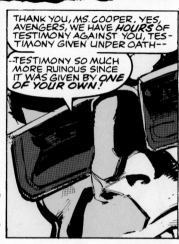

THANK YOU, MS. COOPER. YES, AVENGERS, WE HAVE HOURS OF TESTIMONY AGAINST YOU, TESTIMONY GIVEN UNDER OATH--

--TESTIMONY SO MUCH MORE RUINOUS SINCE IT WAS GIVEN BY ONE OF YOUR OWN!

WHAT!

WHO IS THE LYING BLACKGUARD?

WHO?!

WHAT KIND OF LOUSE WOULD SMEAR US LIKE THAT?

THE INFORMANT'S IDENTITY IS CLASSIFIED INFORMATION, PENDING CORROBORATION BY A SECOND PARTY WE BELIEVE WILL SOON COME FORWARD.

YOU WILL BE CONFRONTED BY YOUR ACCUSER AT THE TRIAL ITSELF.

IF I MAY, HENRY, I'D LIKE TO APOLOGIZE TO THE AVENGERS FOR THE TREATMENT THEY RECEIVED TODAY, BUT THESE ARE SERIOUS CHARGES, AND...

WE GET THE IDEA, RAYMOND. THAT'LL BE ENOUGH.

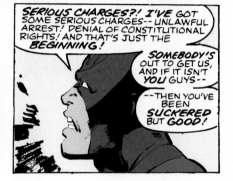

SERIOUS CHARGES?! I'VE GOT SOME SERIOUS CHARGES-- UNLAWFUL ARREST! DENIAL OF CONSTITUTIONAL RIGHTS! AND THAT'S JUST THE BEGINNING!

SOMEBODY'S OUT TO GET US, AND IF IT ISN'T YOU GUYS--

--THEN YOU'VE BEEN SUCKERED BUT GOOD!

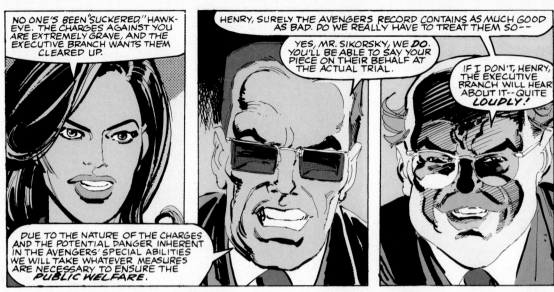

NO ONE'S BEEN "SUCKERED," HAWK-EYE. THE CHARGES AGAINST YOU ARE EXTREMELY GRAVE, AND THE EXECUTIVE BRANCH WANTS THEM CLEARED UP.

HENRY, SURELY THE AVENGERS RECORD CONTAINS AS MUCH GOOD AS BAD. DO WE REALLY HAVE TO TREAT THEM SO--

YES, MR. SIKORSKY, WE **DO**. YOU'LL BE ABLE TO SAY YOUR PIECE ON THEIR BEHALF AT THE ACTUAL TRIAL.

IF I DON'T, HENRY, THE EXECUTIVE BRANCH WILL HEAR ABOUT IT--QUITE **LOUDLY!**

DUE TO THE NATURE OF THE CHARGES AND THE POTENTIAL DANGER INHERENT IN THE AVENGERS' SPECIAL ABILITIES WE WILL TAKE WHATEVER MEASURES ARE NECESSARY TO ENSURE THE **PUBLIC WELFARE.**

AND AS THE HEARING PROGRESSES, A SYMBOL OF AMERICA PONDERS WHAT IS GOING ON ABOUT HIM...

...AND WONDERS WHAT HIS NEXT MOVE IS TO BE.

WHILE, ACROSS THE CONTINENT, IN THE CITY WHICH IS ITSELF A SYMBOL OF AMERICA...

...ANOTHER COSTUMED ADVENTURER FACES HARSH **ACCUSATIONS.**

WHEN COOPER INSISTED WE TAKE YOU, AN OUTSIDER, INTO FREEDOM FORCE, I HAD DOUBTS--BUT I WAS WILLING TO GIVE IT A SHOT.

BUT I SAW HOW YOU **HESITATED** DURING THE BATTLE TODAY, SPIDER-WOMAN. IT COULD HAVE COST US A VICTORY. AND WE CANNOT **AFFORD** TO HAVE THE GOVERNMENT LOOK WITH DISFAVOR UPON US.

PERHAPS YOU THINK THAT BECAUSE WE USED TO BE OUTLAWS, YOU'RE TOO GOOD TO WORK WITH US.

IF THAT'S THE CASE-- **LEAVE.** BUT DON'T FORGET THE **HANDSOME SALARY** YOU'RE PAID. AND DON'T FORGET THAT FREEDOM FORCE MAY NOT ALWAYS BE WORKING **WITHIN** THE LAW.

YOU WOULD THEN HAVE SOME VERY DANGEROUS ENEMIES.

I'M SORRY, MYSTIQUE. I WON'T LET IT HAPPEN AGAIN.

I CAN'T STAND THIS MUCH LONGER.

I CAN'T STAND THIS ANYMORE! EVERYTHING YOU'RE SAYING IS THE EXACT *OPPOSITE* OF EVERTHING AMERICA STANDS FOR.

YOU'RE TELLING US WE'RE *GUILTY* UNTIL PROVEN INNOCENT! BUT THAT'S *WRONG!* THAT'S *INJUSTICE!*

YOU SEND OUT THUGS TO ARREST US, WITHOUT SO MUCH AS THE COURTESY OF A PHONE CALL OR TIME TO PREPARE FOR THIS HEARING!

YOU TELL US WE'VE BEEN ACCUSED OF CRIMES--MANY OF WHICH YOU WON'T EVEN *NAME*-- BUT YOU WON'T *ALLOW* US TO CONFRONT OUR ACCUSER!

WELL, I WONDER IF THE PRESIDENT *REALLY* KNOWS WHAT'S GOING ON HERE--HOW PERSONAL *VEN-DETTAS* ARE BEING CARRIED OUT UNDER THE FALSE LABEL OF *JUSTICE!*

I BELIEVE IN THE AMERICAN DREAM. BUT *THIS*...THIS IS SOME SORT OF *NIGHTMARE!*

AWRIGHT, *CAP!*

WAY TO GO, AVENGER!

AN ORATION WORTHY OF AN *OLYMPIAN,* CAPTAIN!

YOU SURE TOLD THOSE STUFFED SHIRTS!

THANKS, CAP.

ENOUGH! ENOUGH!

THE CHEERLEADERS CAN PUT THEIR *POM-POMS* AWAY! ORDER! *ORDER!*

I'M SURE WE WERE ALL *MOVED* BY CAPTAIN AMERICA'S LOVELY SPEECH.

WHEN FULL CHARGES ARE BROUGHT, AVENGERS, YOU WILL BE FREE TO ENGAGE LEGAL COUNSEL. UNTIL SUCH TIME, BY DECREE OF THIS DULY EMPOWERED PANEL, YOU ARE ALL REMANDED TO *FEDERAL CUSTODY.*

AND, WHEN *WILL* THE TRIAL TAKE PLACE?

WE'RE NOT SURE YET, WASP. BUT DON'T WORRY--.YOU'LL BE THE *FIRST* TO KNOW.

AND NOW, I DECLARE THIS HEARING ADJOURNED. GUARDSMEN--TAKE THE AVENGERS TO... THE *VAULT.*

NOT FAR FROM THE SCENE OF THE HEARING--DEEP INSIDE ANOTHER OF THE MIGHTY PEAKS OF THE ROCKIES-- THERE SITS THE NEW, TOP SECRET U.S. GOVERNMENT CONTAINMENT CENTER FOR SUPER-POWERED CRIMINALS.

THE *VAULT.*

MANNED BY A LARGE CREW OF HIGHLY TRAINED GUARDSMEN, IT GLEAMS WITH NEWNESS AND HUMS WITH POWER.

IN OPERATION LESS THAN A WEEK, IT AWAITS ITS FIRST SHIPMENT OF SUPER-CRIMINALS FROM AROUND THE COUNTRY. ELEVEN OF ITS CELLS, HOWEVER, ARE NOW FILLED.

CAPTAIN AMERICA IS TRAPPED IN A SMOOTH-WALLED, SPHERICAL CELL THAT SPINS EVERY TIME HE TRIES TO GET A FOOTHOLD.

ALL HIS GYMNASTIC SKILLS AND COMBAT KNOWLEDGE ARE USELESS.

HERCULES' CELL IS LINED WITH TWO FOOT THICK *ADAMANTIUM,* WHICH WILL NOT YIELD, EVEN TO A GOD.

WHAM WHAM

THE WASP HAS BEEN SEARCHING HER CELL CONTINUALLY FOR A SMALL OPENING TO ESCAPE THROUGH.

THERE IS NONE TO BE FOUND

WITH HIS SWORD TAKEN FROM HIM, NO SPECIAL CELL IS NEEDED TO HOLD THE BLACK KNIGHT.

...AND CAPTAIN MARVEL IS KEPT CONTINUALLY SEDATED BY TRANQUILIZING GAS!

BUT, THOUGH IRON MAN'S ARMOR IS BACK IN WORKING ORDER...

...THE ELECTRI-CITY DRAINING NODULES LINING HIS ROOM CREATE A POWER-GRID THAT SAPS ALL HIS SUIT'S ENERGY, LEAVING HIM BARELY ENOUGH TO SIT UP.

AS IF KEEPING MY DUAL PERSON-ALITY UNDER CONTROL WASN'T ENOUGH! I COULD GO MAD! NO CAT LIKES TO BE COOPED UP! ME ESPECIALLY!

I DON'T KNOW WHO I WANT TO CLAW WORSE-- GYRICH, OR THE CREEP WHO BETRAYED US!

SOME LEADER I TURNED OUT TO BE! DISSEN-SION COST US THE BATTLE! I BLEW IT.

AT LEAST SIKORSKY INTERVENED SO WE WOULDN'T HAVE TO UNMASK YET...

HE'S THE ONLY ONE I THINK ISN'T TOTALLY OUT TO GET US.

I BET HAWK'S REALLY BLAMING HIMSELF FOR THIS. I WISH I COULD TELL HIM HE'S WRONG.

WE COULD'VE WON-- CAP ESCAPED! IT WAS HIS GOOD SOLDIER ATTI-TUDE THAT KEPT HIM FROM GOING TO GET HELP.

NEARBY, WONDER MAN IS SUSPENDED IN A STASIS-FIELD THAT EFFECTIVELY PARALYZES HIM!

SOMEBODY'S GOING TO PAY FOR THIS.

AND, HENRY PYM...

WELL, NOW I REMEMBER WHY I QUIT THE COS-TUMED ADVENTURER BIZ! BUT, RETIRED OR NOT-- I'M STILL IN AS DEEP AS ANYBODY.

AND, AT NEW YORK CITY'S AVENGERS MANSION, THE EAST COAST TEAM'S BUT-LER, EDWIN JARVIS, FIELDS DISTRESS CALLS FOR THE MISSING AVENGERS.

I'M SORRY, THE AVEN-GERS ARE AWAY...UH... ON A CONFIDENTIAL MISSION.

WHERE CAN THEY BE? ARE THEY EVEN ALIVE?

I WISH THE FANTAS-TIC FOUR WERE HERE! THEY'D BE ABLE TO HELP.

AND THE LUXURIOUS GROUNDS OF THE WEST COAST AVENGERS COMPOUND ARE SILENT SAVE FOR THE ROAR OF THE NEARBY SURF.

A HALF-MILE ABOVE THE AVENGERS' CELLS, OUTSIDE ONE OF THE SEALED ENTRANCES TO THE VAULT...

GIN.

AW, NUTS. I WAS ONE CARD AWAY.

ANOTHER HAND.

ABOVE THEM, HIDDEN IN THE SHADOWS, A LONE FIGURE WATCHES.

OKAY, SMART GIRL. YOU KNEW THE AVENGERS WERE PRISONERS AND YOU SNUCK INTO MYSTIQUE'S FILES TO FIND OUT WHERE THIS PLACE IS...

THEN YOU EVEN TRAIPSED BACK ACROSS THE COUNTRY TO GET HERE. THE QUESTION NOW IS -- WHAT HAVE I COME HERE FOR?

I GUESS I CAME HERE TO PLAY HEROINE -- TO TRY AND HELP THE AVENGERS... SOMEHOW!

BUT I FORGOT A COUPLE OF SIMPLE THINGS... LIKE, THERE'S ONLY ONE OF ME -- AND I DON'T HAVE ANY KIND OF PLAN!

NOT TO MENTION MYSTIQUE'S THREATS.

BUT HOW CAN I LIVE WITH MYSELF IF I DON'T DO ANYTHING FOR THE AVENGERS...? OR AM I OVERREACTING?

MAYBE IT'S LIKE MYSTIQUE SAID... MAYBE THE FEDS ARE JUST ACTING TOUGH.

I-I CAN'T RISK EVERYTHING I'VE GOT. NOT YET. I HAVE TO GO BACK -- SEE WHAT HAPPENS. IF I'M REALLY NEEDED, I CAN COME BACK -- MAYBE EVEN WITH HELP.

THERE'S TOO MUCH AT STAKE! MYSTIQUE HAS ONE ON ME.

BUT AS SPIDER-WOMAN PREPARES TO DEPART, HER FOOT TRIGGERS A CONCEALED SECURITY DEVICE!

LIGHTS BLARE! SIRENS EXPLODE INTO HIGH-PITCHED WAILINGS!

AARRROOOOOOO

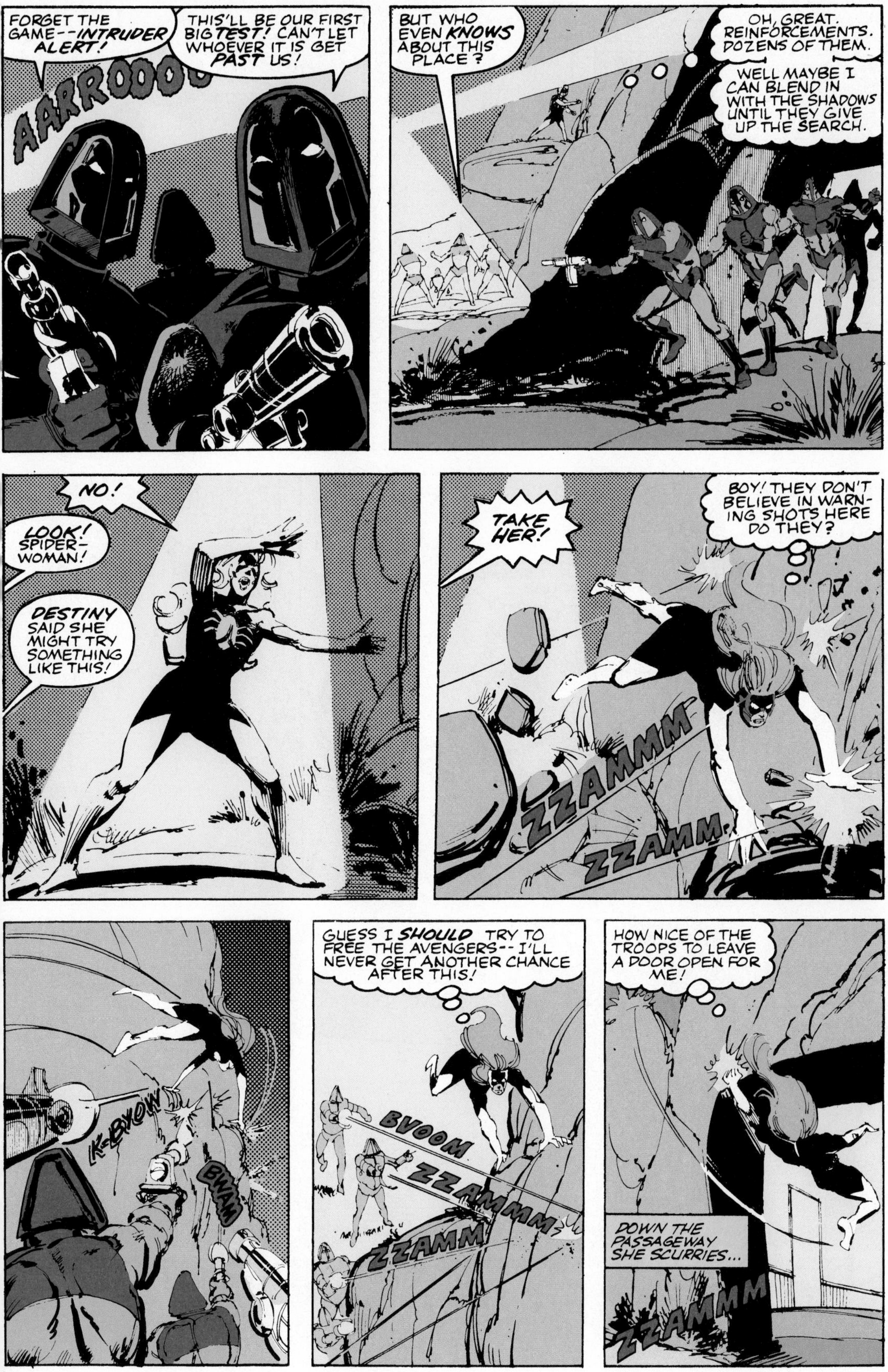

FORGET THE GAME--INTRUDER ALERT!
THIS'LL BE OUR FIRST BIG TEST! CAN'T LET WHOEVER IT IS GET PAST US!
AARROOOO
BUT WHO EVEN KNOWS ABOUT THIS PLACE?
OH, GREAT. REINFORCEMENTS. DOZENS OF THEM.
WELL MAYBE I CAN BLEND IN WITH THE SHADOWS UNTIL THEY GIVE UP THE SEARCH.
NO!
LOOK! SPIDER-WOMAN!
DESTINY SAID SHE MIGHT TRY SOMETHING LIKE THIS!
TAKE HER!
BOY! THEY DON'T BELIEVE IN WARNING SHOTS HERE DO THEY?
ZZAMMM
ZZAMM
K-BYOW
BWAM
GUESS I SHOULD TRY TO FREE THE AVENGERS--I'LL NEVER GET ANOTHER CHANCE AFTER THIS!
BVOOM
ZZAMMMM
ZZAMM
HOW NICE OF THE TROOPS TO LEAVE A DOOR OPEN FOR ME!
DOWN THE PASSAGEWAY SHE SCURRIES...
ZZAMMM

... COMING SHORTLY TO AN ELEVATOR SHAFT, EASILY FORCING THE DOORS TO OPEN...

I'LL BET THAT THE PRISONERS ARE KEPT *DOWN BELOW.*

DESCENDING THE CABLE...

... SPIDER-WOMAN FINDS HERSELF IN THE GUARDSMEN'S *LOCKER ROOM...*

SHEESH. THE BOSS'LL HAVE MY *HEAD* FOR BEING LATE. CAN I HELP IT IF I *SLEPT* THROUGH THE SIRENS?

I'M SURE YOUR BOSS WILL UNDERSTAND, FRIEND.

HE'LL PROBABLY BE LESS UNDERSTANDING ABOUT YOU LETTING AN INTRUDER GET AHOLD OF YOUR *WEAPON...*

S-SPIDER-WOMAN!

I WANT INFORMATION. WHERE ARE THE AVENGERS?

AND I'LL *KNOW* IF YOU'RE LYING.

NOT REALLY. BUT IT *SOUNDS* TOUGH.

C-CORRIDOR SIX-- DIAGONALLY ACROSS FROM HERE. B-BUT YOU'LL NEVER GET PAST THE *SECURITY* THERE.

THANKS. NOW CLOSE YOUR EYES. IT'S *NAP* TIME.

WHAM

SOON, OFF CORRIDOR SIX...

THIS *HAS* TO BE WHERE THEY'RE BEING HELD. THERE'RE MORE GUARDS HERE THAN I CAN COUNT.

BUT THAT GUY WAS *RIGHT.* I'LL NEVER GET PAST *SECURITY* HERE.

ON THAT VIDEO CONSOLE-- THE AVENGERS IN THEIR CELLS! AND A BANK OF *CONTROLS* NEXT TO THE SCREENS...!

LOOK ALIVE, MEN! THE REPORT IS THAT *SPIDER-WOMAN'S* INFILTRATED THE FACILITY.

SHE'S PROBABLY HEADING DOWN *HERE!*

GOOD GUESS, SHERLOCK! HI, GUYS!

GOT TO MOVE FAST!

*WHAM*

*BLAM*

YEOW! MY KNUCKLES!

GOT TO TAKE OUT SOME OF THIS MACHINERY--!

*RRIII-RRR*

THAT SHOULD DISRUPT THE CONTROLS OF THE AVENGERS' CELLS.

I'M MESSING *SOMETHING* UP, THAT'S FOR SURE!

*KRAAAKLE*

*PWOOMP*

*BZZZZ*

HERE, FELLAS! CATCH!

*BWAAMMM*

I'VE LOST THE ELEMENT OF *SURPRISE.* THESE GUYS'RE GONNA START REVVING UP THEIR GUARDSMEN SUITS AND HITTING ME HARD!

TIME FOR ME TO MAKE MYSELF *SCARCE!*

HOPE I WAS ABLE TO ACTUALLY DO SOME *GOOD* FOR THE AVENGERS--

--CAUSE I'VE SURE JUST SCREWED UP MY *OWN* LIFE!

AND SPIDER-WOMAN'S ACTIONS *HAVE* HAD SIGNIFICANT EFFECT...

THE FEEDING SLOT--*OPENING?* BUT MEALTIME WAS JUST AN HOUR AGO.

AND THE BACK-UP PARTITION HASN'T SLID INTO PLACE!

LOOKS LIKE A *PERFECT ESCAPE ROUTE.*

LOOKS LIKE A PERFECT *SET-UP*-- SO THEY CAN CLAIM THEY HAD TO *KILL* ME WHILE I WAS TRYING TO ESCAPE!

OR IT *COULD* JUST BE A SYSTEMS MALFUNCTION...

GOT TO RISK IT--!

WELL, SO FAR I HAVEN'T BEEN BLASTED TO ATOMS BY LASERS. MAYBE IT *ISN'T* A TRAP.

GOT TO FREE THE OTHERS SOMEHOW.

CAP'S CELL!

IT'S SEALED WITH THE SAME ELECTRO-LOCKING SYSTEM ALL OUR CELLS ARE.

I GUESS IT'S TIME FOR ME TO--

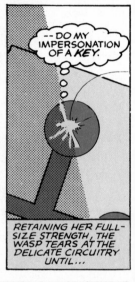

--DO MY IMPERSONATION OF A *KEY.*

RETAINING HER FULL-SIZE STRENGTH, THE WASP TEARS AT THE DELICATE CIRCUITRY UNTIL...

*ARRGH!* MUST'VE TOUCHED A WRONG *WIRE!* CURRENT FLOWING THROUGH ME!

WHOA! THAT *SMARTS!*

WASP! HOW DID YOU GET FREE--?

I'M NOT SURE...

...BUT WE'VE GOT TO FREE THE *OTHERS* NOW!

AS REPREHENSIBLE AS ALL THIS IS--

--I STILL HAVE A HARD TIME WITH THE IDEA OF BREAKING OUT!

THIS *IS* THE U.S. GOVERNMENT WE'RE DEALING WITH--ALBEIT NOT ITS MOST *PLEASANT* SIDE.

CAP... I UNDERSTAND YOUR PROBLEM. BUT YOU SEE THE *PERVERSION* OF LAW AND JUSTICE HERE.

LET'S TRY TO GET OURSELVES AND THE OTHERS OUT--THEN WE CAN DECIDE WHAT THE RIGHT THING TO DO IS--

--AS *FREE* MEN AND WOMEN.

OKAY, JAN. YOU'VE MADE YOUR POINT. LET'S GET *STARTED*.

THE WASP SHRINKS DOWN AND, CAREFUL NOT TO SHOCK HERSELF AGAIN, TAKES CARE OF THE LOCK ON HERCULES' CELL...

*CAPTAIN!* MY THANKS--

KEEP IT DOWN, HERCULES. LET'S MOVE.

WONDER MAN'S CELL IS OPENED.

*ZOUNDS!* SIMON IS *TORTURED* BY THOSE BEAMS OF LIGHT.

THEY SHALL TORTURE HIM *NO MORE!*

SMA-AASH

UNH... TH-THANKS, HERC...

N-NEED A SECOND TO CATCH MY BREATH...

YOUR STRENGTH WILL RETURN TO YOU NOW--AND WE'LL HAVE *NEED* OF IT ALL TOO SOON.

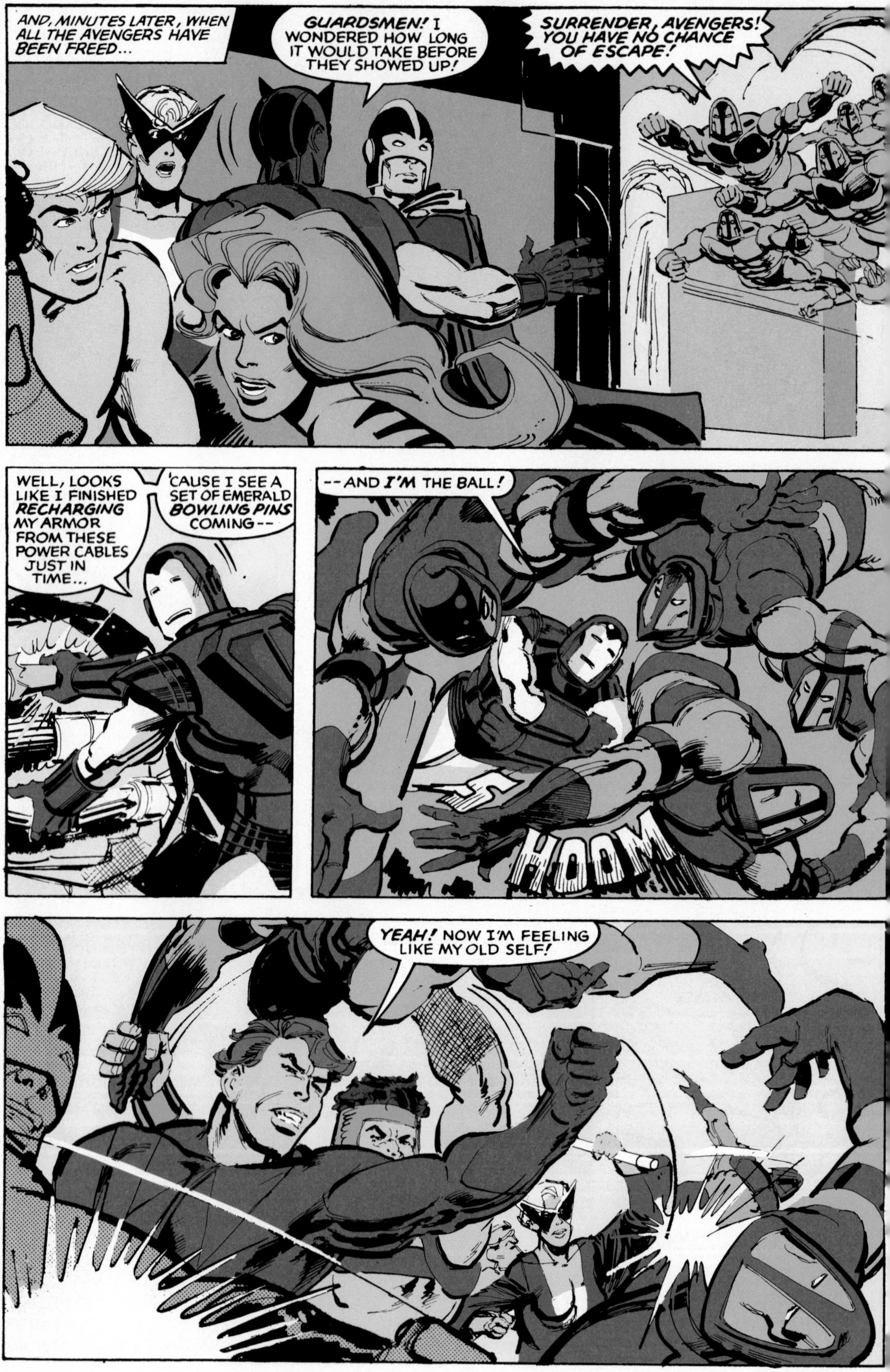
AND, MINUTES LATER, WHEN ALL THE AVENGERS HAVE BEEN FREED...
GUARDSMEN! I WONDERED HOW LONG IT WOULD TAKE BEFORE THEY SHOWED UP!
SURRENDER, AVENGERS! YOU HAVE NO CHANCE OF ESCAPE!
WELL, LOOKS LIKE I FINISHED RECHARGING MY ARMOR FROM THESE POWER CABLES JUST IN TIME...
'CAUSE I SEE A SET OF EMERALD BOWLING PINS COMING--
--AND I'M THE BALL!
HOOM
YEAH! NOW I'M FEELING LIKE MY OLD SELF!

IN MY ELECTRIC FORM I CAN GIVE THEM THE SHOCK OF THEIR LIVES--*NO!*

IT'S NOT WORKING!

THEIR SUITS ARE TOO WELL *INSULATED*--

--BUT THERE MIGHT BE ONE WAY TO STOP THEM QUICKLY *AND* COMPLETELY.

AND, AS IRON MAN TURNS A SMALL DIAL ON HIS GLOVE...

EEEEEEEEEE

THAT *SOUND*--!

MY EARS!

SORRY, FOLKS, YOU'LL HAVE TO ENDURE THAT HIGH-PITCHED WHINE FOR A FEW MORE SECONDS--

--BECAUSE, IF I'M RIGHT, IT'S GOING TO MAKE THINGS A WHOLE LOT *EASIER* FOR US!

CAN'T MOVE-- MY ARMOR'S *FROZEN* UP!

MINE TOO!

AS *TONY STARK,* I DESIGNED THE PROTOTYPE FOR THESE SUITS. WHEN THE GOVERNMENT REPRODUCED THEM...

...THEY ALSO, UNKNOWINGLY, DUPLICATED THE *FAIL-SAFE* DEVICES I INSTALLED SO IT COULDN'T BE USED AGAINST ME.

THANK HEAVEN FOR BUREAUCRATS.

MEANWHILE, CAPTAIN MARVEL, IN THE FORM OF INVISIBLE RADIO WAVES, SEARCHES THROUGHOUT THE COMPLEX FOR THE AVENGERS' WEAPONS.

BINGO!

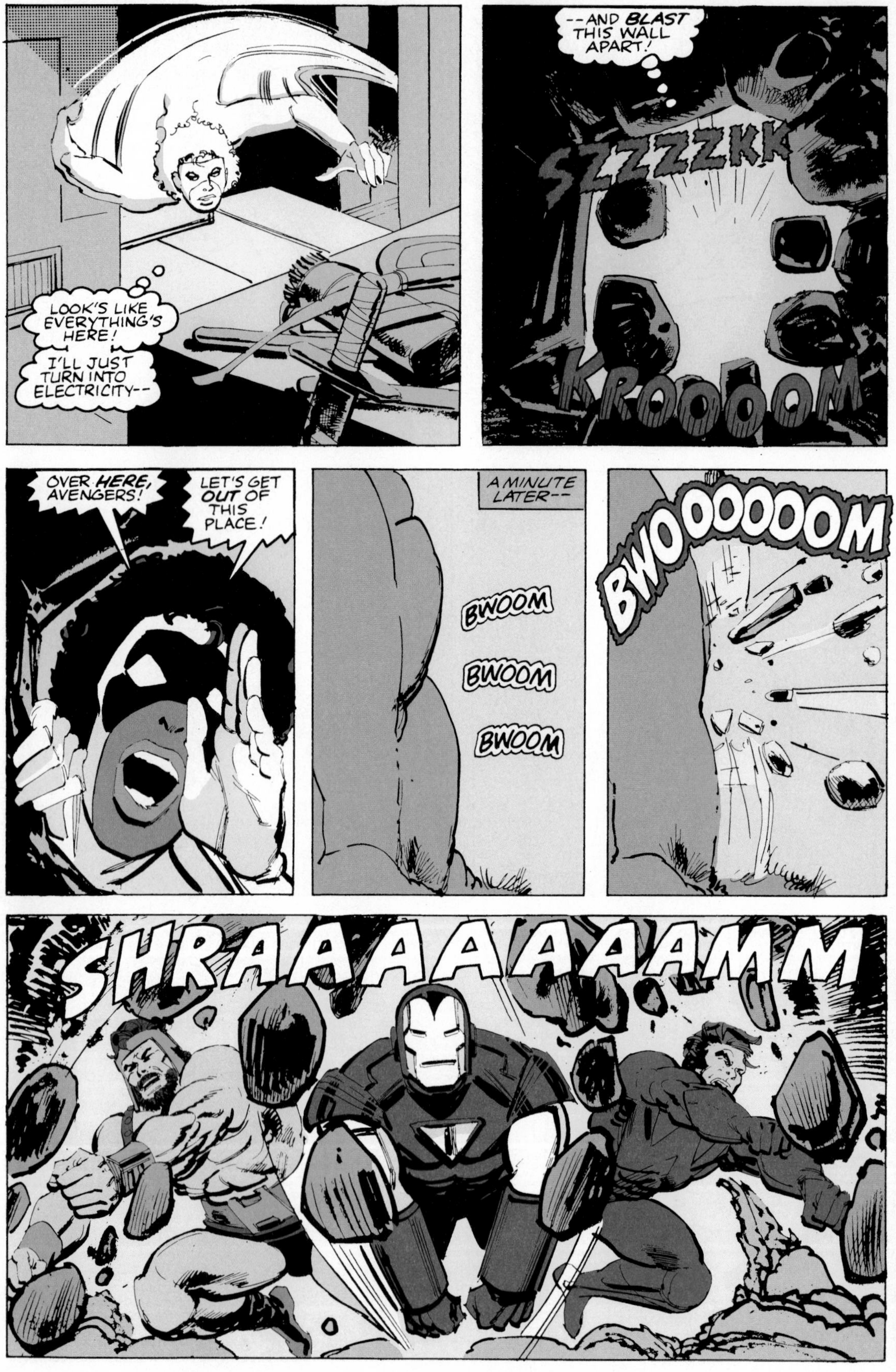
LOOK'S LIKE EVERYTHING'S HERE!
I'LL JUST TURN INTO ELECTRICITY--
--AND BLAST THIS WALL APART!
SZZZZKK
KROOOOOM
OVER HERE, AVENGERS!
LET'S GET OUT OF THIS PLACE!
A MINUTE LATER--
BWOOM
BWOOM
BWOOM
BWOOOOOOM
SHRAAAAAAAAMM

AS THE AVENGERS POUR OUT OF THE HOLE IN THE CLIFFSIDE--

-- CAPTAIN MARVEL PASSES THROUGH AND DISRUPTS THE VAULT'S ELECTRONIC SYSTEMS BEFORE SHE FOLLOWS.

THERE! NOW IT'LL BE THAT MUCH HARDER FOR THEM TO TRACK US.

STAY ON FOOT, YOU GUYS! YOU'RE TOO EASILY DETECTABLE IN THE AIR.

THERE THEY GO. I GUESS I DID HELP THEM GET FREE.

IT WAS PRETTY STUPID OF ME TO ACT WITHOUT A BETTER PLAN. THAT'S A LESSON I'LL HAVE TO REMEMBER.

STILL, I'M GLAD I DID WHAT I DID. I JUST HOPE I HAVEN'T SCREWED MY LIFE UP COMPLETELY.

I SURE DON'T HAVE MUCH FUTURE WITH FREEDOM FORCE. WONDER IF I HAVE WHAT IT TAKES TO BE AN AVENGER...?

LOOKS LIKE WE'RE ACTUALLY GONNA MAKE IT!

BOY, DO I WANT TO CLAW THAT GYRICH'S EYES OUT!

EASY, TIGRA. WE'LL HAVE OUR DAY.

MEANWHILE...

WELL, WHAT ARE YOU ALL *STANDING* THERE FOR?! FIND THE AVENGERS!

BUT, BOSS-- OUR SUITS'RE STILL STIFF-- AND ALL THE VAULT'S *TRACKING DEVICES* ARE DOWN.

THEY COULD BE *ANYWHERE* BY NOW. THEY'RE THE *AVENGERS!*

A SHORT TIME LATER...

...A DARKENED CAVE ENTRANCE STANDS AS IT HAS FOR THOU- SANDS OF YEARS, BARELY NOTICEABLE TO ANY WHO CHANCE PAST IT.

BUT THE AVENGERS, DESPERATE FOR SHELTER, FOUND IT. AND, DEEP INSIDE THE TWISTING CAVERNS...

...THE FALSELY ACCUSED TEAM PLANS BY THE FLICK- ERING LIGHT OF ONE OF HAWKEYE'S FLARE ARROWS...

THEN IT'S *AGREED*--

--OUR FIRST PRIORITY IS TO FIND OUT *WHO* BETRAYED US AND *WHY.*

THEN WE CAN DECIDE ON OUR COURSE OF ACTION!

FOR WE ARE AVENGERS, AND ONE WAY OR ANOTHER WE WILL HAVE--

# VENGEANCE!

TO BE *CONCLUDED* IN THE PAGES OF THE *FIRST WEST* COAST AVENGERS ANNUAL! ON SALE IN TWO WEEKS! *DO NOT MISS IT!*

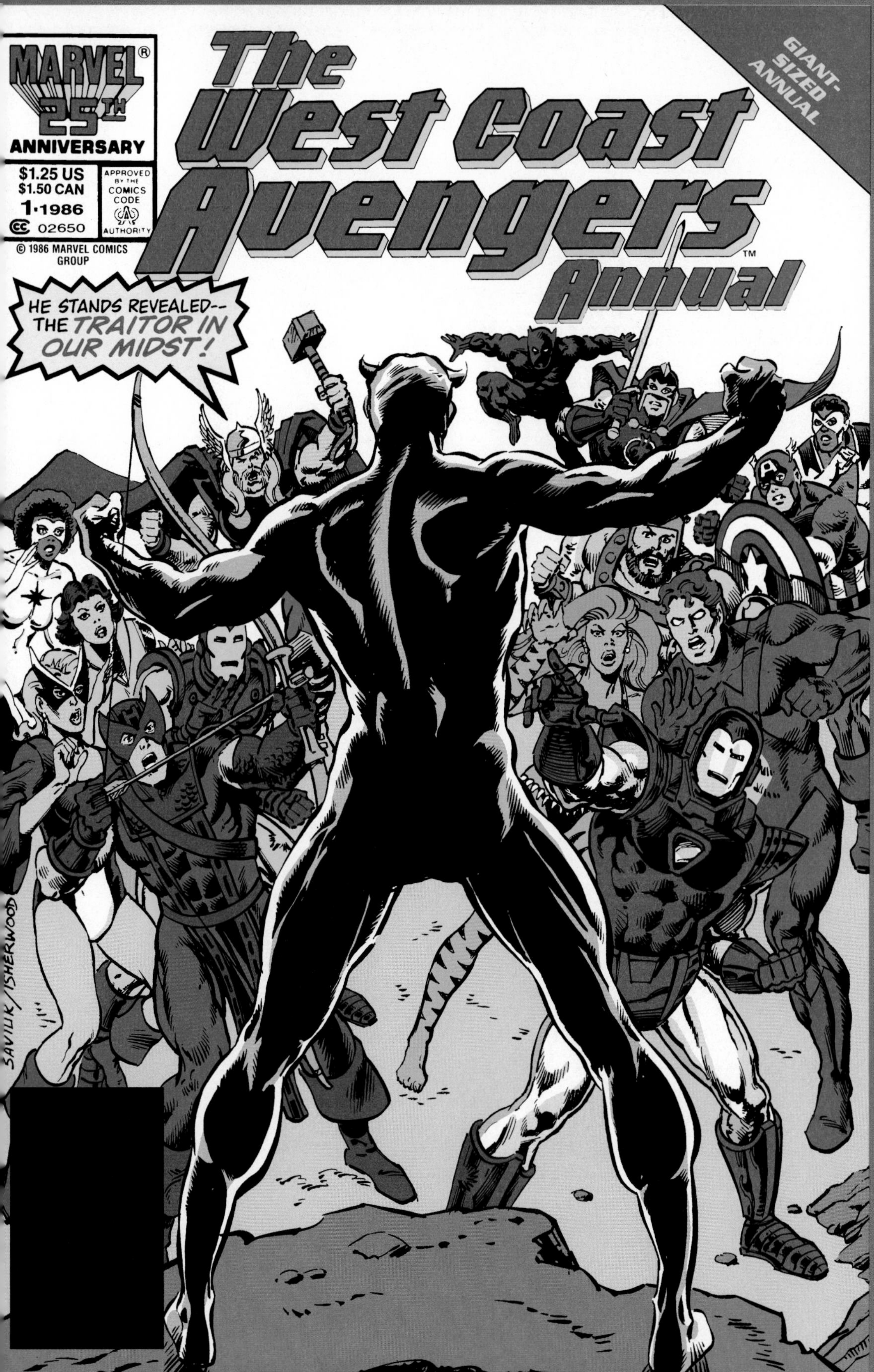

MARVEL® 25TH ANNIVERSARY
$1.25 US
$1.50 CAN
1·1986
02650
APPROVED BY THE COMICS CODE AUTHORITY
© 1986 MARVEL COMICS GROUP
The West Coast Avengers Annual™
GIANT-SIZED ANNUAL
HE STANDS REVEALED-- THE TRAITOR IN OUR MIDST!
SAVIUK/ISHERWOOD

# The WEST COAST AVENGERS

IN AVENGERS ANNUAL #15, NOW ON SALE, THE COMBINED FORCES OF THE EAST AND WEST COAST AVENGERS WERE CAPTURED BY THE GOVERNMENT, ACTING ON FALSE CHARGES SUPPLIED BY-- AN AVENGER!

NOW, HAVING ESCAPED INTO THE ROCKY MOUNTAINS, ELEVEN VERY ANGRY HEROES ARE READY TO FIND OUT WHO LIED ABOUT THEM-- AND GET SOME SATISFACTION!

# ONE OF OUR OWN!

STEVE ENGLEHART        MARK BRIGHT        GEOF ISHERWOOD        TOM ORZECHOWSKI        PETRA SCOTESE
SCRIPT-- CO-PLOTTERS-- PENCILS                    INKS                            LETTERS                      COLORS

DANNY FINGEROTH          MICHAEL HIGGINS              MARK GRUENWALD              JIM SHOOTER
THE FING                       MANAGING EDITOR                    EDITOR                      EDITOR IN CHIEF

HAWKEYE! THEY'VE BROADENED THEIR SEARCH TO THE *WOODS!*

I *FIGURED* THEY WOULD, CAPTAIN MARVEL! SEE WHAT I *FOUND* US!

FUNNY TO USE HER *FULL NAME*-- BUT "*CAP*" IS *CAPTAIN AMERICA* TO ME--

--AND SHE SURE DOESN'T LOOK LIKE A "*MARV*"!

I CAN GIVE US A LITTLE *LIGHT*--!

WISH YOU *WOULDN'T.* LET'S LEAVE THINGS *DARK*-- LIKE MY *HEAD*, GETTING US *INTO* THIS MESS!

*EASE UP*, CLINT! YOU ONLY AGREED TO ACCEPT A *GOVERNMENT ORDER!*

THE ONE WHO GOT US *INTO THIS--*

--WAS THE AVENGER WHO *BETRAYED* US!

I'VE SCANNED THE CAVE WITH MY *SENSORS*, HAWK-EYE! WE'RE *ALONE*-- AND I'LL KEEP AN *ELECTRONIC EAR* COCKED FOR ANYBODY GETTING TOO *CLOSE!*

BUT WE MUSTN'T *TARRY OVERLONG*, IRON MAN!

HERCULES WANTS *VENGEANCE*, AND IN *FULL MEASURE*, ON THE *VIPER* IN OUR MIDST!

NOBODY'S *ARGUIN'*, HERC! SO LET'S *FIGURE IT OUT!*

I TRUST EVERYBODY *HERE*-- AND THAT, FOR YOU *EAST COASTERS*, INCLUDES *HANK PYM*, WHO'S PROVED HIMSELF WITH *US!* *

NO QUESTION *ABOUT* IT!

*HE SUFFERED A BREAK-DOWN IN *AVENGERS* #217.

BUT WHOEVER *DID* DO IT KNOWS OUR OPERATION *THOROUGHLY*-- AND KNOWS ENOUGH *ABOUT* US TO SUPPLY ONLY ACCUSATIONS WE CAN'T *DISPROVE!*

SO, DISTASTEFUL AS IT *IS...* LET'S GO DOWN THE *LIST!*

"IT CAN'T BE *THE THING* BECAUSE EVEN THOUGH HE *AGREED* TO JOIN US, HE NEVER *DID*-- *

"--AND AGENT GYRICH SAID *DEFINITELY* THE TRAITOR WAS AN *AVENGER!*

*WEST COAST #10.

"WE HUNG OUT WITH A LADY NAMED *FIREBIRD* RECENTLY, BUT SHE, uh, NEVER EVEN GOT *ASKED* TO JOIN! *

* *WEST COAST* #4-9.

"MOONDRAGON...

"WELL, MOONDRAGON NEVER JOINED... AND NOW SHE'S *DEAD!*"*

*DEFENDERS #152.

"HELLCAT NEVER JOINED! SHE TOOK UP WITH THE *DEFENDERS,* AND THEN RETIRED TO MARRY *DAIMON HELLSTROM*-- AFTER HE GOT OUT FROM UNDER BEING THE *SON OF SATAN!* *

*DEFENDERS #125.

"SO THEN WE GET TO THE *ACTUAL MEMBERS--!*

"THE OLD *MS. MARVEL* CHANGED HER NAME TO *BINARY* AND SPLIT FOR *DEEP SPACE!*"

**X-MEN #174.

*THE UNUSUALLY QUIET WASP NOW STEPS FORWARD!*

"WE LEFT *STARFOX* OUT THERE, TOO-- IN THE *ANDROMEDA GALAXY!* *

*AVENGERS #261.

"THE *HULK* IS IN NO POSITION TO RAT ON ANYBODY--*"

* SEE HULK #324.

"-- AND OUR MOST *RECENT* RECRUIT, THE *SUB-MARINER,* HAS LEFT OUR RANKS ON A PER-SONAL QUEST...

"*MANTIS* BECAME THE *CELESTIAL MADONNA,** AND I CAN'T PICTURE ANYBODY THAT *COSMIC* WORKING THROUGH *AGENT GYRICH!*

*GIANT-SIZE AVENGERS #4.

"JOCASTA WAS BUILT BY *ULTRON-8,* BUT SHE WAS NEVER *EVIL*--

"--NEVER ACTUALLY *JOINED* US--

"-- AND *SACRIFICED HERSELF* IN THE END--"

*MARVEL TWO-IN-ONE #93.

"-- AS DID THE *SWORDSMAN,* WHEN HE SAVED *MANTIS'S* LIFE! "*

*GIANT-SIZE AVENGERS #2.

SO THAT LEAVES...

...THOR, VISION, SCARLET WITCH, QUICKSILVER, SHE-HULK...

...BLACK PANTHER... ...BLACK WIDOW, THE ALTERNATE IRON MAN...

...BEAST... AND THE FALCON! IS THAT EVERY-BODY?

A NICE SHORT LIST-- BUT WE'VE GOT TO CONTACT THEM ALL!

WHO WOULD HAVE THOUGHT I'D LIVE TO SEE HAWKEYE TAKING COMMAND--

--AND EVERYONE LISTENING?

WE'LL SPLIT UP! MOST OF THEM ARE NEAR NEW YORK, SO WE SHOULD MEET BACK AT A PLACE I KNOW UPSTATE!

IF NOTHING ELSE, IT'LL BE LESS DRAFTY--!

AND SO, AS DAWN'S EARLY LIGHT BEGINS TO SWEEP ACROSS THE CONTINENT, THE HUNT BEGINS!

CAPTAIN MARVEL TAKES OFF FOR THE MOON, TO CHECK ON QUICK-SILVER!

ONE IRON MAN FLIES HIGH ENOUGH TO SEND A STRAIGHT-LINE SIGNAL TO THE WEST COAST--

--AND ANOTHER IRON MAN-- JIM RHODES!

I DON'T WANT TO TRUST A SATELLITE, RHODEY!

BUT TONY, YOU KNOW I GOT MY HEAD ON STRAIGHT AGAIN!*

I WOULDN'T BETRAY YOU NOW!

I KNOW! THIS IS LESS AN INVESTIGATION--

*IRON MAN #195.

--THAN AN INVITATION!

YOU MEAN--YOU WANT ME TO SUIT UP AGAIN, AND JOIN YOU?

THAT'S EXACTLY WHAT I MEAN!

BOSS-- YOU TWISTED MY ARM!

AND IN MANHATTAN--

RRROW! YOU GUYS DON'T FOOL AROUND WHEN YOU BUILD A HEADQUARTERS, DO YOU?

SAYS THE WOMAN WHO LIVES ON A HOLLYWOOD STAR'S ESTATE!

ANYWAY, I DIDN'T *BETRAY* YOU, TIGRA-- AND I'M FAR LESS AN *AVENGER* THAN A MEMBER OF THE *FANTASTIC FOUR*, THESE DAYS!

*SURE*, SHE-HULK! I NEVER REALLY THOUGHT YOU *DID!*

IT'S HARD TO IMAGINE *ANYBODY* ON OUR LIST TURNING TRAITOR--!

--BUT *I'M* NOT ON THE LIST-- AND MY *CAT SIDE* ALMOST SUCCUMBED TO *GRAVITON*, JUST THE *OTHER DAY!* *

I'M SO *CLOSE* TO *LOSING CONTROL*-- BUT I *HAVEN'T YET!* AND I *WON'T*---

WHAT, *REED?* I DIDN'T *HEAR* THAT!

I SAID, THE FF CAN *HELP* YOU, TIGRA!

NO... WE HAVE TO DO THIS *OUR-SELVES!*

*WEST COAST #13, NOW ON SALE.

*WAKANDA--*

THIS IS *GRAVE NEWS*, MY FRIEND!

BUT REST ASSURED, THE *BLACK PANTHER* HAS SWORN TO AID THE AVENGERS *WHENEVER* THEY CALL ON HIM!

ONLY MY *PEOPLE* HAVE A GREATER *CLAIM* ON ME!

*GREAT*, T'CHALLA! WHEN CAN WE EXPECT---

I'M ON MY WAY, HAWKEYE!

*MANHATTAN AGAIN--!*

BY YMIR'S *FROST-COVERED BEARD*, ART THOU *MAD?*

I CREATE A *NEW SECRET IDENTITY* AS *SIGURD JARLSON*-- I ENTRUST *ONE AVENGER* WITH MY ADDRESS--

--THOU COM'ST HITHER TO ASK MY *AID*--

--AND *THEN* THOU WOULDST CONSUME *FRIED FOWL* ERE RETURNING TO OUR *ALLIES!*

BY MY TROTH, OLYMPIAN! EVERY TIME I CONSIDER THEE A *FULL-FLEDGED GOD*, THOU *REMINDEST* ME OF THY *HALF-HUMAN HERITAGE!*

IT HAS BEEN A *LONG NIGHT*, THOR!

I NEED *STRENGTH* TO EXACT *REVENGE!*

I NEED STRENGTH TO DEAL WITH *THEE!*

*TAP TAP TAP*

SORRY-- I GAVE AT THE *OFFICE!*

HI, CAP!

HI, FALC!

DOESN'T ANYTHING *SURPRISE* YOU?

NOTHIN' *YOU* CAN DO! NOT AFTER BEIN' YOUR *PARTNER* ALL THOSE YEARS!

WELL, IF YOU WANT TO BE MY PARTNER *AGAIN*--

--MINE, AND THE *AVENGERS'--!*

THAT'S WHAT *HAPPENS* WHEN YOU BECOME A *SOCIAL WORKER*-- ALL THE *DERELICTS* WANT YOUR *HELP*--!

AND, ON THE LOWER EAST SIDE--

--SO, HANK, WE RAN DOWN THE ENTIRE LIST, AND AS SILLY AS IT CERTAINLY MUST BE, THE NAME OF THE BEAST WAS THERE TO BE CHECKED!

I UNDERSTAND, JAN---

I KNOW YOU'RE BACK WITH YOUR OLD FRIENDS IN THE X-FACTOR GROUP-- PROBABLY NEVER EVEN THINK ABOUT US IN THE AVENGERS--

NO, NO---

-- BUT I HAVE TO ASK---

-- AND I'D LIKE TO ANSWER, SWEET LADY!

AS YOU MIGHT IMAGINE, A SMART MUTANT STAYS AS FAR AWAY FROM THE GOVERNMENT AS HE CAN--

--AND THOUGH IN NORMAL TIMES I'D RUSH TO PROVIDE YOU WITH MY SERVICES, I'M REASONABLY CONSUMED BY OUR OLD/ NEW TEAM JUST NOW!

BUT IF YOU REALLY NEED ME--!

NO, THAT'S OKAY!

STAY WELL!

UPPER EAST SIDE--

...BUT WE'VE BOTH BEEN SPIES, MOCKINGBIRD! SURELY YOU SEE THAT THIS COULD ALL BE AN EXERCISE IN DISINFORMATION!

YOU DON'T HAVE TO BE BORN RUSSIAN TO KNOW BIG GOVERNMENT! GYRICH HAS HAD YEARS TO FERRET OUT A FACT HERE, A FACT THERE--

NO, NATASHA-- HE WAS TOO SPECIFIC TO BE GUESSING!

HOWEVER, IF YOU DON'T WANT TO HELP--!

I DIDN'T SAY THAT!

SO THIS IS THE WOMAN HAWKEYE MARRIED-- HAWKEYE, THE MAN I CAME TO AMERICA FOR!*

SHE'S PRETTY!

*TALES OF SUSPENSE #57.

SO THIS IS CLINT'S FIRST LOVE!

SHE'S PRETTY!

ALEXI-- CLINT-- MATT-- IN THE END, THE BLACK WIDOW KEPT NONE OF THEM!*

SHALL WE GO?

*ALEXI IS HER DECEASED HUSBAND. MATT, OF COURSE, IS DAREDEVIL.

LEONIA, NEW JERSEY--

I NEVER EXPECTED TO BE BACK SO SOON, BRO!

I KNOW YOU AND WANDA HAVE *BETTER* THINGS TO DO THAN *CRUSH THE AVENGERS!* FRANKLY, I TOOK THIS ASSIGNMENT *PRIMARILY* TO LOOK IN ON MY NEW *NEPHEWS!**

YOU'RE VERY *WELCOME,* SIMON-- THOUGH I WISH YOUR VISIT WEREN'T IN RESPONSE TO SUCH... UNHAPPY EVENTS!

YES--*TOMMY* AND *BILLY* HAVE MADE US FAR MORE *SENSITIVE* TO THE *DANGERS* OF THE WORLD!

AS YOU KNOW, *BILLY* CAN'T BE DETECTED BY ANY *INSTRUMENT,* SO HIS BIRTH WAS A *COMPLETE SURPRISE!* IT'S LUCKY I'M IN *GOOD HEALTH--*

--AND EVEN *THEN,* HER RECOVERY HAS BEEN *SLOW!*

YOU'LL *UNDERSTAND* THAT WE CAN'T JOIN WITH THE AVENGERS AT THIS *TIME!*

*SURE!* YOU FOUR JUST TAKE CARE OF *YOURSELVES,* AND LEAVE THE *WORLD* TO US! IF I HAVE ANYTHING TO SAY ABOUT IT--

--IT'LL NEVER BOTHER YOU OR YOURS *AGAIN!*

'BYE--!

*WONDER MAN (LIKE YOU, WE HOPE!) WAS HERE FOR THE BIRTHS IN VISION/WITCH #12.

OH VIZH! IT CAN'T BE ...*HIM!*

NOT *HIM!*

...CAN IT...?

AND SO THE SEARCH CONCLUDES--!

ONE HOUR LATER, IN A CABIN NEAR CHICHESTER, NEW YORK--

CAN IT BE... *HIM?*

THERE BE *SIXTEEN* OF US *HERE!*

*FOUR MORE* ACCOUNTED FOR!

THEN...

247

QUICKSILVER IS NOT ON THE *MOON*--!

WELL, HE'S NOT THE *LEAST* LIKELY SUSPECT, FOR CERTAIN! HE NEVER *WAS* ONE OF THE *GROUP*!

YOU DIDN'T *KNOW HIM* THE WAY *I* DID, TONY! WHEN THE AVENGERS WAS JUST *HIM* AND *WANDA*, CAP AND ME--

--WE WERE A *SOLID TEAM*!*

*BEGINNING WITH THE IMMORTAL *AVENGERS* #16.

INDEED, CLINT BARTON! AND YOU FOUR MADE THE *ORIGINAL* AVENGERS VERY *PROUD*!

THUS, I *REJECT* THIS ASSUMPTION OF *PIETRO'S* GUILT--

-- AND TURN ONCE MORE TO THE MAN WHO MADE US *MOST ASHAMED*-- HANK PYM!

NO, THOR! HE *COULDN'T*!

HEY! IT'S A *FIGHT*!

248

HANK AND I WERE ORIGINAL AVENGERS TOO, YOU KNOW! UNLIKE THE *REST* OF *US*, HE DIDN'T TURN OUT TO BE *SUITED* FOR OUR KIND OF LIFE, AND IN TRYING TO KEEP UP A *FRONT*, LOST HIS *WAY* FOR A WHILE!

BUT ONCE HE *FACED* THE FACT THAT HE WASN'T A SUPERHERO BY NATURE, HE *RECOVERED*-- AND *RETIRED*!

OUR *MARRIAGE* RETIRED THEN, AS WELL--

-- BUT I *KNOW* THIS MAN, INSIDE AND OUT, AND I AGREE WITH HAWKEYE *ABSOLUTELY*--

-- HANK IS *NOT* GUILTY!

BUT THEN WHO *IS*?

I AM!

BALDER'S BLOOD! IT IS QUICKSILVER!

YES! THE *FASTEST MAN ALIVE!* AND *GUILTY, GUILTY, GUILTY*--

--OF *VENGEANCE!*

WHY YOU *SLIME-SUCKING SCUM*--!

I WENT TO *BAT* FOR YOU!

WAIT, HAWKEYE! I WANT TO HEAR THE REASON *WHY!*

WHY? WHY *NOT?* YOU SAID IT YOURSELF--

--I WAS *NEVER* ONE OF THE *GROUP!* I WAS NEVER ONE OF *ANY* GROUP!

I GAVE YOU ALL A MAN CAN *GIVE* HIS COLLEAGUES-- MY *TRUST*--

-- AND YOU *BETRAYED ME* JUST LIKE *EVERY-ONE ELSE* HAD *BETRAYED ME!*

THAT'S CRAZY!

Oh YES! THAT'S WHAT YOU PEOPLE ALWAYS SAY! "PIETRO'S CRAZY!" "PIETRO'S PARANOID!"

BUT WHO'S PARANOID WHEN YOUR FATHER IS MAGNETO, AND HE ENSLAVES YOU AND YOUR SISTER IN HIS BROTHERHOOD OF EVIL MUTANTS?*

*X-MEN #4.

WHO'S PARANOID WHEN YOU ESCAPE THAT LIFE AND JOIN THE AVENGERS, "EARTH'S MIGHTIEST HEROES"--

--AND A SYNTHETIC "HERO" SEDUCES YOUR SISTER, AND THE OTHER "HEROES" SUPPORT HIM INSTEAD OF YOU?

QUICKSILVER-- I DON'T KNOW YOU, BUT--

NO-- TO KNOW SOMEONE YOU MUST CARE!

WHEN I WAS INJURED IN OUR BATTLE WITH THE SENTINELS-- GRAVELY INJURED-- *

-- THE "HEROES" RAN AWAY AND LEFT ME TO DIE!

THAT'S NOT TRUE!

WE DIDN'T KNOW WHERE YOU WERE! *AVENGERS #104.

AND I WAS RESCUED BY CRYSTAL, OF THE INHUMANS, WASN'T I? CRYSTAL, TO WHOM I GAVE THE LOVE MY SISTER THREW AWAY!*

WE WERE MARRIED!** WE MOVED TO THE MOON!***

BUT THAT WAS THE FINAL TRAP! AS A MUTANT IN THE REAL WORLD, I WAS AN OUTCAST-- BUT AS A MUTANT IN THE CLOSED SOCIETY OF INHUMANS, I WAS THE ONE-AND-ONLY ALIEN!

CUT OFF! COMPLETELY CUT OFF--!

* FF #131.
** AVENGERS #127.
*** FF #240.

AND THEN MY WIFE BETRAYED ME, TOO-- FOR A CHEAP FLING WITH A REAL-ESTATE SALESMAN! AND MY SISTER--

--MY SISTER BETRAYED ME! TRIED TO MAKE ME FORGIVE!*

BUT I DO NOT FORGIVE!

*VISION/WITCH #10.

I DO NOT FORGIVE ANY OF YOU! I SET GYRICH ON YOU, AND IF HE BETRAYS ME TOO, BY FAILING TO DESTROY YOU--

--I'LL DO IT MYSELF!

MYSELF-- THE ONLY ONE I CAN TRUST!

I HAVE AN ARMY BEHIND ME, AVENGERS, AND WE SHALL DESTROY ALL YOU STAND FOR! THREE THINGS MARK YOU AS I KNEW YOU--

--THE CIRCUS WHERE YOU FIRST FOUGHT SIDE-BY-SIDE, TO BECOME THE AVENGERS--

--THE MANSION, WHERE I FIRST JOINED YOU--

--AND THE INSTALLATION IN AUSTRALIA WHERE YOU LEFT ME TO DIE!

IN THOSE THREE PLACES, YOU'LL PAY FOR WHAT YOU'VE DONE!

THE MAN IS MADDER THAN LOKI--!

PIETRO-- WE CAN HELP YOU--!

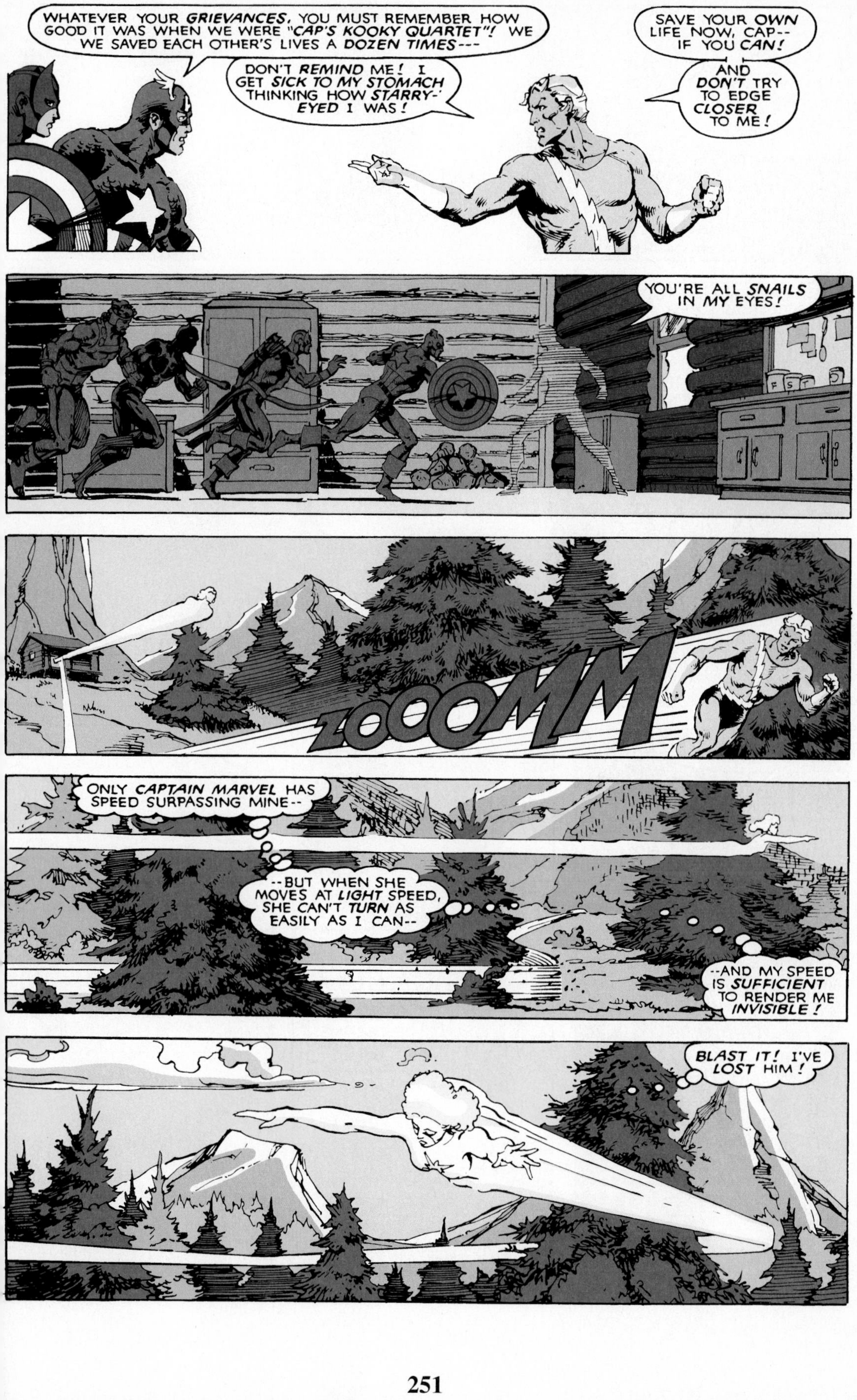
WHATEVER YOUR GRIEVANCES, YOU MUST REMEMBER HOW GOOD IT WAS WHEN WE WERE "CAP'S KOOKY QUARTET"! WE WE SAVED EACH OTHER'S LIVES A DOZEN TIMES---
DON'T REMIND ME! I GET SICK TO MY STOMACH THINKING HOW STARRY-EYED I WAS!
SAVE YOUR OWN LIFE NOW, CAP-- IF YOU CAN!
AND DON'T TRY TO EDGE CLOSER TO ME!
YOU'RE ALL SNAILS IN MY EYES!
ZOOOMM
ONLY CAPTAIN MARVEL HAS SPEED SURPASSING MINE--
--BUT WHEN SHE MOVES AT LIGHT SPEED, SHE CAN'T TURN AS EASILY AS I CAN--
--AND MY SPEED IS SUFFICIENT TO RENDER ME INVISIBLE!
BLAST IT! I'VE LOST HIM!

MADNESS! ALL MY *LIFE* HAVE I WATCHED IT PLAGUE NOBLE *ASGARD!*

I KNOW *TOO WELL* THE DANGER OF A *BROTHER GONE MAD*-- AND I TELL YE *NOW*, AVENGERS--

--PIETRO IS *OUR* BROTHER AS SURELY AS HE'S *WANDA'S!*

CAPTAIN AMERICA-- IRON MAN-- WE AND THE WASP MUST AWAY *AT ONCE* TO THE POINT WHERE THE AVENGERS *BEGAN!*

NO, THOR-- THAT'S THE *OLD* TEAM, AND WE'VE JUST GOTTEN OUR TWO *NEW* TEAMS OPERATING THE WAY WE *WANT* THEM!

I'LL STICK WITH THE *WEST COASTERS!*

DITTO FOR THE *EAST COASTERS*, BLONDIE!

ESPECIALLY SINCE YOU DIDN'T INVITE *HANK* TO JOIN YOUR TEAM!

WE'LL HEAD FOR OUR *MANSION*--!

BUT, JAN-- *GYRICH* WILL HAVE IT *COVERED!*

IT'S NOT LIKE THERE'S AN *ALTERNATIVE*, CAPTAIN!

WE'LL TAKE THE *CIRCUS*, IN THE *SOUTHWEST*--

"--AND THE LATE-COMERS GET *AUSTRALIA!*"

AND, SOON, THE *THREE GROUPS* OF FIVE TAKE OFF IN *THREE DIRECTIONS*--

--LEAVING ONLY *HANK* BEHIND!

THOR HOLDS A *GRUDGE!* I NEVER KNEW...!

BUT THAT'S NOT IMPORTANT NOW. THERE'S SOMETHING I MUST DO!

252

# CHAPTER TWO

# CARDINAL SINS

THEY WAIT IN CENTRAL PARK-- AND THEY FEAR NONE OF ITS MYRIAD DANGERS...

THEY ARE-- --GEMINI--

--CANCER--

--TAURUS--

--AND ARIES!

--OF THE ZODIAC CARTEL!

I CAN'T SEE THIS AT ALL! THERE ARE TWELVE OF US ALREADY IN ZODIAC--WHY SHOULD WE WORK WITH THIS QUICK-SILVER?

BECAUSE HE'S LIVED ON THE MOON, ARIES-- AND THE MOON IS PRECIOUS TO ME!

WE'VE NEVER LEFT EARTH IN ALL OUR LIVES!

WE DON'T HAVE LIVES, CANCER!

WE'RE LIFE-MODEL DECOYS, CRAB-MAN! A MAN NAMED SCORPIO MADE US!* WE'VE EVOLVED SINCE THEN-- RECREATED OURSELVES, BY OURSELVES--

--BUT NO MATTER HOW GOOD WE GET, WE'LL NEVER BE-- ALIVE!

LIGHTEN UP, TAURUS! YOU MAY LIKE TO GET MAD, BUT GEMINI'S GOT OTHER IDEAS!

CRUNCH

*DEFENDERS #50

GENTLEMEN!

HEY! THE BOSS!

WE'LL SEE!

CAN WE GO GET MY HANDS ON SOME AVENGERS, NOW?

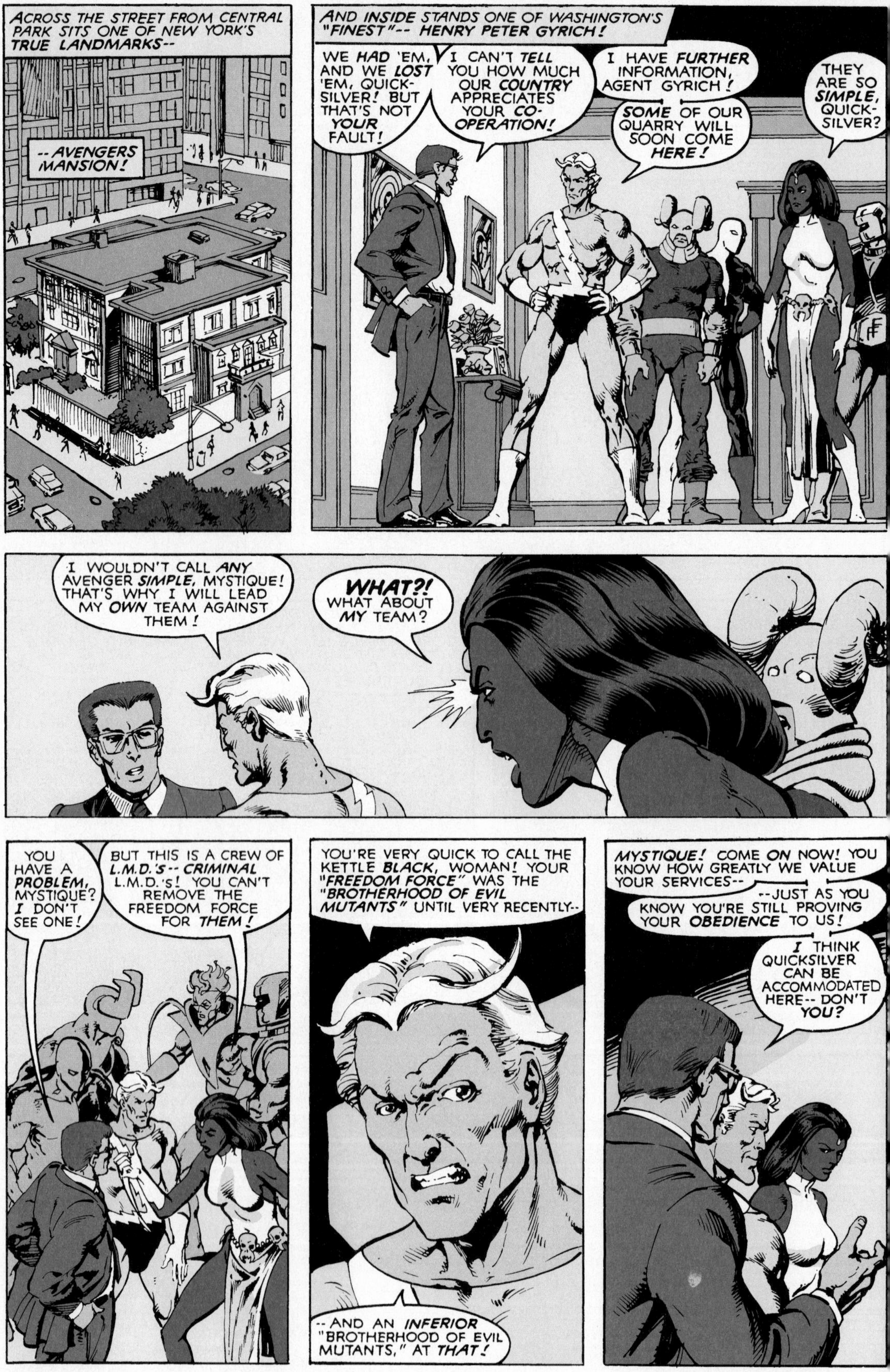

ACROSS THE STREET FROM CENTRAL PARK SITS ONE OF NEW YORK'S TRUE LANDMARKS--
--AVENGERS MANSION!
AND INSIDE STANDS ONE OF WASHINGTON'S "FINEST"-- HENRY PETER GYRICH!
WE HAD 'EM, AND WE LOST 'EM, QUICK-SILVER! BUT THAT'S NOT YOUR FAULT!
I CAN'T TELL YOU HOW MUCH OUR COUNTRY APPRECIATES YOUR CO-OPERATION!
I HAVE FURTHER INFORMATION, AGENT GYRICH!
SOME OF OUR QUARRY WILL SOON COME HERE!
THEY ARE SO SIMPLE, QUICK-SILVER?
I WOULDN'T CALL ANY AVENGER SIMPLE, MYSTIQUE! THAT'S WHY I WILL LEAD MY OWN TEAM AGAINST THEM!
WHAT?! WHAT ABOUT MY TEAM?
YOU HAVE A PROBLEM, MYSTIQUE? I DON'T SEE ONE!
BUT THIS IS A CREW OF L.M.D.'S-- CRIMINAL L.M.D.'s! YOU CAN'T REMOVE THE FREEDOM FORCE FOR THEM!
YOU'RE VERY QUICK TO CALL THE KETTLE BLACK, WOMAN! YOUR "FREEDOM FORCE" WAS THE "BROTHERHOOD OF EVIL MUTANTS" UNTIL VERY RECENTLY--
--AND AN INFERIOR "BROTHERHOOD OF EVIL MUTANTS," AT THAT!
MYSTIQUE! COME ON NOW! YOU KNOW HOW GREATLY WE VALUE YOUR SERVICES--
--JUST AS YOU KNOW YOU'RE STILL PROVING YOUR OBEDIENCE TO US!
I THINK QUICKSILVER CAN BE ACCOMMODATED HERE-- DON'T YOU?

HE DID IT!

NOT SO LOUD!

YOU NEEDN'T WORRY-- MY REPORT WILL GIVE YOU FULL CREDIT FOR THE ORIGINAL CAPTURE!

TAKE THE BACK WAY OUT!

JUST ONE FIRE-BURST! JUST ONE!

ONE NEED NOT KNOW DESTINY TO KNOW THE CONSEQUENCES OF THAT, PYRO!

OUR PART IN THIS DRAMA IS DONE!

GUARD POST ONE-- THIS IS GYRICH!

STILL QUIET, SIR!

ONCE WE TAKE POSSESSION OF A PLACE, IT STAYS TOOK, SIR.

THAT'S "TAKEN," POST ONE!

ALL RIGHT, AVENGER-- I'M TURNING RESPONSIBILITY OVER TO YOU WITH THE SITUATION SECURE!

YOU FOOL-- SECURE? HARDLY!

I KNOW THE AVENGERS...

"...AND I KNOW HOW THEY'LL TRY TO GET IN!"

255

I'VE REACHED THE HATCH!

GREAT!

I'M VERY GLAD WE DIDN'T RUSH TO TELL GYRICH ABOUT OUR SUBMARINE TUNNEL!

AYE! WON'T HE BE SURPRISED--

-- WHEN WE CLIMB STRAIGHT INTO HIS UGLY FACE?

!

!

!!

AVENGERS ASSEMBLE!

RIDING ON RADIO WAVES, CAPTAIN MARVEL'S VOICE IS DIGITALLY CRISP AND CLEAR!

HERCULES HAD NO TIME TO DRAW A *BREATH*, AND HE DOESN'T HAVE HIS *AIR MASK*-- BUT NEITHER DOES THE MAN HE'S *FIGHTING!*

*DOESN'T* THAT *HORN-HEAD* NEED TO BREATHE?

I COULD HOLD AIR IN MY LUNGS FOR *OVER AN HOUR*-- IF I *HAD* ANY AIR!

I *MUST* REACH THE SURFACE, IF ONLY FOR A *MOMENT*--!

*DANE'S* DROWNING, *TOO!* I *TOLD* HIM THE ARMOR WOULD HAMPER HIS ABILITY TO HOLD HIS BREATH!

I'LL--

*WHA*--? THERE'S *PIETRO*, ABOUT TO THROW--

FULL

PURGE

--THE *PURGE SWITCH!*

HE SWIMS SO *FAST* HE CAN GET *IN AND OUT* BEFORE HE *NEEDS* TO DRAW A BREATH--

PURGE

--BUT *WE'LL* BE SUCKED BACK INTO THE *RIVER!*

CAP'S GOT *HERCULES* AND *B.K.,* BUT THE TWO OF THEM WILL DROWN *LONG* BEFORE WE REACH *OPEN WATER--*

-- UNLESS I *CARVE* US A *SHORTCUT!*

THE PRESSURE WILL DRAW THE WATER *BEHIND* ME--

-- VERY *NICELY!*

*QUICK THINKING,* CAPTAIN *MARVEL!*

I *HAD* TO BE *QUICK,* CAP! OUR FRIENDS COULDN'T HAVE LASTED *ANOTHER* MINUTE!

I WOULDN'T PUT THAT THOUGHT IN THE *PAST* JUST YET, MARVEL!

*CANCER, GEMINI* AND I ARE STILL COMMITTED TO YOUR DESTRUCTION-- IN A *MINUTE,* OR *LESS!*

I'VE HAD *ENOUGH* OF YOUR THREATS, PIETRO!

COME ON, AVENGERS!

WASP?!

DID YOU FORGET I'M *TEAM LEADER*, CAP?

WE THOUGHT YOU *DROWNED*, JANET VAN DYNE-- BUT YOU, *TOO*, HAVE NOT ESCAPED YOUR *FATE!*

I'M A *WATER SIGN*, WASP!

YES, BUT *WHAT ELSE* ARE YOU? NOT THE CANCER THE *AVENGERS* CAPTURED, *THAT'S* FOR SURE! *

*AVENGERS #120-122.

I REMEMBER *POLICE REPORTS* OF A *NEW* ZODIAC, CREATED AS *L.M.D.'S!* *

YOU'RE *ASTUTE*, CAPTAIN! THAT'S *EXACTLY* WHO THEY ARE!

AREN'T *YOU* THE GUY WHO THINKS ALL MEN ARE "*CREATED*" EQUAL, WINGHEAD?

I HAVE *NO SECOND THOUGHTS* ABOUT BEING AN INCARNATION OF THE *GEMINI FORCE*--

YOU MEAN-- YOU'VE ALLIED YOURSELF WITH PEOPLE WHO AREN'T EVEN *ALIVE*?

*CAPTAIN MARVEL ONCE WORKED FOR THE NEW ORLEANS *HARBOR PATROL*.

--WITH ITS ABILITY TO *EXPAND!*

PLANG

EXPAND ALL YOU *WANT*, MISTER!

THE GREATEST BATTLES IN *HISTORY* HAVE BEEN FOUGHT AND WON BY *UNDERDOGS*!

DAVID vs. GOLIATH-- AMERICA vs. THE BRITISH EMPIRE--

--AND *CAPTAIN AMERICA* vs. A *BLOWHARD*!

PLOW

SLOK

SIZE MEANS *NOTHING*! ONLY A *WILL* TO *LIVE*--

--WHICH AN *L.M.D.* CAN'T *POSSIBLY* KNOW!

PLEASE-- YOU'RE *RIGHT*! I'VE *CHANGED MY MIND* ABOUT BACKING QUICKSILVER!

WHAT KIND OF A TRICK IS *THIS*?

NO *TRICK*! I'VE JUST *REVERSED* MYSELF!

WE'RE *ALL* INCARNA- TIONS OF OUR *SIGNS*!

GEMINI, YOU WISHY-WASHY *WIPEOUT*! CHANGE YOUR MIND *AGAIN* AND FIGHT--

ARRRGH!

WATER CONDUCTS A *WASP STING* WONDERFULLY, MOON-MAN!

AND SO YOUR DREAMS OF DESTRUCTION COME TO AN *END*, QUICKSILVER!

YOU SAID I DIDN'T *KNOW* YOU, BUT I'VE SEEN YOU IN *ACTION* NOW--

-- AND I *LEARN* WITH THE SPEED OF *THOUGHT*!

OOOPS! HE'S HEADING INTO ONE OF THOSE *OLD BUILDINGS* SCATTERED THROUGHOUT THE PARK!

SOME *WHEELER-DEALER* OF THE *NINETEENTH CENTURY* BUILT A *SUMMER HOME* OR SOMETHING-- AND NOW I'M FACED WITH *TWENTY DIFFERENT TUNNELS!*

ONCE I START CHASING HIM THROUGH *HERE*, WE'LL LOOK LIKE A *MARX BROTHERS* MOVIE ON A *RUNAWAY PROJECTOR!*

BA-LAMM

AND *THAT*-- THAT'S NOT THE *ZODIACS* ANY MORE--

--IT'S *GYRICH* AND HIS *FEDERAL MARSHALLS!*

IT IS TIME FOR HERCULES TO LEND A HAND IN THIS BATTLE!

I SHALL PROVIDE US SOME *SHELTER.*

I WOULDN'T SAY YOU WEREN'T *PULLING YOUR WEIGHT*, OLYMPIAN!

NO...

PTING

...BUT WE *SHOULDN'T* BE *HIDING!* WE SHOULD BE *OUT FRONT*, IN *COMBAT!*

NOT IF IT WOULD MEAN OUR DEATHS, HERC. BESIDES-- AS MUCH AS I DESPISE *GYRICH*, HE'S NOT OUR *REAL* ENEMY!

*PIETRO'S* THE *KEY* TO THIS!

AVENGERS-- GIVE UP RIGHT NOW!

BELIEVE ME, I STILL HAVE ALL THE AUTHORITY I NEED TO ISSUE THIS ORDER!

LET'S GET OUT OF HERE! HE MAKES ME SICK!

I'LL ONLY HAVE TO STRIKE HIM ONCE...!

NO, HERC! THAT'S AN ORDER!

FOLLOW ME, AVENGERS! AND PRAY THAT THE OTHER TWO TEAMS HAVE BETTER LUCK THAN WE DID!

GONE! EVEN CAPTAIN AMERICA DEFIED ME!

BUT IT ONLY GOES TO PROVE WHAT I'VE ALWAYS SAID-- WE HAVE TO CONTROL THESE SUPER-TYPES, FOR THE COMMON GOOD!

AND WE WILL, MEN! YOU CAN TRUST ME ON THAT!

RIGHT...

DING DONG

I HOPE I'M NOT DISTURBING YOU...

NO, HANK-- WE HAVEN'T BEEN ABLE TO SLEEP!

I CAN GUESS WHY YOU'VE COME...!

# CHAPTER THREE

# FIXED ASSETS!

MONUMENT VALLEY, ARIZONA-- AN INDIAN *HOLY SPOT*--

--A JOHN WAYNE *HOLY SPOT!*

TODAY, A *BLOT* ON THE *LANDSCAPE!*

LOOK! HE'S NOT EVEN *BREATHING* HARD!

IT'S *TRUE*, THEN! YOU INTEND TO LEAD *ALL THREE* ZODIAC CLUSTERS!

MY HAT'S *OFF* TO YOU!

THAT'S WHAT HE *SAID* HE WOULD DO, LEO!

MY WORD IS MY *BOND*, LEO-- UNLIKE THE *MAJORITY* OF MANKIND!

MOST *ASSUREDLY!* STILL, *LIBRA* WOULD SUGGEST YOU NEED A *CO-CAPTAIN* IN EACH CLUSTER!

YOU CAN'T DO EVERYTHING *YOURSELF!*

Oh NO?

*NORMAL* MEN "*CAN'T*" DO WHAT THEY WANT TO DO-- BUT I AM *NOT* A "*NORMAL MAN*"!

I AM AS FAR BEYOND "*NORMAL MEN*" AS-- AS--

-- AS "*NORMAL MEN*" ARE BEYOND YOU, ZODIAC! BUT YOU MAKE A *GOOD MILITIA!*

LISTEN, I DON'T MEAN TO *PRY*, BUT WHAT'S YOUR STAND ON NORMAL *WOMEN?*

YOU LOST YOUR *WIFE*, AM I *RIGHT?* COULDN'T WORK IT OUT--?

AND I'LL *NEVER* WORK IT OUT *AGAIN*, VIRGO! MARRIAGE WAS A *MISTAKE*-- IT DIVERTED MY *ENERGIES!* I COULD HAVE LOST MY *PURITY!*

FLESH IS A RUNNER'S *ENEMY!* ANYWAY, LET'S GET TO THE *CIRCUS!*

IT WANDERS THROUGH THE WEST-- A JUNIOR COMPETITOR FOR OVER ONE HUNDRED YEARS TO RINGLING BROTHERS, BARNUM & BAILEY!

BUT IN THE SMALLER TOWNS WHERE BRIGHT LIGHTS ARE FEW AND FAR BETWEEN, THE *KEIBLER CIRCUS* HAS ALWAYS DELIVERED AN EVENING OF *THRILLS!*

TONIGHT IS NO EXCEPTION!

WHAT TH--!

BUT-- THERE'S NO *NET*--!

SCREAMS ERUPT FROM THE SEATS AS, UNDERNEATH--

GO, MY *BRETHREN!* CLAIM THIS REALM FOR YOUR *OWN!*

SHOW THEM WHY *LIONS* TOGETHER ARE CALLED A *PRIDE!*

WITHIN THE ENVELOPING BIG TOP--CHAOS, CONFUSION, AND CACOPHONY!

THIS IS LIKE THAT TIME WHEN I WAS A KID!

THE TIME THE *HULK* TORE IT UP WITH THE--

--AVENGERS, MISTER!

AND I REMEMBER IT EVEN BETTER THAN YOU DO--OUR FIRST TIME TOGETHER! *

*RAISE YOUR HAND IF YOU'VE EVER READ AVENGERS #1.

I ONLY REMEMBER HOW MUCH TROUBLE CAT-PEOPLE HAVE CAUSED ME, LEO!

YOU'RE MY MEAT TONIGHT!

CARE TO DANCE--?

LOOK! IT'S WONDER MAN!

AND I'VE GOT THE BIG CHEESE IN MY SIGHTS, TIGRA!

PIETRO, I KNOW IT'S NOT EASY TO TURN GOOD AND STAY TURNED-- BUT WE STARTED TOGETHER!

WE CAN STILL KEEP IT GOIN'-- TOGETHER!

WHAT DO YOU KNOW OF TOGETHERNESS, HAWKEYE?

YOU'VE QUIT THE AVENGERS MANY TIMES!

QUITTING AND SELLING OUT ARE TWO DIFFERENT THINGS!

HURRY UP, SCORPIO! BLOW ME OUTTA HERE WHILE HE'S TALKIN'!

ANYWAY, I'M MARRIED TOO, NOW! THAT'S TOGETHERNESS! AND I COULD NEVER DO THIS TO MOCKY!

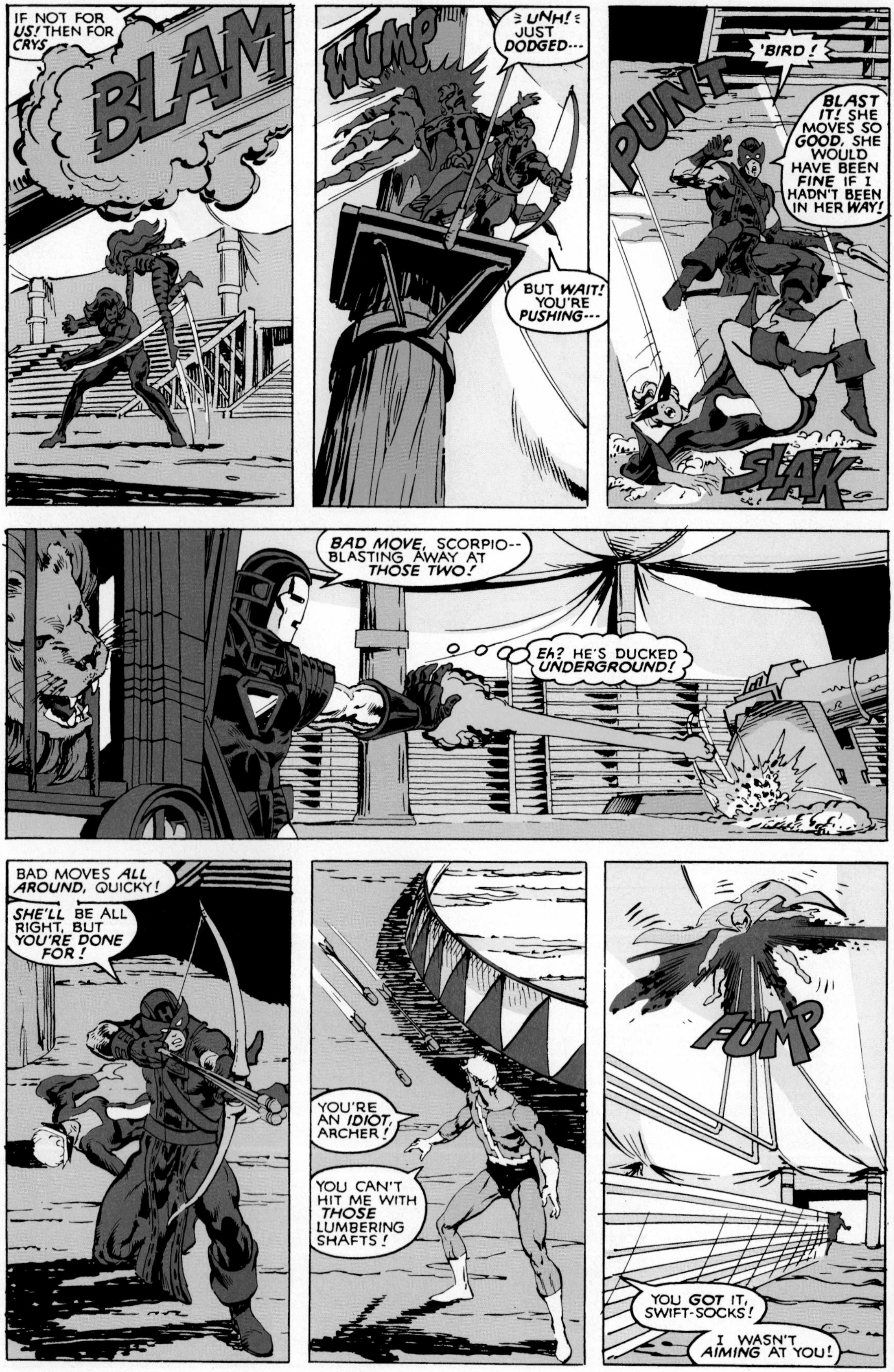
IF NOT FOR US! THEN FOR CRYS
BLAM
WUMP
UNH! JUST DODGED---
BUT WAIT! YOU'RE PUSHING---
'BIRD!
PUNT
BLAST IT! SHE MOVES SO GOOD, SHE WOULD HAVE BEEN FINE IF I HADN'T BEEN IN HER WAY!
SLAK
BAD MOVE, SCORPIO-- BLASTING AWAY AT THOSE TWO!
Eh? HE'S DUCKED UNDERGROUND!
BAD MOVES ALL AROUND, QUICKY!
SHE'LL BE ALL RIGHT, BUT YOU'RE DONE FOR!
YOU'RE AN IDIOT, ARCHER!
YOU CAN'T HIT ME WITH THOSE LUMBERING SHAFTS!
FUMP
YOU GOT IT, SWIFT-SOCKS!
I WASN'T AIMING AT YOU!

NOW WHAT ABOUT *YOU*, LADY?

I'VE GOT NO *DEATH WISH*, HAWKEYE!

BUT *I'VE* GOT *DEATH*-- IN THE FORM OF MY *SCORPION'S NEUROTOXIN!*

BACK IT UP, BOSS! THE ANIMALS ARE *CAGED*, SO IT'S *MY TURN* ON CENTER STAGE!

*FOOL!* THIS TOXIN CAN DROP *YOU* AND EVERY *ELEPHANT* YOU JUST *CARRIED!*

Uh... YEAH--

DO--

--TELL!

*PLOW*

*KRUK*

AND I'LL TAKE OVER *HERE*, TIGRA!

SHE'S *TIRED*-- FROM FIGHTING *LEO*, OR *HERSELF?*

SHE'S *GOT* TO RESOLVE HER *DUAL IDENTITY* SOON, OR GO MAD!

HOW'RE YOU *DOING*, WONDER MAN--?

WONDER MAN?!!

HAWKEYE!

IT... WEARS OFF--!

LOOK OUT--

267

TOO *LITTLE* AND TOO *LATE*, HAWKEYE!

WHA--? CAN'T MOVE THE *ARMOR!*

IT'S AN *ENERGY SIPHON* I MADE UP, TIN MAN! *I'M* GOOD WITH MACHINES, TOO!

YOUR TEAM GOT *MOST* OF MY TEAM, BUT IT'S ALWAYS THE ONE YOU *OVERLOOK* THAT GETS YOU IN THE *END!*

YOU *SAID* IT!

NOW *EAT* DIRT!

PUNK

Uh... TIGRA... IF YOU GET THIS *MACHINE* OFF MY BACK, I CAN GET AFTER *QUICKSILVER!*

IRON MAN, THAT COOL BREEZE IS HALFWAY TO *AUSTRALIA* BY NOW!

WE MIGHT AS WELL WAIT FOR *WONDY, HAWK* AND *MOCK* TO RECOVER, SO WE CAN FOLLOW HIM AS A *GROUP*-- AND--

OH! I WAS *GOING* TO SAY I WANTED TO *PLAY* WITH MY *PREY*--!

MEANWHILE--

WANDA? WHERE *ARE* YOU?

RIGHT HERE-- *HONEY!*

THERE ARE BOTTLES FOR THE BOYS-- IN THE FRIDGE!

I'VE GOT TO GO TO HIM---

NOT ON YOUR *LIFE!*

# CHAPTER FOUR

# MUTANT MELTDOWN!

SOMEWHERE IN *DREAMTIME*, THE AUSTRALIAN OUTBACK CONTINUES ALMOST UNCHANGED-- UNTOUCHED BY MAN--

-- BUT IN YEARS *PAST*, IT WAS TOUCHED BY THE *SENTINELS*, THAT STRANGE CORPS OF ANTI-MUTANT ROBOTS--

--WHEN THEY BUILT AN *"ANTHILL"* AS THEIR SECRET HEADQUARTERS! *

*AVENGERS #103.

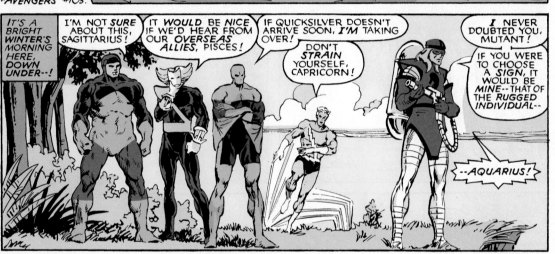

IT'S A *BRIGHT WINTER'S MORNING* HERE, *DOWN UNDER*--!

I'M NOT *SURE* ABOUT THIS, SAGITTARIUS!

IT *WOULD* BE *NICE* IF WE'D HEAR FROM OUR *OVERSEAS ALLIES*, PISCES!

IF QUICKSILVER DOESN'T ARRIVE SOON, *I'M* TAKING OVER!

DON'T *STRAIN* YOURSELF, CAPRICORN!

*I* NEVER DOUBTED YOU, MUTANT!

IF YOU WERE TO CHOOSE A *SIGN*, IT WOULD BE *MINE*--THAT OF THE *RUGGED INDIVIDUAL*--

--AQUARIUS!

I HAVE NO USE FOR *INDIVIDUALS* WHEN THEY DIS-RUPT THE *PLAN*, QUICKSILVER!

YOU'VE RUN *HALFWAY* AROUND THE *WORLD*! YOU'RE *TIRED*!

TIRED OF *FAILURE* BY YOUR FELLOW *REPLICANTS*, CAPRICORN!

THE AVENGERS HAVE BEATEN THEM *BOTH* TIMES, DESPITE MY *BEST EFFORTS*--

--BUT *YOU FOUR* AND I HAVE *ONE LAST CHANCE* TO RUB THEIR *NOSES* IN THEIR *PAST*!

*TIRED?* NOT *ME!* NOT WHEN *TRIUMPH* IS WITHIN MY GRASP!

MOMENTS LATER--

**BLAK**

ALL RIGHT, AUSSIES! WE KNOW YOU TOOK THIS BUNKER OVER FOR *GOVERNMENT RESEARCH*, BUT *WE'RE* TAKING IT FOR *ZODIAC* NOW! ANY *BACKTALK* AND WE'LL SLAP YOU *SILLY!* ANY *VIOLENCE* AND WE'LL--

--WE'LL--

I DON'T *GET* IT! WHERE *IS* EVERYBODY?

**PLANG**

THAT HAMMER!

THE HAMMER OF--

YES, *THOR*-- AND *FOUR REJECTS!* UNLIKE THE *WEST* AND *EAST COAST* TEAMS, THESE FIVE HAVE NEVER *WORKED TOGETHER!*

AND THE "IRON MAN" IS ONLY A *STAND-IN!*

MISTER, I WAS *NEVER* A *STAND-IN*-- OR A *REJECT!* IT TOOK ME A *LONG* TIME TO *LEARN* THAT TRUTH, BUT NOW THERE'S *NO DOUBT* OF IT!

I'M *NUMBER TWO* WHEN IT COMES TO THE *ARMOR*, BUT I'M *STILL* ALL THE IRON MAN *WE'LL NEED* TO TAKE YOU!

YOU'LL HAVE TO *SHOW* ME THAT!

THE FIRST HURLING WAS A *WARNING*, PISCES! THOU SHOULDST HAVE PAID IT *HEED!*

MANY OF US HAVE DUTIES WHICH KEEP US FROM *FULL-TIME* AVENGERS MEMBERSHIP, ZODIAC! OUR STATUS IS OUR *CHOICE!*

EVEN IF *I'VE* ONLY PARTICIPATED IN A *FEW* CASES--

WOP

--I APPRECIATE THE *HONOR* OF MEMBERSHIP--AND THE *RESPONSIBILITY!*

AND *SOME* OF US JUST FOUND OUT WE DON'T LIKE *CROWDS* WHEN WE GO TO *WORK!*

I LIKE THE *WIDE-OPEN SPACES* MYSELF, FALCON!

THAT'S WHY *SAGITTARIUS THE ARCHER* DECIDED HAWKEYE SHOULDN'T *MONOPOLIZE* THE *ARROW BIZ!*

YOU MAY'VE *DECIDED* IT, MAN, BUT THAT DON'T MAKE IT *REAL!*

YES, FALCON-- SOME OF US DON'T LIKE *CROWDS!*

AND YET-- -- SOME OF US MAY HAVE PUSHED THE PURSUIT OF FREEDOM *TOO FAR!*

YOU GOT A *LONG WAY* TA GO TA THREATEN THE *HAWK!*

*PLOK*

*UNHH!*

SINCE THE DAY I *DEFECTED* TO THE *WEST,* I'VE *EXEMPLIFIED* THE CULT OF THE *INDIVIDUAL*-- ESPECIALLY IN MY RELATIONSHIP WITH *MATT MURDOCK!*

AND NOW, IN *MATT'S HOUR OF NEED---*

HEY, WIDOW, YOU'RE GONNA *INSULT* ME IF YOU DON'T GET YOUR MIND BACK ON *BUSINESS!*

*WHUPP!*

OF COURSE, THE *REAL* REASON I WANTED YOU TO FIX ON ME--

-- WAS TO GIVE *AQUARIUS* TIME TO DELIVER HIS *ELECTRO-BLITZ!*

AS *QUICK-SILVER SAID,* THESE PEOPLE DON'T KNOW HOW TO *WORK TO-GETHER* LIKE--

*WAGHHH!*

IF ONLY *MEN* WOULD BE AS SILENT AS THE *BEASTS!*

THANKS, *PANTHER!* THAT SHOULDN'T HAVE BEEN *NECES-SARY!*

NAY-- BUT E'EN *THOR* HATH HIS MIND *ELSE-WHERE!*

THE VAST CHANGES IN THE *REALM ETERNAL*-- THE ASCENSION OF *BALDER* TO THE *GOLDEN THRONE*-- AND MOST OF ALL--

THOOM

-- THE DAMAGE TO MY *FACE* WHICH THIS *BEARD* CAN BARELY *HIDE AWAY!*

I AM ONE WHO DOTH *REVEL* IN THE GATHERING OF AVENGERS-- YET THIS IS *NOT* THE TIME I WOULD HAVE *CHOSEN* FOR'T!

BLAM

CREEEK

SO LET THIS BATTLE *CEASE!*

YOU-- YOU'RE PULLING THE *COMPUTER* DOWN-- WITHOUT EVEN *TRYING!*

I NEVER *DREAMED---*

FA-VOOM

REACTOR 3

ALWAYS THE ZODIAC FALLS IN *DEFEAT!* THEY *COULD* BE *GREAT,* GIVEN *TIME* AND *LEADERSHIP,* BUT I USED THEM TOO *QUICKLY!*

IT DOESN'T *MATTER!* MY PLAN *ALLOWED* FOR THIS *CONITINGENCY!*

THERE WAS A *BETTER* REASON THAN *NOSTALGIA* TO END OUR BATTLES IN THIS *INSTALLATION!*

YOU'VE BEEN RUNNING LIKE A *RABBIT,* BLUE BOY--

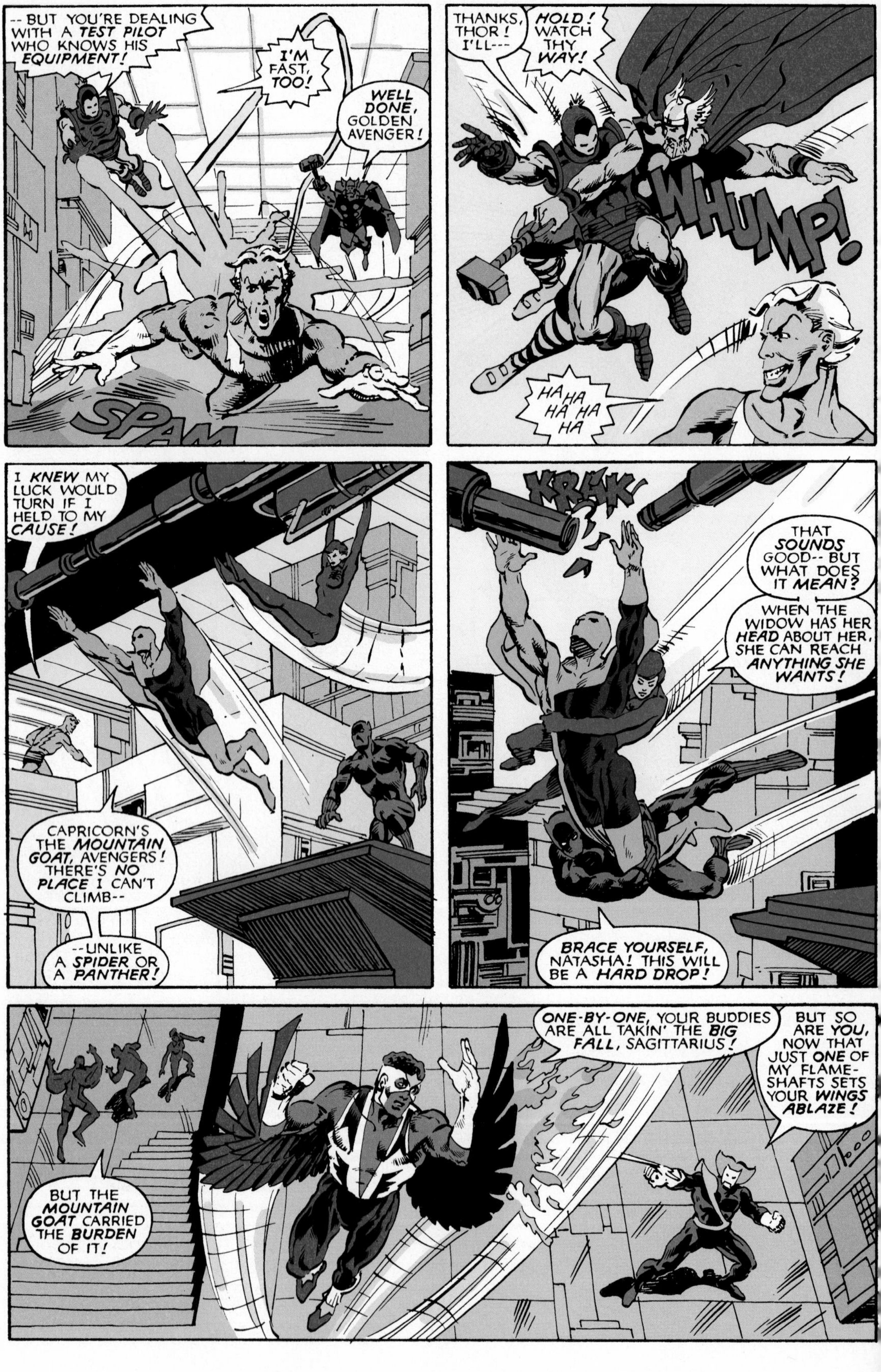
-- BUT YOU'RE DEALING WITH A TEST PILOT WHO KNOWS HIS EQUIPMENT!
I'M FAST, TOO!
WELL DONE, GOLDEN AVENGER!
SPAM
THANKS, THOR! I'LL---
HOLD! WATCH THY WAY!
WHUMP!
HA HA HA HA HA
I KNEW MY LUCK WOULD TURN IF I HELD TO MY CAUSE!
CAPRICORN'S THE MOUNTAIN GOAT, AVENGERS! THERE'S NO PLACE I CAN'T CLIMB--
--UNLIKE A SPIDER OR A PANTHER!
KRAK!
THAT SOUNDS GOOD-- BUT WHAT DOES IT MEAN?
WHEN THE WIDOW HAS HER HEAD ABOUT HER, SHE CAN REACH ANYTHING SHE WANTS!
BRACE YOURSELF, NATASHA! THIS WILL BE A HARD DROP!
BUT THE MOUNTAIN GOAT CARRIED THE BURDEN OF IT!
ONE-BY-ONE, YOUR BUDDIES ARE ALL TAKIN' THE BIG FALL, SAGITTARIUS!
BUT SO ARE YOU, NOW THAT JUST ONE OF MY FLAME-SHAFTS SETS YOUR WINGS ABLAZE!

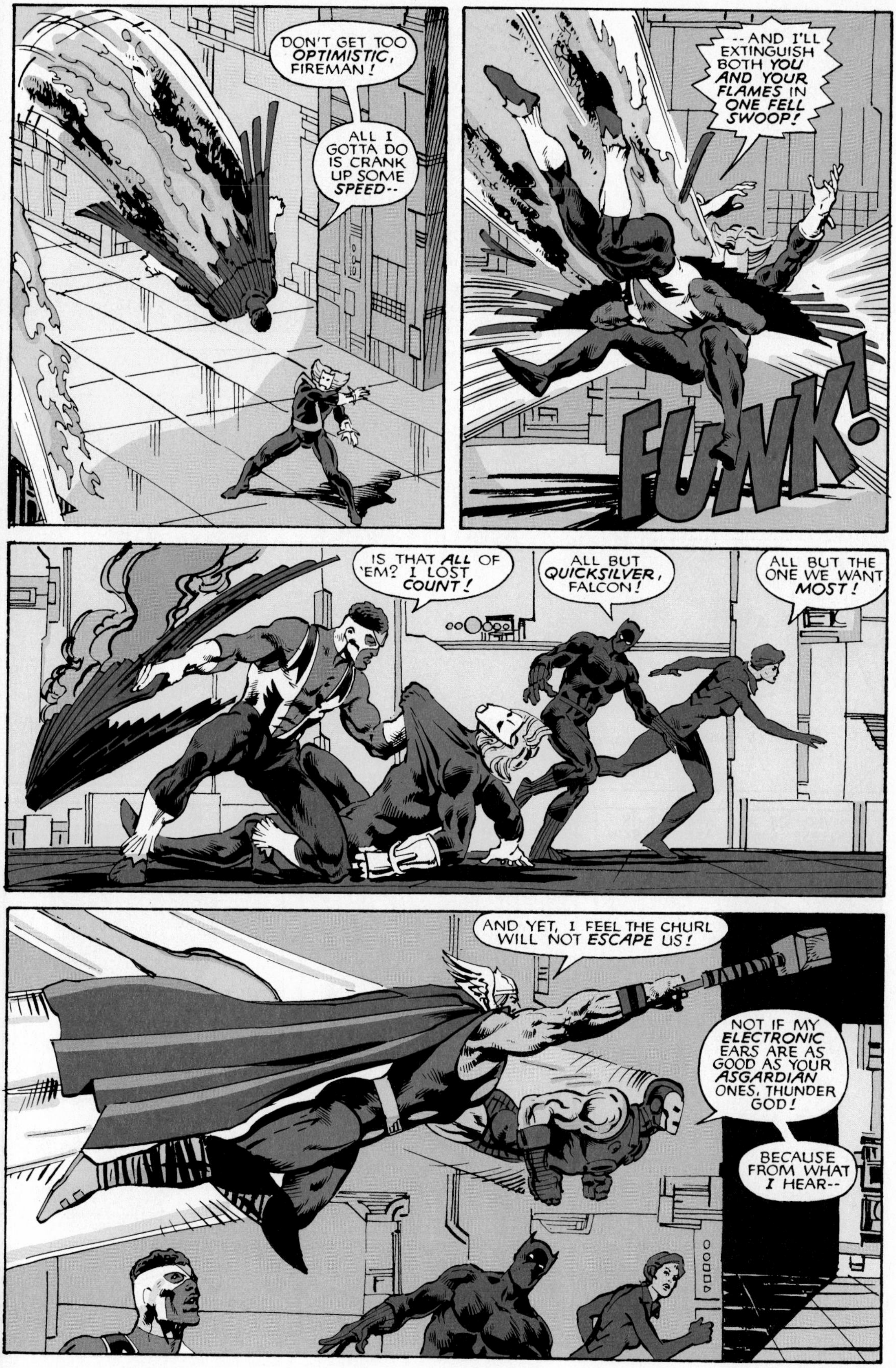
DON'T GET TOO OPTIMISTIC, FIREMAN!
ALL I GOTTA DO IS CRANK UP SOME SPEED--
--AND I'LL EXTINGUISH BOTH YOU AND YOUR FLAMES IN ONE FELL SWOOP!
FUNK!
IS THAT ALL OF 'EM? I LOST COUNT!
ALL BUT QUICKSILVER, FALCON!
ALL BUT THE ONE WE WANT MOST!
AND YET, I FEEL THE CHURL WILL NOT ESCAPE US!
NOT IF MY ELECTRONIC EARS ARE AS GOOD AS YOUR ASGARDIAN ONES, THUNDER GOD!
BECAUSE FROM WHAT I HEAR--

--THE *REST* OF THE *AVENGERS* HAVE ARRIVED!

HOW'S IT *GOIN'*, GUYS? THE *ZODIACS WE* CAPTURED HAVE SPILLED THE BEANS TO *GYRICH!*

HE'S GRINDING HIS TEETH DOWN TO *NUBS*, BUT WE'RE *CLEAR!*

STILL, I WANT MY HANDS ON *QUICK---*

*AAAGH! POWER--!*

POWER COURTESY OF THE *AUSTRALIAN GOVERNMENT* -- BUT NOW *MINE!*

YOU *KNEW* THIS WAS A *RESEARCH INSTALLATION*--

--BUT YOU *DIDN'T* KNOW THE RESEARCH WAS FOR A WAY OF DEFENDING AUSTRALIA WITH-OUT *NUCLEAR WARHEADS!*

THEY DEVELOP *PARTICLE-BEAM* WEAPONS HERE--

--WEAPONS JUST AS *DEADLY*, YET *DIRECTABLE*--

--AND IF THAT'S WHAT IT *TAKES* TO SECURE MY *REVENGE*, THEN *SO BE IT!*

*GOODBYE,* AVENGERS-- AT *LAST!*

STOP, PIETRO!

Wha--?

THE VISION!

WHATEVER YOU CONTEMPLATE IS FUTILE! ONE SQUEEZE IS ALL IT TAKES!

CAP! YOUR SHIELD AND MY ARROWS--!

HE'D HAVE TIME TO REACT BEFORE WE HIT HIM, HAWKEYE!

I CAN NAIL HIM WITH MY REPULSOR RAYS!

AYE, BUT THAT MIGHT CAUSE HIS FIST TO CLENCH!

I WARN YOU, SYNTHEZOID, AN ATTACK--

I DO UNDERSTAND, PIETRO! THAT'S WHY I BRING ONLY A ... GIFT!

CAPTAIN MARVEL! I NEED YOUR HELP!

STAY BACK! EVEN YOU AREN'T FAST ENOUGH--!

THE GIFT IS IN THIS RUBY, PIETRO.

WANDA CREATED IT, BECAUSE SHE STILL BELIEVES IN YOU-- HER ONLY BROTHER!

SHE WANTED TO BRING IT HERSELF, BUT I DON'T HAVE HER FAITH!

STILL, HERE IT IS-- FOR AS I SHINE MY FOCUSED SOLAR BEAM THROUGH THE RUBY--

--AND CAPTAIN MARVEL ADDS HER LASER RAY--

-- I GIVE YOU THE FIRST HOLOGRAMS OF MY SONS--

--YOUR NEPHEWS, BROTHER-IN-LAW!

YOU CLAIM YOU HATE EVERYONE ON *TWO WORLDS*-- YOUR *WIFE*, YOUR *SISTER*, YOUR *FORMER TEAM*--

--BUT CAN YOU TRULY HATE THESE TWO *INNOCENTS*, WHOSE *FATHER*-- AND *MOTHER*-- YOU WILL HAVE TO MURDER TO ESTABLISH YOUR *CLAIM*?

*TOMMY* AND *BILLY* NEED THEIR *UNCLE*, PIETRO-- JUST AS YOUR *OWN* CHILD NEEDS HER *FATHER!* WHATEVER WE *ADULTS* HAVE DONE TO YOU---

ENOUGH--!

ENOUGH!!

IN JUST *THAT* SHORT A TIME, HE'S *LOST* TO THE *DISTANCE*-- ALMOST AS IF HE WERE *NEVER* *THERE* IN THE FIRST PLACE--

--BUT SIXTEEN AVENGERS KNOW HE *WAS!*

I'M SORRY I DIDN'T ARRIVE *EARLIER*, BUT WE WEREN'T CERTAIN OF THE *SITUATION* UNTIL *HANK PYM* CAME TO US!

*PYM*-- BROUGHT THEE INTO *THIS*?

NO ONE'S MORE *SENSITIVE* THAN *HANK*, THOR!

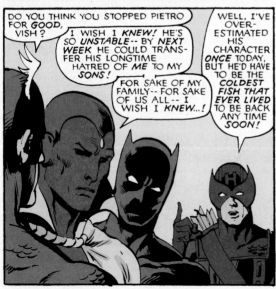

DO YOU THINK YOU STOPPED PIETRO FOR *GOOD*, VISH?

I WISH I *KNEW!* HE'S SO *UNSTABLE*-- BY *NEXT WEEK* HE COULD TRANSFER HIS LONGTIME HATRED OF *ME* TO MY *SONS!*

FOR SAKE OF MY FAMILY-- FOR SAKE OF US ALL-- I WISH I *KNEW...!*

WELL, I'VE OVER-ESTIMATED HIS CHARACTER *ONCE* TODAY, BUT HE'D HAVE TO BE THE *COLDEST FISH* THAT *EVER LIVED* TO BE BACK ANY TIME *SOON!*

SOOOO... I'D LIKE TO REMIND YOU ALL OF THE MUCH *BETTER* REASON WE GOT TOGETHER THIS WEEKEND!

BACK BEFORE THE *KIBITZERS* SHOWED UP, WE WERE GONNA PLAY US SOME *SERIOUS SOFTBALL!*

--ANDICHOOSETHORFORMYTEAM!

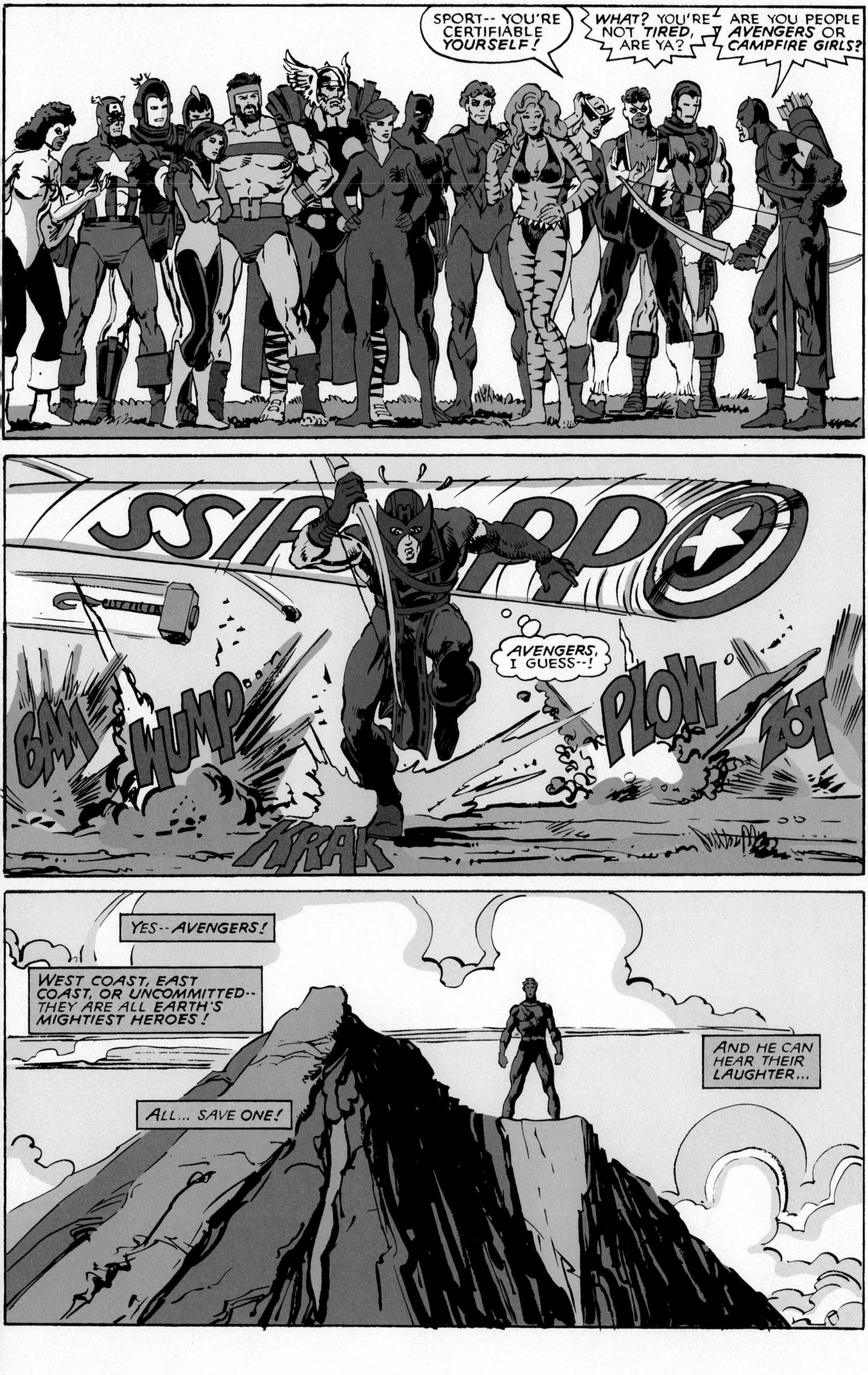
SPORT-- YOU'RE CERTIFIABLE *YOURSELF!*
*WHAT?* YOU'RE NOT *TIRED*, ARE YA?
ARE YOU PEOPLE *AVENGERS* OR *CAMPFIRE GIRLS?*
*AVENGERS*, I GUESS--!
BAM
WUMP
KRAK
PLOW
ZOT
YES-- AVENGERS!
WEST COAST, EAST COAST, OR UNCOMMITTED-- THEY ARE ALL EARTH'S MIGHTIEST HEROES!
ALL... SAVE ONE!
AND HE CAN HEAR THEIR LAUGHTER...